TALKING movies

TALKING MOVIES

TALKING movies

Contemporary World Filmmakers in Interview

JASON WOOD

WALLFLOWER PRESS

LONDON & NEW YORK

First published in Great Britain in 2006 by
Wallflower Press
6a Middleton Place, Langham Street, London W1W 7TE
www.wallflowerpress.co.uk

Cover images:
Beau travail (*Good Work*, Claire Denis, 1999)
Japón (*Japan*, Carlos Reygadas, 2002)
L'emploi du temps (*Time Out*, Laurent Cantet, 2001)
Batalla en el cielo (*Battle in Heaven*, Carlos Reygadas, 2005)
La niña santa (*The Holy Girl*, Lucrecia Martel, 2004)
Amores perros (*Love's a Bitch*, Alejandro González Iñárritu, 2000)
Dirty Pretty Things (Stephen Frears, 2002)
Where the Truth Lies (Atom Egoyan, 2005)
All the Real Girls (David Gordon Green, 2003)

A catalogue record for this book is available from the British Library.

ISBN 1-904764-90-8 (pbk)
ISBN 1-904764-91-6 (hbk)

Book design by Elsa Mathern

Printed by Replika Press Pvt Ltd., India

Contents

Acknowledgements

I must first of all extend my appreciation to the directors who agreed to be interviewed for the pieces that would eventually come to form this book.

My gratitude is also expressed to the below individuals and organisations, many of whom allowed the reproduction of previously published materials:

Nigel Algar, Yoram Allon (Wallflower Press), Geoff Andrew (*Time Out*), Eileen Anipare (Ion Productions), Artificial Eye, John Atkinson (*Kamera*), BBCi, Oliver Berry (*Kamera*), Rosa Bosch, Nick Broomfield, the Cambridge Film Festival (Tony Jones), Will Clarke, Walter Donohue (Faber and Faber), Andi Engel (*Enthusiasm*), Gareth Evans (*Vertigo*), Nick James (*Sight and Sound*), Steve Jenkins, Richard T. Kelly (Faber and Faber), Rob Kenny, Moira McDonagh (Artificial Eye), Suzanne Noble (Icon), Optimum Releasing, Andrew Pulver (*The Guardian*), David Shear and Verena von Stackelberg.

My final thanks are to my family: Nicky, Felix and Rudy. As always, their patience and understanding is astonishing.

Preface

So much is written about the cinema now, and so little of it of real worth. It wasn't always so. Once upon a time, before countless entirely unremarkable people became famous simply for wanting to be famous, there were far fewer movie magazines than now, and far fewer articles dealing with movie-related matters in the newspapers. True, there were always gossip rags and yes, there were always film reviews, but it's only in the last two or three decades that the media in general have become fanatically obsessed with stars and box-office performance and the next hyped-up Hollywood hit. I recall the late, great British film critic Tom Milne telling me how easy it used to be to secure an interview with a director or visit the set of a film; when Alfred Hitchcock was filming *Frenzy* in London, apparently, there was no lengthy list of hacks begging for the privilege of watching the master at work. Now, however, journalists regularly sell their souls – or at least whatever critical integrity they may have – in return for a paltry 15 or 20 minutes in the company of a currently fashionable juve lead… and, of course, half-a-dozen or more fellow scribes also crowded around the same table at a high-profile press junket.

And the outcome of these ludicrously brief encounters? Most often, utter drivel. For one thing – and I speak from personal experience, having long ago subjected myself to a few of these round tables in Cannes (never again!) – there simply isn't the time to create any kind of properly meaningful dialogue in the company of so many other journos all keen to ask as many questions as possible. (I won't even allow myself to be distracted here by horrendous memories of the seemingly ubiq- uitous 'critic' who always insists on kicking off the proceedings with: 'So, maestro, when are you going to come to Budapest?' Actually, of course, the hack is not really Hungarian, but discretion demands I conceal the offending person's identity by changing the name of the city to which the interviewee is invariably invited.) For another, many of the attendant press are either barely familiar with the interviewee's work – one could, if one were so inclined, prepare nothing at all for such a gathering and simply record the responses to questions put by others – or they are anxious only to secure soundbites of the most mind-numbing triviality. And then there's the problem of the interviewees themselves. If they're young Hollywood actors, they've usually been very carefully trained by PRs to give specific, fixed answers that allow for no honesty or insight whatsoever, let alone any controversy or scandal. And if they are old and experienced enough to be regarded by the publicity folk as sentient beings sufficiently sensible to be permitted to speak their own minds, they are probably tired of hearing the same silly questions over and over again in – literally – hundreds of interviews.

Small wonder, then, that so much of what we now read, hear and see in the media about filmmaking is dull, repetitive, predictable and hollow, having little connection to the realities of creative thought and activity as practised by most filmmaking personnel. If you're going to find out anything of real value about filmmaking from an interview, the interviewer has to have enough time – one-to-one time – with the interviewee, not only to ask all the questions he/she considers most important with regard to the topic in hand but to establish some kind of rapport; the most fruitful interviews – at least in this writer's experience – are those where a real two-way dialogue is established. In order for that to happen, it's essential that the interviewer is properly familiar with the work of the interviewee. Being well prepared for the conversation in terms of having done adequate research immediately beforehand is the minimum required of the interviewer; ideally, he/she should know the interviewee's work so well that he/she can respond at once to anything the interviewee says. And that is the kind of knowledge that comes from a real and passionate enthusiasm both for cinema in general and for the work under discussion in particular.

Too often, these days, you get the impression that the writer has interviewed someone from the film world not out of any genuine interest in that person's work, but simply in order to meet someone famous. Such a charge, clearly, could never be made against this book of interviews conducted by Jason Wood. Not only does the author always direct his questions to the work, but the people he has interviewed are of interest primarily because of that work, not because of a particularly high public profile. This is no self-celebrating souvenir of glamorous meetings with particularly well-known men and women; it's a collection of unembellished transcriptions of informed, intelligent, down-to-earth conversations with hard-working filmmakers about the creative decisions they made, why they made them, and what the consequences of those decisions were. In each case, you get a real sense of people talking movies – actually thinking about cinema, rather than simply requiring and providing the usual trite soundbites.

As noted above, the transcriptions are to all intents and purposes unembellished, and are added to with a thumbnail sketch of the interviewee's career by way of introduction. Nevertheless, while Wood himself never offers any comments on his subjects' personalities, I'd argue that those personalities do emerge to some degree from the interviews. Some filmmakers, like Guillermo del Toro and Alejandro González Iñárritu, give lengthy, detailed, very open responses; others, like Nuri Bilge Ceylan or Stephen Frears, are more succinct, even slightly guarded, the former as engagingly to-the-point as his films, the latter displaying a wry sense of humour that typifies his disarmingly modest attitude to the director's role and function. The impression one gains of Claire Denis is of a thinker as erudite and subtle as her films, but also of someone very pragmatic; Hal Hartley, too, comes across as someone whose theoretical approach to movie-making is consciously and carefully counterbalanced by an awareness of the need to deal with certain logistical realities and to communicate with the viewer. And then there is Jan Svankmajer, a fiercely independent thinker whose comments on his work are as original, idiosyncratic, uncompromising and intellectually rigorous as his films.

Those seven names alone give an idea of the range of work covered in this book. Every continent on the planet is represented; animation and documentary are included alongside live-action fiction, be it art-house, experimental or (comparatively) mainstream. Those of the opinion that cinema is dying should (re-)visit the work of the filmmakers gathered together for this volume. Just take the time to look beyond Hollywood, and you'll find that, as an art form, the cinema is still in surprisingly robust health.

Geoff Andrew
London
October 2006

Introduction

The following interviews are compiled from what amounts to over ten years of conversing with film directors for various film and print sources. One or two – John Sayles and Bruce Weber for example – are more up to date, a chance few words at festivals hastily expanded with an eye to inclusion in this compendium.

The criteria for whittling these many dialogues down to thirty-one interviews to form *Talking Movies* was relatively simple: primarily the filmmakers should be those whose work is clearly defined by a singular or unique vision and who have therefore over relatively recent years – and of course Stephen Frears, Jan Svankmajer and John Sayles go back quite a while longer – made a significant contribution to the contemporary filmmaking landscape. It was also my intention to select on the basis that the subjects be as diverse and eclectic as possible. This was in order to hopefully provide insights into how filmmaking practices and aesthetics differ according to the social, political and cultural environments that inform them. Finally, I wanted to avoid 'star' directors, and instead give a forum to those whose work may ordinarily find little favour within a media increasingly infatuated by box-office grosses, glitzy premieres and the notion of cinema as a purely populist entertainment vehicle for performers with marquee value.

Without exception I found each of the directors contained in this volume to be passionate, intelligent and lucid about their craft; open to debate and willing to discuss the myriad interpretations that a subjective art such as film inspires. I very much hope that you find them to be equally illuminating and engaging.

1

Susanne Bier

Born in Denmark in 1960, Susanne Bier studied at the Bezalet Academy of Arts & Design in Jerusalem and read architecture in London before enrolling for the film direction course at the National Film School of Denmark. *De Saliges Ø* (1987), Bier's graduation film, won first prize at the Munich film school festival and was subsequently distributed by Channel Four.

Finding immediate success in Denmark with her features *Freud Flytter Hjemmefra* (*Freud Leaving Home*, 1990), *Det Bli'r i Familien* (*Family Matters*, 1993), *Pensionat Oscar* (*Like it Was Never Before*, 1995) and *Sekten* (*Credo*, 1997), Bier's major breakthrough came with *Den Eneste Ene* (*The One and Only*, 1999). A comedy about the fragility of life, the film won a clutch of Danish Film Academy awards and established Bier's relationship with actor Paprika Steen. The film remains one of the most successful domestic films ever released in Denmark.

A sidestep from the easy going charm of *Livet är en schlager* (*Once in a Lifetime*, 2000), *Elsker dig for evigt* (*Open Hearts*, 2002) brought Bier's work to much wider international attention. Acutely observed and beautifully written by Bier and Anders Thomas Jensen, the film is a perceptive and painful exploration of broken lives and interconnected tragedies. Made under Dogme regulations, the film also marked a move towards a more minimalist aesthetic.

Since the completion of *Open Hearts* Bier's reputation has continued to ascend with the harrowing *Brødre* (*Brothers*, 2004) and the emotional and engaging *Efter Bryllupet* (*After the Wedding*, 2006).

Also the maker of shorts, music videos and commercials, Bier is currently completing *Things We Lost in the Fire*, an American project starring Halle Berry and Benicio del Toro. The tale of a recent widow who invites her dead husband's troubled best friend to live with her and her two children, the film looks set to continue Bier's intelligent mediation on pain, tragedy and atonement.

This interview took place in 2002 on the release of Bier's *Open Hearts* and originally appeared in *Projections 13* (Faber and Faber, 2004).

Jason Wood: Could you begin by talking about how you first became involved in film directing and some of your motivations for doing so?

Susanne Bier: I studied comparative religion for a while and then I studied architecture and whilst I was studying architecture I became much more interested in elements more along the lines of movies, such as set design. Then I became more interested in the people within the walls that I would design and began reading scripts. I applied as a set designer to the National Film and Television School in the UK and while I was at the interview I told them that I was undecided as to whether I wanted to be a set designer or a director, and they told me that I should go home and think about that. Very soon after I applied as a director for the National Film School of Denmark. I am not like many of the male directors who have been film fanatics all their lives.

JW: Were there any particular directors or film figures at this time who did exert an influence over you?

SB: I was incredibly influenced at that time by directors such as Antonioni who used architecture very significantly. Eventually, as I progressed through film school I became very interested in the American directors of the 1970s. I think that if one is to talk about Dogme and that particular sensibility then we are heavily indebted to the 'movie brats' and what those American directors did for cinema in the 1970s. I think that what they are aiming for and what we are also aiming for is some kind of deeper sense of realism and a deeper sense of dealing with somebody's truthful world.

JW: Were you also influenced by the tendency amongst many of the directors of this period to concentrate more on character than on adhering to formulaic narrative conventions?

SB: Very much. I was very interested in films such as *Dog Day Afternoon* [1975]. On its most simplistic level this is a film about a bank robbery but if you look at other films about bank robberies this is not classically what they look like. This was a movie where they were incredibly focused on characters; I was very influenced by that. I was also very influenced by the notion of a character being beyond the narrative.

JW: *Open Hearts* explores the notion of the fragility of life and the shifting sands on which modern life and relations are built. You have stated that this theme became even clearer to you when shooting the film in the post-11th September climate. The current situation in Iraq I think further emphasises this.

SB: We wrote the script before the events of 11th September but shot it after the events so while we were working on the film this notion of fragility became very strong, especially I think for our actors. The screenwriter Anders Thomas Jensen and I actually met through my own very strong personal sense of potential catastrophe. I think that this has to do with being Jewish and having a sense of history where the impossible is a possibility. I think Anders also has this sense of potential catastrophe so this was very close to us. The events of 11th September have really altered most people's perception of fragility and on a grand scale. On that day, if you happened to be late for your train you survived, whereas if you just happened to go into the office early you were dead.

JW: There are moments that are both emotionally and physically shocking. Joachim [Nikolaj Lie Kaas] being struck down by a car, Niels [Mads Mikkelsen] deciding that he is going to leave his wife. These moments frequently seem to come out of the blue, acting almost as a slap in the face for the audience. Was this intentional?

SB: I felt that the accident had to happen just like this. As for Niels leaving his wife, I think that this is how these things actually happen. In these situations you do things that are not necessarily planned and actions become more definite than you intended them when you actually started talking. These situations are the kind where you realise after you have taken a major action the longer-term implications of what you have actually done. Telling somebody that you love them is the same; the words often just happen to fall out of your mouth. These kinds of situations are often fake; telling a person that you are leaving them is often fake because there is this assumption that you have planned it and it is not always like that. In fact, the act of telling somebody that you are leaving them is often more shocking for the person doing the leaving than it is for the receiver.

JW: To return to the accident sequence, how difficult was the accident to set-up. It avoids histrionics which I think makes it all the more harrowing.

SB: Well in terms of practicalities Nikolaj obviously went through the scene with a stunt man in order that he didn't hurt himself. That was basically it. There are no effects at all and I was initially scared and anxious that it wouldn't be enough and would lack impact and simply not work. Actually I also feel that it is much harsher than had there been lots of technical effects. From a technical perspective I am perhaps most proud of this scene.

JW: Nikolaj Lie Kaas has perhaps the most difficult acting task in playing a paraplegic. How did you help him and what specific technical issues did the scenario present?

SB: We had a specialised nurse who deals with such injuries and patients with us all the time in order for it to be right. This is why in some scenes he is on his back and in others he is on his side. The nurse also helped shape the way in which we show Joachim being encouraged to deal with the reality of his situation. It was then up to Nikolaj to administer the performance, obviously acting only with his face. I was keen that he avoided some of the usual histrionics that are common when actors play invalids.

JW: The film marks Sonja Richter's screen debut as Cecile. What convinced you that she would be right for the part and how did you help her find and develop her character?

SB: I had a casting agent audition thirty or so actors for the part and then from this I auditioned the best seven or so actors myself. As soon as she came into the audition I thought, I really hope she is good because she is the one I want. She had frailness and yet a kind of strength. She was very confident in herself in working with the more experienced actors and certainly wasn't timid. Sex scenes can be intimidating for an actor doing them for the first time but Sonja handled them extremely well and threw herself into it with a lot of authority.

JW: You convey very economically the distinctions between the somewhat staid marriage between Niels and Marie [Paprika Steen] and the subsequent

burgeoning relationship between Niels and Cecile.

SB: It was a very fine balance because I wanted the wife to be attractive and I wanted the marriage to be a good marriage. I didn't want it to be a dead marriage but on the other hand I did want it to be the kind of marriage where you could still feel lonely somehow. What often happens is that you find patterns with one another and that the gap between you can actually grow without anybody noticing because everything seems to be fine. Marie seems to be in charge of everything but I think Niels has been feeling increasingly lonely whilst still performing the functions of family life. With Cecile he is suddenly given a new chance to define himself and find out who he is after he has grown up. For Niels this offers an injection of life that proves irresistible.

JW: How deep was your involvement with Jesper Winge Leisner's score?

SB: I worked quite closely on this and the score was actually composed before shooting. Because of the Dogme rules the majority of the music comes out of Cecile's headphones so all the songs were composed in advance. I was keen that the slower ballad, the one which is played the most and which is associated with Cecile was slightly slower than Leisner's original concept. I wanted it to capture who she is and as soon as I heard it I thought, yes, that's her.

JW: The film uses a very distinct palette. The sombre greens of the hospital, contrasted with the more sensual oranges and reds of Cecile's apartment.

SB: The natural lighting that was there and available to us dictated this. If you use a lot of candles, as Cecile does, you do get a very warm, reddish hue. It was also a way of offering juxtaposition between the comforting interiors and the harsh exteriors that are a reality of a Scandinavian winter. We wanted to push this element. Also, we Danes simply use lots of candles, the days are so short so we have to have a way of making it cosy.

JW: How did the raw emotions with which *Open Hearts* deals contribute to the shoot?

SB: When you shoot a Dogme film you have a very small crew so everybody is part of a scene and the mood of the scene is very much the mood of the set so yes, certain days were very painful. The two or three days over which we shot the disintegration of the marriage which features arguments and recriminations were quite tough and there was a certain amount of relief that we had finished with this painful period. Also, as a director if you want that honesty that you desire from a scene and from your actors you do also have to live within the content of a specific scene.

JW: There seems to be a very natural bond between the actors. How did you encourage this?

SB: Well Paprika and Mads are quite friendly off-screen and I am also on quite close terms with both of them. I often find that actors are far too polite to be really familiar with one another. Sonja and Nikolaj did not know each other but I think this was an advantage because their on-screen characters had the crispness and spontaneity of a relatively new relationship. It was important that they weren't too familiar.

JW: With regards to the smaller crew, did you enjoy working within the more intimate Dogme parameters?

SB: I have never worked with huge crews but I had certainly not worked with as minimal a crew as this before. The rule of working only with available lighting of course reduces the crew immediately and also there are other people that are not on set who normally would be, such as costume, make-up etc. Everybody has such big responsibilities on a Dogme film, the actors bring their own clothes in each morning and the fact that everybody carries this intense responsibility often gives the movie an edginess that I find very satisfying. *Open Hearts* is the most exhausting film I have ever made but also certainly the most exciting. There is no waiting around on a Dogme film so you are able to shoot all the time. This makes it vivid and invigorating but there is an explosion of energy that ultimately makes it exhausting because of that.

JW: How does the actual process of making a Dogme film unfold? Are there various approvals that are required?

SB: There was a Dogme office that is now closed but nothing has to be approved. You submit yourself to the vow of chastity and then you follow the rules. The question of obeying the rules is itself a question of interpretation because any ruling is a matter of interpretation. The Dogme rules are also very much open to interpretation as is the whole political content. Making a Dogme film is a political act somehow because it is saying that movies, and then in a broader sense art, has to deal with your own world. I think that the most important role in that sense is that of the director not assuming any sort of aesthetics, of not loading the movie with an aesthetic. I think that this is an impossible rule to adhere to because any artistic decision is an aesthetic decision, when you make a cut this is an aesthetic decision. Having said that, for me it is also the most important rule because psychology must be beyond anything else. In a traditional film there may be the temptation to dress the actors in certain colours in order to create a specific visual effect. For example in many Bergman films the actors all wear very natural colours. You cannot do that here because the actors bring all of their own clothes themselves and choose whatever they find to be particularly suitable for their character. You can't put an aesthetic above psychology.

JW: *Open Hearts* has a realist aesthetic that can be attributed to the Dogme practice of production, particularly the use of hand-held camera. This is particularly good for highlighting the moments of intimacy and awkwardness between characters. Was this one of the enticements for working within the Dogme format?

SB: I had been talking to Peter Aalbaek Jensen at Zentropa about making a Dogme film for a few years but didn't feel that I had the right story. It was after we had made the first version of the script that both Anders Thomas Jensen and I thought that it would be extremely suited to a Dogme film because we felt that the storyline would gain from being forced into reality. One of the Dogme rules of course is that the camera has to be hand-held so this was a consideration. For me it was very important to have elements in the film that did not adhere to rational aspects of storytelling but which did embody the psychological space between the characters.

JW: Did you find any of the Dogme rules prohibitive?

SB: I do find the rule that the sound has to be produced at the same time as the image prohibiting. I understand that it prevents the director from indulging in filmic stunts but the problem is that while shooting it becomes very complicated. For example, if you have some extras talking in the background and you want real sounds from them it has to be produced at the same time as the more important dialogue in the foreground. This makes the actual process of shooting in terms of sound incredibly inflexible and actually opposed to the realness of the Dogme credo.

JW: Are you contemplating working again under the Dogme regulations?

SB: Yes I am because I don't feel that I have investigated it all the way through.

I feel that I want to take it further.

JW: Somewhat in contrast with the Dogme realist aesthetic are the inserts of daydream sequences where Cecile imagines Joachim's hand moving towards hers.

SB: We wanted some kind of media for the characters to act upon impulses in a way that they were unable to actually do. For example, Cecile really wanted to touch Joachim and him to reach out and touch her and so the Super-8 sequences were a means of allowing this to happen. In the original cut there were many more and quite extreme instances of these fantasy sequences. I wanted them to be almost real but not completely real. I find these sequences offer a feeling of relief. I very much like the scene where Joachim moves his hand. There was a lot of discussion about this because it almost feels as if it is too much.

JW: The opening and closing images of the film shot using a heat sensitive camera intrigued me. What were your intentions here?

SB: I wanted an image that would have the characteristic of an X-ray and this was the closest we could get. Because it was winter it worked extremely well because the area was so cold and the bodies were so hot. We had this camera with us throughout the shoot and used the technique quite a lot but in the end we realised when editing that it became disturbing within the actual narrative because you went continually in and out of the fiction. Therefore we used it only at the opening and closing of the film. It also worked well here because there were lots of people, heightening the effect.

JW: And why was this X-ray effect so important to you?

SB: It was my way of saying that these people could be any one of us. I had the feeling that once you take away the actual faces of people we are all alike on the inside and the events that occur within the film could happen to anyone.

JW: Did the film radically alter during editing?

SB: It did change a lot. Eventually it did become the movie we felt it was going to be whilst writing the script but the first cut was three hours long and felt very monumental. The first cut was very arty in a way and certainly very heavy; it didn't really capture the light that exists amongst the sadness. I invited eight or nine friends who also work in the film industry and whose opinions I respect and they kept saying no, you mustn't cut it down but I knew that this version was not the film I wanted. I wanted something that didn't impose the themes upon the audience; it contained them but did not overwhelm you with them.

JW: In Denmark you are best known for your comedies. *Open Hearts* treads a very fine balance between comedy and tragedy and has a humour that evolves from the reality of the situation. The recently paralysed Joachim having difficulties using the electronic page-turning device for example.

SB: I do think that life is a balance between tragedy and comedy. My earlier work, including the comedies, does have a sadness to it. True, they are more funny than sad but both elements are present. I could never make a purely 'sad' film because I do not believe that life is like that. I have always have a hard time with certain Scandinavian movies where a lonely woman stands and cries silently by a window. I think that the scene with the book you mention is very truthful, life can be like that. For me, humour can be a way of understanding tragedy. I personally understand tragedy much better through dark humour than I do through the heavy movies I was subjected to all through my childhood.

JW: Your mention of the woman at the window crying reminds me of the refreshing way in which *Open Hearts* handles the theme of infidelity. You avoid the cliché of the vengeful spouse and that of the lust-addled husband.

SB: I don't approve in real life of the vindictive bitter woman. The only person you are actually really harming is yourself. Also, to paint all men as bastards … life is not really like that. One of the things about growing up is that realising that people and situations are not black and white. These kind of representations in cinema have nothing to do with life.

JW: Your work has been critically and commercially successful in Denmark. How much does this mean to you personally?

SB: Well, I had flu when they were giving out the Bodils and I thought about staying away. I want to be indifferent and cool about it but as the evening approached I starting to put on my good clothes and began to get all excited. I was incredibly happy to receive my award and cannot really pretend that it doesn't matter. It doesn't however in any way influence what I will do next. It is also important for me that the movies I make do have an audience. I believe that cinema is a mass medium. Obviously, I am not saying that I would not make a film that I knew was only going to meet a very small audience.

JW: *Open Hearts* has also been the most internationally widely released of your films so far. Is it a natural desire for you as a director that as a measure of success your next project be released in a similarly expansive manner?

SB: Yes and no because I also do think that as a Dane it is incredibly important for me to make movies that are for Danish people. I don't necessarily feel that a sign of development is to have my films released to increasing numbers in terms of a world audience. It would be fantastic to make a film that does appeal to people all across the world but it is also important to remain true to one's roots. You do not have to necessarily have to remain rooted to them but it is important not to lose them.

JW: Do you have ambitions to shoot outside of Denmark?

SB: It is not an ambition that I actively cultivate but I would like to do that. I also think that my way of telling stories could and does apply to people outside of Denmark because the cocktail of sentiment and humour that you find in my work is not culturally and nationally specific.

JW: The theme of family and the imperfections of the family unit come across very strongly in your most recent work and is, I think, a theme that recurs in many of the films of your compatriots, Thomas Vinterberg's *Festen* [*The Celebration*, 1998] and Annette K. Olesen's *Små ulykker* [*Minor Mishaps*, 2002] for example.

SB: I recognise this also. I think that what Dogme films have done, and I recognise that *Minor Mishaps* is not a Dogme film, is deal with families in a state of dysfunction. I guess that in the western part of the world this is a very pertinent problem. In fact the problem goes deeper and is one relating to our difficulty in defining our identity and reaching out for new identities. We are living still with notions of eighteenth-century ideals of what relationships should capture and families should contain and yet we are living such different lives. These movies reflect upon the new directions in which we are going.

JW: There is a high regard for films and filmmakers coming out of Denmark. Do you see this as a particularly fertile period?

SB: It's a fantastic time. We have been so incredibly lucky to have a combination of good reviews and strong audiences. Pretty much all of the directors you are referring to have emerged from Danish film school. We have this new education and a new sense of the importance on the script, the story and a questioning of the stories the directors want to tell and why. This started at the film school in the beginning of the 1980s and has borne its fruit now. I also think that another important factor is that a lot of these directors, like myself, did not necessarily begin as film fanatics but had other experiences in life. This, I believe creates and contributes to diversity.

JW: How do you view this whole process of talking about your films as opposed to actually physically making them?

SB: There is a depressive element to it because you want to continue your creative investigation but I also have a very pragmatic view because I do consider it as part of the wider process and as much fun of the rest of it is, this is very much a part of it.

* * *

Laurent Cantet

With *Ressources humaines* (*Human Resources*, 1999) and *L'Emploi du temps* (*Time Out*, 2001) writer-director Laurent Cantet, born in Melle, Deux-Sevres in 1961, established himself as one of French cinema's leading realists and analysts of social discontent.

Prior to *Human Resources*, a deeply realist look at class mobility and tension that focuses on the effects of a factory worker's son achieving white-collar status, Cantet had graduated from Paris's acclaimed IDHEC film school and produced two shorts, *Tous a la Manif* (1993; winner of a Prix Jean Vigo) and *Jeux de Plage* (1995). Moving into longer productions, Cantet directed the made-for-television *Les Sanguinaires* (1997) for the '2000 Seen By...' series before completing his César-winning feature debut. The film also won the New Directors Prize at the San Sebastian Festival and the Fassbinder/ Discovery Prize at the European Film Awards.

A further exploration of the disparity between work and home that dips beneath the veneer of the everyday, *Time Out* tells the story of a respectable family man who loses his job and then invents a web of lies to keep the truth from his family. Co-written with Cantet's editor and occasional writer Robin Campillo, the film skillfully portrays the abandonment of responsibility and the residual accumulation of pressure and tension.

Released in 2006, Cantet's third feature is *Vers le sud* (*Heading South*), an investigation of sex tourism set in a beach resort in late-1970s Haiti, under the dictatorship of Duvalier. Basing their script on three stories by the Haitian writer Dany Laferrière, Cantet and Campillo sensitively but trenchantly look into a complex nexus of sexual and political issues.

This interview took place in 2001 and originally appeared in *Enthusiasm 06* in spring 2003.

Jason Wood: How did the idea for *L'Emploi du temps* develop?

Laurent Cantet: First of all there was *Ressources humaines* and I wanted to develop this idea of how each of us defines ourselves within the world of work. It seemed an interesting idea to continue working on. I also had the desire to follow the idea of a lie being gradually built up and then to put face to face the virtuality of the lie and the virtuality of the world Vincent [Aurélien Recoing] is trying to escape from.

JW: The work environment you create in *L'Emploi du temps* differs from the one you created in *Ressources humaines* in that here you deal with executives and middle management. You still retain, however, your authenticity. Did you spend a lot of time visiting these faceless offices and watching the mechanics of the work place?

LC: I simply look at things that are next to us and that we walk by daily. When you are attentive and on the look out, you sense things which you gradually pick up. For example, the scene where Vincent visits the modern office where he purports to have a meeting and views the workers in their daily tasks, we wanted this scene to be both real but also like an advert, perhaps for something like a temping agency. We wanted to give a feeling that this character would walk through this advert with the same unreal sensation as the tasks that he is viewing.

JW: Vincent seems powerless to halt the façade he constructs. Events and reality gradually spill out of his control with a snowball effect.

LC: I wanted initially the first moments of his little adventure to be under control and quite carefully mastered and then gradually he finds the story taking him over so that he is obliged to react in the instant.

JW: For the first fifteen minutes or so we are unsure as to how much of

Vincent's world is fantasy. It is initially conceivable that he is going to a high-powered new job in Geneva. Was this the ambiguity you sought?

LC: Very much. We really wanted the lie to be understood little by little, much as the way in which Muriel [Karin Viard] grasps it little by little. Right from the beginning we very carefully distilled the information so that the story was able to move forward and not just be a chronicle of a wandering. We wanted to go from a simple, ordinary world of the family with defined spaces of houses and schools and then gradually to slide towards the description of a mental space as opposed to a physical one. In the writing you cannot really trust this, it is something that you have to wait to see if it has worked once you get the rushes.

JW: The almost final scene where Vincent pulls into the field and seems to stride off into the darkness is very affecting. It continues the notion of ambiguity, which concludes with the ending of the film where the sense that Vincent has got his life back on track gradually fades with his job interview. His eyes indicate that all is not well.

LC: For me the ending is tragic. Vincent will not be able to find any happiness whatsoever in this new life and he clearly knows it. His desire to answer the questions in the interview is his last lie. All avenues for escape are now closed to him. He won't have the strength even to dream. For me it is a slow suicide on a very low gas.

JW: You contrast greatly the natural environment – the chalet, the river by which Vincent sits – with the environment of the workplace.

LC: Above all we wanted Vincent's special adventure to give him pleasure. We also wanted this pleasure to be discreet and quite minimal; it revolved around having the time purely to enjoy just existing. We wanted to achieve the idea of him entering the landscape as if by osmosis.

JW: Your films offer perceptive commentaries on the relationships between fathers and sons. This is obviously a subject that intrigues you.

LC: I think the father/son relationship is the one that perhaps most forms us. It's also important that in both my films the father represents the social norm but also I try to detail the affectionate side of the relationship as I feel this to be very important. I'm always interested to see the relationship between the intimate and the social and how one can contaminate the other.

JW: The sons always seek approval. Which is I think something we all do in real life.

LC: This is not necessarily true of Julian [Nicolas Kalsch] in *L'Emploi du temps*.

JW: I feel that he is also seeking approval in his own way but you also, in a very affecting scene, show the effects of when this approval, or bond between the father and the son and indeed the whole family is taken away. This sequence must have been difficult to film.

LC: It was. It was the scene that was thought about most during the film and we re-modelled it a lot. We had to re-adjust and re-shoot when we saw certain elements were not working.

JW: In your work you deal in very accurate and perceptive terms with contemporary neuroses concerning work and job security.

LC: This film is slightly different in that unlike the characters in *Ressources humaines* Vincent is not a victim of the dole; he even negotiates his unemployment. I really didn't want him to be seen as a shameful person on the dole.

JW: I agree, he's not been made redundant but it's still a result of the pressure of maintaining his status and keeping himself and his family in the style to which they have become accustomed.

LC: It is in that sense maybe that the alienation concerning work is the same as in my previous film.

JW: There are so many emotions one feels toward Vincent: empathy, sympathy etc. There are also moments where he exploits his friends and one feels revulsion for him. Yet he lacks the true capacity for 'evil'. For example, he feels great guilt after financially exploiting his friends.

LC: I have the impression that the film is always with him without me judging him at any time. We were keen to make him go through different states and the feelings that I personally feel for him vary enormously. There are moments where I feel that he is a true hero and others where I no longer want to even follow him. I hope however that there is always some empathy.

JW: Vincent is a character with whom I am sure many can identify, as are many of the circumstances in your films. You unflinchingly deal with some of the most pressing issues in society.

LC: What I enjoy is to have discussions after a film and I often marvel at how passionate these debates can be because I think that people do recognise themselves or moments in their lives. I take much satisfaction from the fact that people are starting to think as they watch the film.

JW: Did the critical success of *Ressources humaines* and the chord that it struck place a huge amount of expectation upon you?

LC: I actually wrote *L'Emploi du temps* before *Ressources humaines* and I also very heavily invested myself in *L'Emploi du temps* from a very early stage, even during the promotion for my first film so I was always completely in the action and never really looking back. I don't really feel the pressure of the audience; the pressure comes from me because I do not want to fail the film. Each time I finish a work I merely think that I have enjoyed a marvellous stroke of luck.

JW: Your films focus very much not only on the family but also on the community. They are political in many ways.

LC: This is important to me. I am not a militant but I want very much to be involved in what surrounds me. To make these films is certainly a way of dealing with my relationship to politics. This relationship is similar to that which any of my contemporaries may have; it is no longer purely about slogans and manifestos. With this film I did want to move more towards a cinema of fiction whilst continuing to ensure that the context had a documentary element about it.

JW: The film features a fantastic performance from Aurélien Recoing.

LC: Aurélien is first and foremost a great theatre actor, who has worked with many great theatre directors such as Patrice Chereau. He has done a few smaller parts in film. Aurélien's face immediately projected itself onto the character I had written and we met and we worked together for quite a while, even before I took the decision to cast him.

JW: He has the ability to convey great emotion through the simplest of facial gestures.

LC: He has a great technique as an actor. We also, as I said, worked together for a very long time to capture these details. In fact, we worked together from May but the film didn't begin shooting until January the next year. Aurélien lived this character during these many months and did not do anything else during this time.

JW: Serge Livrozet, who plays the smuggler is also very good.

LC: Interestingly, he is not an actor. First of all he started by being a thief and spent ten years in prison where he read and wrote and thought a lot and became a militant anarchist.

JW: His character introduces to the film a real humour, especially in the dinner-party sequence with Vincent's family.

LC: I think that in that particular sequence he does a similar thing to Vincent; he transposes his professional abilities into his actual life and his lies. It's true, I did want this scene to be slightly comic, and it also makes Muriel's looks during this sequence more moving and effective in terms of pathos. She does not for one moment believe the tales she is being told.

JW: I must also compliment you on your choice of music. Jocelyn Pook's score feels perfect.

LC: Initially I was not going to use any music. I thought that music would only come from Vincent's car radio and would be used to pierce his little bubble. As I watched the rushes I realised how well the music worked and that it could still be used to pierce Vincent's world. I had never used music in my work before and had no idea how to work with a musician and I was initially resistant to using music. I was, however, wary of adopting too puritan a position. Jocelyn was involved right through the editing process and I was impressed with how she used music to underline the interior aspect of the film and composed sounds to take us inside Vincent's head. Her music also captures the idea of a nightmare from which we sometimes cannot go forward.

***

Nuri Bilge Ceylan

Born in 1959, Nuri Bilge Ceylan studied filmmaking for two years at the Mimar Sinan University in his native Istanbul after originally gaining a BSc in Electrical Engineering from Bosphorus University .

Ceylan's first major short film, *Koza* (*Cocoon*, 1995) attracted significant interest at the Cannes Film Festival and he made his debut feature two years later with *Kasaba* (*The Small Town*, 1997). Told in four parts from the perspective of two children, *Kasaba* describes relationships between members of a Turkish family. The first part, in a primary school, shows the 11-year-old daughter facing feelings of shame as she tries to adapt to the school's social life and its difficulties. The second part shows the girl with her brother, and their journey to the cornfield where their family are waiting. As they pass through the countryside, they encounter the mysteries of nature and wildlife. In the third part the brother and sister witness the complexities and darkness of the adult world. The fourth part takes place at their home. Based on an autobiographical story by the director's sister, Emine Ceylan, the film offers a vibrantly sensitive, intimate and evocative portrait of an extended family living in a remote Aegean village.

Mayis Sikin Tisi (*Clouds of May*, 1999) tells the story of Muzaffer, who returns to his native town to make a movie. His father, Emin, is dedicated to saving the small forest he cultivates on his property from confiscation by the authorities. Muzaffer's cousin, Saffet, a young town-dweller whose efforts are all doomed to failure by bad luck – or by his own rebelliousness – dreams of going to Istanbul. Muzaffer sets about recruiting family and friends to work on his film. The film is told with subtle comedy and charm, and inscribed with beauty and a reverence for the lives of its characters.

Ceylan's first two features certainly established a clear working methodology and sensibility in their dealing with the estrangement of the individual, the relative monotony of life and issues regarding communication. Generally casting non-professional actors, many of whom are family members, Ceylan also calls upon his background as a photographer, acting as his own cinematographer and imbuing his minimalist and relatively low-budget tales of everyday life with a crisp visual aesthetic. All of these elements came to fruition and wide international attention with *Uzak* (*Distant*, 2002) the tale of a successful commercial photographer struggling to come to terms with the growing gap between his artistic ideals and his professional obligations. Clinging to the melancholic and obsessive routines of his solitary life, the photographer's world is thrown into confusion when a distant relative arrives from the country. The two men struggle to make any kind of connection.

Since this interview took place in 2003, when the director was in town to promote *Uzak* at the London Film Festival, Nuri Bilge Ceylan has completed *Iklimler* (*Climates*, 2005), a moving and sharply observed drama that charts the breakdown of a relationship with precision and intelligence.

Jason Wood: Could you begin by commenting on the fact that on *Uzak* you mutli-task; shooting, editing and directing. Where did you learn so many different skills?

Nuri Bilge Ceylan: I was a photographer before. I started photography at fifteen years old. And I have the kind of personality that likes the technical things actually. And also I am an electrical engineer so... But it's not because I don't trust anybody. I have ideas about all these things and I know the things that I don't need. I don't like many people around during the shooting so that's why I do as much as I do. I keep the crew very small. If I find a cinematographer he will want an assistant and many lights, which I also don't like. I work with very few lights, available light mostly.

JW: Did you study at film school?

NBC: After finishing university I wanted to study in London, but it was very expensive and so I went back to Turkey to study cinematography for two years. It was actually a four-year course but after two I left because I think the actual process of filmmaking is more important in terms of gaining an education.

JW: The central character in *Uzak* is a photographer. Had you always wanted to make a film that dealt with this subject?

NBC: Well, it was for practical reasons because I shoot shutter film in my house and there was a studio there so I could use it if I made the character a photographer. It could have been something else, it wasn't that important.

JW: So you actually shot in your house?

NBC: Yes. And also I used my car. I thought, why not? And it was cheaper that way.

JW: You must be a producer's dream because you keep costs to a minimum. You do everything yourself and even use your own location and props! How did the idea for *Uzak* come to you and how did you begin to map out the two central characters in the film, Mahmut and Yusuf?

NBC: Actually at first I wanted to make a film about two photographers because these kind of problems happened to me ten years ago. But to be able to shoot the character of Mahmut better I decided to put an opposite, younger character in. This is Yusuf.

JW: Your first two films – *Kasaba* and *Mayis sikintisi* – are set in rural locations. *Uzak* begins in the country before moving into the city. How did you find the differences in filming in the rural areas and the more urban landscape? Did you like the different themes that this introduced?

NBC: For me it's not a big difference. The only difference is that in the city there are more people walking around so you have to tackle this problem. It was also cheaper to film in the city because I think everybody was staying in their own houses.

JW: Also there is the difference between someone from a small town and some-one from a bigger city because the character of Mehmet was originally from this town, and he's kind of changed, his ideals have kind of altered. Was that something you wanted to explore by having Yusuf come and show him how to change?

NBC: Actually most of the people living in Istanbul are originally from the country. There is a huge migration to Istanbul because everything is there; all the money, all the business, everything. So everybody's dream, every young person's dream, is to come to Istanbul to find work or to find a better life. So the subject matter is quite typical for Turkey. It happens to everybody.

JW: There is a line where Yusuf says, 'This place has changed you.' Are you saying that living in a city and in an urban metropolis can have a kind of corrupting influence on people's characters?

NBC: I think so, because in life you have to help each other because of the conditions. Sometimes in the villages the mosque is also the school. But in the city, if you have the opportunities and if you earn enough money you begin to be reserved. Firstly, you don't like to want something from others and in return you begin not to give anything to others. So you start to live in your own apartment like a prison.

JW: The other thing I think the film does very well is to highlight the harsh economic realities of the situation. They talk in the movie about the fact that the local factory has closed down and that entire families have lost their work, hence coming to the city. Was it important to you that you did address the economic realities of life in Turkey?

NBC: Well that was not my first interest actually but I needed a reason for the young boy to come to the city. In those days there was a future crisis in Turkey and it influenced everybody's life, not only the poor people but the rich people also. I am interested in the inner life of the people but this fact came as a result of the background of Yusuf.

JW: I think that that the moment where Mahmut rediscovers the silver watch he believed Yusuf to have stolen is pivotal.

NBC: He wanted to take advantage of this situation in the relationship because he wanted Yusuf to feel guilty. By means of that Mahmut can be more powerful.

JW: Mahmut seems to be paralysed by apathy and there's a great sequence where he is on a shoot and sees this perfect photo opportunity with the sun and mountains and he asks Yusuf to set up the camera but then says, 'No, fuck it.'

NBC: I think this scene would illustrate the type of character that he is. I know this situation very well because I was a photographer. When you are in your car in the countryside you always see something to shoot but the motivation or the urge, that's the degree of your love of your art and it determines whether you stop and shoot it or not. I wanted to show that the distance between his ideals and his real life is growing. So this scene would help me to do that whilst also typifying photographers.

JW: This moment also hints at the film's humour, as does Mahmut becoming stuck in his own mousetrap and when he switches from pornography to an arty Tarkovsky film to avoid detection.

NBC: It's not an intention to be humorous, it was more a reflection of how I see life. Even in the most tragic situations I see humour. Humour can underline tragedy better if they are together; they are like a sister and brother. I also stepped in this kind of mousetrap but I never laughed at it. When you look from outside it is funny and I think with our life, if you are living alone in a house for a long time, habits and our obsessions begin to be funny because of the type of society we live in. In the house we relax and we live without masks.

JW: We've touched on the reference to Tarkovsky in *Uzak*. Is he a major influence?

NBC: I am the sum of everything that has influenced me in my life. My observations, my own life, other films, everything. Tarkovsky is one of the filmmakers that has influenced me but even more than Tarkovsky I would cite Ozu. Not only with his films but also with his decisions. As a filmmaker he became more and more sophisticated and in his final films reduced things such as camera movement to the bare minimum. The subject matter also narrowed and this kind of attitude especially influenced me. Also, I think Ozu has a great amount of compassion for his characters and for people in general.

JW: Is the editing process one that you particularly enjoy? Most directors I talk to find it to be so.

NBC: It is the same for me because it is here that I can really be alone. You have to deal with many kinds of people during shooting. In the script you are also alone but I am not very successful with that; it is the most difficult part for me. In editing it is real joy. I can also work at night; so I like it the most.

JW: Did the film drastically change during the editing process?

NBC: Yes, it changed a lot. Actually there were many more scenes that I found un-necessary in the editing stage.

JW: What sort of scenes did you edit?

NBC: They were more about the relationships of the characters. For instance there was a small nephew and a birthday scene. There was also a murder in the apartment upstairs. It felt like something from an action movie and didn't suit *Uzak* at all. What this sequence did do, however, was provide the motivation for Mahmut and Yusuf going together on the photography trip. Now they go without any specific reason.

JW: The film is beautifully composed. I've never seen Istanbul in snow. I was reminded of Kiarostami in the way you position your figures within their landscapes.

NBC: I don't plan these things that far in advance. For me, you get in a car and then begin to search with the actors and the crew the best way to shoot a scene. I improvise where to put the camera depending upon the locations and am not specific in this regard in the shooting script. I try to find a focal point for the camera and then begin to rehearse.

JW: There are not a huge amount of close-ups; you allow the camera to simply observe and allow things to unfold.

NBC: In my first film there was a lot of close-ups but with time I instinctively began to like them less. I think you should have a good reason for close-ups. If I can do it without a cut I prefer to do it without a cut but I am not obsessive about not cutting and so the scene should be a master shot. Again, I decide these instinctively and on location, not beforehand in the script.

JW: I did like the cut to a close-up of the keys Yusuf returns. It was such a melancholic moment. You get the sense that something has passed between these two people that will never be regained.

NBC: Actually, I wrote it and shot it more after he leaves the house but in the editing I think the keys were enough and if it's enough you don't need other things. I prefer to tell the story in the most minimalist way.

JW: For me I think the overriding feeling of the film is one of sadness. Do you consider it this way?

NBC: I put a little hope in the last scene. Mahmut smokes the cigarette that he refuses to smoke when originally offered to him. His smoking again can mean maybe again he is ready to change and perhaps has the potential to do so. Perhaps this is a sign of hope.

JW: I also found Mahmut's relationship with his ex-wife to be quite poignant. He follows her to the airport prior to her departure for a new life and then can't bring himself to actually say 'goodbye'. There's a wonderful shot where she spots him hiding behind a pillar and he jumps back behind it. Did you think he was aspiring to any kind of reconciliation?

NBC: Actually, he left his wife because he thought much more interesting things were going to happen in his life and she began to appear as an obstacle to him; I think many men in Turkey and in the world are like this. It's a kind of hope for him but if they come together again it will not work out I'm sure. He will be the same man.

JW: Are there autobiographical elements to the film?

NBC: Of course, yes. It's perhaps the most autobiographical film of mine. You can assume that about 40% of it is autobiographical. The script came out of my own experience and also my observations of my friends.

JW: Were the two lead actors – Muzaffer Özdemir and Mehmet Emin Toprak – ones you had considered or was there a long audition process?

NBC: These were actors who I also worked with on my previous films. I know them very well but on this film I wanted to work with different actors. I wanted the character of Yusuf [Toprak] to be younger at first and I put an ad in the newspaper and I tried many more people for that role. And for the photographer [Özdemir], I wanted to use someone else and made many test shots.

JW: Did you enjoy working with a combination of professional and amateur actors in this film?

NBC: Yes. In this film there are professionals as well, which is something I wanted to try as I've infrequently worked with trained professionals. The ex-wife, for instance, the janitor and also the lover of the photographer are all professional actors. But I think I prefer amateurs. Their responses are very good and they give themselves to the subject very seriously and with a lot of energy.

JW: And do you allow them to contribute to the script?

NBC: I don't show them the script as I want to see what they can do first. I show them the situation and what kind of things they should talk about and in the rehearsal I like to see what kind of things they can do, where they can imagine something I couldn't and if I don't like it I begin to change things. We try to find another balance in the scene and we come to a conclusion together. But I think amateurs can create a very nice style that you never imagine.

JW: How did the tragic death of Mehmet Emin Toprak affect you and did you see the major award he received for acting as recognition of his acting talents?

NBC: He was not only my actor but also my cousin and that increased my suffering in those days. After he received the prize in Cannes it was even more poignant.

JW: And, of course, the film also won a major prize in Cannes in its own right. As a filmmaker beginning to attain a reputation on an international level, how important are these festivals in bringing your work to a wider audience?

NBC: Actually I don't like to talk about my films too much but of course the festivals help a lot with regards to selling the film. This is especially true of Cannes. For this kind of film festivals are the best place for recognition and no one would even hear about the film without a festival as a platform. Cannes is a very strong festival, even if you don't win, because everyone is there. Also, more producers take interest in your work and you can find funding much easier.

JW: Do these festivals and awards bring compromise? You strike me as someone who cherishes their independence.

NBC: I've always produced my own films and I always put the money up myself without asking anyone else. But fortunately because I make low-budget films I always make a profit so I've never had a problem. There are more offers now to co-produce and things like that but I'm not sure. I am thinking about that. I finish the script and then decide what I can do.

JW: Would you consider working outside Turkey?

NBC: I am sure I want to make films in Turkey only.

JW: One sequence in *Uzak* that I particularly wanted to talk about before we conclude is the dream sequence where you play with the film speed.

NBC: Yes, there is one dream sequence for Yusuf where he sees a light in the room; also I manipulated the sound. It's actually not exactly a dream. There is a time between dreaming and waking where you don't understand what is happening but of course I shot this scene with half the frames per second. Something strange is going to happen. I wanted to add some kind of mystery to the scene because I wanted to separate it from the film. And I wanted to use only the objects in the room to express a sense of mystery.

JW: This may seem strange but the two central characters stayed with me after the film and I'm trying to work out why that happened. Are you able to speculate as to what will become of these characters?

NBC: Yusuf will find a solution. For Mahmut, I believe nothing will change, as I personally don't think much changes in life. If this was a Hollywood film I am sure they would contact each other but I don't want to alter the reality of things.

* * *

Guillermo del Toro

Born in Guadalajara, Mexico, in 1964, Guillermo del Toro studied scriptwriting with Mexican director Jaime Humberto Hermosillo, and was a founding member of the Film Studies Centre and the Muestra del Cine Mexicano (Mexican Film Festival) in his home town.

Of his numerous shorts (shot on Super-8, 16mm and 35mm) *Doña Lupe* (1985) and *Geometria* (1987) were selected for a dozen international film festivals. Del Toro studied special effects and make-up with legendary SFX artist Dick Smith and for ten years he was dedicated to this work through his company Necropia, where he supervised special effects make-up for several films, including *Bandidos* (1991), *Cabeza de vaca* (1991) and more than twenty episodes of the television series *La hora marcada* (1986), three of which he also wrote and directed. It was through his Necropia company that del Toro met leading producer Bertha Navarro with whom, alongside Laura Esquivel and Rosa Bosch, he formed the Mexico City-based production company Tequila Gang.

Cronos (1993), del Toro's first film as director, won the Critics' Week Award at the 1993 Cannes Film Festival. The film went on to win nine Mexican Academy awards and was recently voted by *Shivers* magazine as one of the best hundred horror films in the history of cinema. Subsequently blending more personal, Latin American projects such as *El espinazo del diablo* (*The Devil's Backbone*, 2001) with bigger-budget studio fare including *Mimic* (1997) and *Blade II* (2002), del Toro recently completed a successful synthesis of personal vision combined with major financing with the comic-book adaptation *Hellboy* (2004). A number of lucrative sequels are already planned.

Screened in the main competition at the 2006 Cannes Film Festival, *El Laberinto del Fauno* (*Pan's Labyrinth*) is a return to Spanish-language productions. A chilling story filled with fantastical creatures that deals with cruelty and repression set against the backdrop of the fascist regime in 1944 rural Spain, Alfonso Cuarón describes the film as 'an explosion of the full potential of Guillermo's mind'.

The interview took place in 2003 and extracts appear in *The Faber Book of Mexican Cinema* (Faber, 2006).

Jason Wood: How did your fascination with horror originally begin?

Guillermo del Toro: In the very beginning I stayed up late without permission from my parents to watch *The Outer Limits*. My brother and I were watching an episode called 'The Mutant' and I got very scared by the make-up that was created for Warren Oates in this episode and I went to my crib petrified. My older brother put two plastic fried eggs over his face and put my mother's stockings over his head and crept into my room. I was so scared. After that, I started waking up at night and would see monsters all around my room. The patterns in the shaggy 1960s carpet became for me a waving ocean of green fingers. I would become so scared that I would need to pee but was too scared to go the toilet and so ended up peeing in my bed. Of course, I was punished for this so I finally said to the monsters that if they allowed me to go to the toilet in the night then I would become their friend. Since this time I have had a very intimate relationship to creatures.

I would also say that being in Mexico I was exposed to a lot of brutal images and situations. I saw my first corpse aged four. It was a highway accident and we were coming back from Lake Chapala and a red car went zooming by and I remember my father saying very clearly, 'they are going to kill themselves' and a few miles later the same car was overturned and there was a guy crying and bleeding on the side if the road. He had a bottle of Tequila in his hand. There was another guy with his butt exposed and he had no head. You could see his head two metres away dangling in the barbed wire fence. That, plus the very gory religious imagery we have in Mexico combined to give me a very intimate relationship with death at a very early age. The fact is that I have a very active imagination and I lived with my grandmother for many weeks in a row and I used to sleep in an old bedroom at the end of a long corridor, and at night I would see in a super slow-motion manner a hand come from behind a closet and then the face of a goat. I could see it, it might have been in my mind but it was incredibly real to me.

JW: Have the films that you have made arrested some of this imagery?

GDT: I still to this day don't know how to be alone. When I met my wife I was for the first time in my life able to sleep in peace. Before that I was an insomniac. But since she has been with me it has been twenty years of peaceful sleeping. It still takes only for me to be alone for my imagination to go into overdrive.

JW: As you grew older did you actively seek out horror movies and horror directors?

GDT: I actually started to get excited by movie stars. My three favourite actors as a child were Boris Karloff, Vincent Price and Peter Cushing. I would start looking for them, as I didn't know anything about directors. I would just seek out the movies that they were in, as I knew that this guaranteed me of being in for some horror. Later, at a slightly older age I started to identify Lon Chaney, Lon Chaney Jr. and all the rest. I was not conscious of the director, but of the type of movie they were.

JW: You took writing classes with Jaime Humberto Hermosillo but then really began your career in special effects and make-up. Was this a result of your horror fascination?

GDT: Doing my short Super-8 films in Guadalajara I didn't have anybody to do effects for me. In fact, I didn't have anybody to do anything for me and was doing the catering, the lighting, the post-sound and just everything. Little by little other people began to ask me to do the effects for their movies. I was involved in a motorcycle accident with my wife that put me in bed for several weeks. I decided then to try and learn the craft professionally in order to gain a little bit of an edge for myself and start preparing for *Cronos*. *Cronos* took me eight years to do and one of the first obstacles that I found when talking to producers was being asked 'well, who is going to do the effects for this movie?' When I replied 'me' they expressed their lack of confidence in my being able to do this level of effects yet. I applied to a course run by effects maestro Dick Smith and during my bed-ridden days I proceeded to do a series of pencil and pen sketches and some very crude make-up effects. Dick told me that he liked my draughtsmanship but that he did not like the sculpting or the appliances. He thought that his course would help me make my movie and so agreed to let me try it. I literally got the course and then got a job at the same time.

JW: Was the course in Mexico or in the US?

GDT: You met with Dick in New York and then you had to practise in Guadalajara. Then you had to meet again for an evaluation after a few months. Anyway, I would meet with producers and agree to do the job for X amount of money which was always just barely enough to pay for materials and barely enough to re-invest in more equipment and materials. Eventually, when *Cronos* started my special effects company – Necropia – had twenty people and offices and was run as a great enterprise but we closed it at the start of *Cronos* because it had served its purpose. To this day, Necropia is a name that I own because I like it; it's my childhood.

JW: Why do you think horror as a genre is again so popular with audiences?

GDT: There is a morbid fascination that is part of human nature; we still secrete this fascination. It is not in everyone but it is certainly within most. I think that there is a thrill in seeing the worst possible outcome of anything. In some of us this manifests in the horror genre, others re-direct it to charity, but there is certainly a reassurance to our well-being to be able to vicariously see the misfortune of someone else. It makes us, I believe, more human to be in contact with our darker side and it is a fact that there was a time when early civilisations believed that the world was created and destroyed every day and every night. This is how strong our fear of the dark is. The other power of the genre is that there is no other that generates images that stay embedded in your mind so strongly. For example, there are millions of people in the world who still will not go in the water because of *Jaws* [1975]. There are millions of others who do not want to pick up a hitchhiker because of *The Texas Chainsaw Massacre* [1974].

JW: How did *Cronos* originally come about?

GDT: I had written *The Devil's Backbone* with the intention of having this script as my theses for Humberto Hermosillo but Hermosillo was very strict on presentation and formatting and did not like the way the script was formatted. Back in those days there were no computers; it was the start of the Corona word processor and only the very rich had it. I had typed my screenplay on my IBM electric typewriter and taken it to Hermosillo for him to read. He took it and threw it in the garbage, telling me that he will not read it until I learn to present my stuff more cleanly. I was so angry and so disappointed that I thought, screw it, I am going to write something else rather than go back and re-write the same script just because the margins weren't right. Looking back, it was not such a big loss because *The Devil's Backbone* evolved into a better movie. Anyway, I told Hermosillo that I was going to write a story in which a young girl gives her grandfather a vampire as a pet. The very first thing that generated the idea was a paragraph in a treatise about vampires where they say that in Europe the vampire first comes to the house and vampirises the family and then goes out to the world. My first impulse, which is not so much in the movie anymore, was to make a critique of the Mexican family in which the father figure returns and sucks them all dry. I started writing this version but found it too dogmatic, as if the thesis was overwhelming both the genre and the feeling of the movie. I said, what if I make it a kind of love story between the granddaughter and the grandfather and very much a story of acceptance? At that moment my grandmother was dying very slowly and I had come to accept and love her despite all our differences and the Catholic fears she had instilled in me as a child. *Cronos* is actually dedicated to her. I started to use the movie quite literally to heal and I do think that movies can have a cathartic effect.

JW: The absence of the father is never made entirely clear by the film.

GDT: It was clearer in the screenplay. The movie was about thirty minutes longer and in these minutes the origin of the missing parents is explained. This segment was really interesting. You know, *Cronos* does not remain one of my favourite movies; it's a sentimental favourite but it could have been so much better had I had a little more experience and had I had the knowledge to bring the whole screenplay to the screen. All the subplot of the father and the granddaughter was very rich and my hope is that one day the screenplay will be published in English. It exists in Spanish but not English. It turns out that the granddaughter's parents died in an accident and the grandfather writes her a letter every week as if it were from them. The letters make out that the parents are still travelling. The grandmother feels that this is insane and that her husband should explain to his granddaughter what being dead means. In the end when she accepts him finally dying, with the knowledge of the full screenplay, it becomes quite a beautiful thing.

JW: As well as critiquing Mexican families, at least in its original form, *Cronos* also comments on the vampiric relationship between Mexico and the US.

GDT: *Cronos* is the prefect example of the feeling that your first movie will also be your last. You try to put everything that you have ever wanted to say about a particular subject in it. I wanted to show the vampiric relationship between the nephew and the uncle and of course the vampiric relationship between Mexico and the United States. This is why the date in the movie – which we see on a newspaper – is 1997, even though the film was made in 1993. I wanted it to be set in a post-NAFTA [North American Free Trade Area] Mexico.

Ultimately I think that it was very accurate in terms of what happened. That is why all the signs that you see in the street are in Chinese, English and Russian. I made a fictional Mexico that was much more cosmopolitan. To me the movie also explores on numerous levels the relationship that characters have with time and age and death. You have the grandmother who refuses to age by trying to fit into the same dress that fitted her last year; you have the millionaire who does nothing but shit and piss all day, living like a Howard Hughes-type recluse in his room but wanting to live forever out of sheer greed. And you have the nephew who wants to change his flesh to become more handsome. The only truly mortal character in the film is the daughter, who does not care about time and is immune to the concept of death. By the same token I wanted to show a vampiric chain that went all the way to the insect locked within the device. That's the ultimate vampire and the ultimate victim. It is locked there like a living filter and is at the same time the master and the slave.

JW: How did you conceive of this device?

GDT: The outside of the device was designed with a painter friend of mine and we sat down together and I explained that I wanted it to be like a Fabergé egg. This is obviously pertinent because the egg is the symbol of immortality and of eternity. We filled the film with images of immortality, for example the serpent that bites its own tail. In early cultures that symbolised immortality. The very shape of the device was intended to remind of a scarab, also a symbol of eternity. There was a time when the producers refused to pay for the construction of the device and I said 'but we absolutely need it! It's the fugue point of the whole perspective of the movie. If you don't have the inside, then you don't have the movie.' I sold my own van and personally paid for the construction of the interior of the device, which was designed completely by me. It was designed to look like a big factory. Microscopic drama has always intrigued me and as a child I would lay on my belly on the patio and watch ants for hours. This entomological fascination goes all the way to the inside of the device, as I wanted to have the point of view of the insect. The insect is based on a prehistoric tic. It was very elegantly designed. I sculpted the tail and my father-in-law mechanised the tail and all the interior pieces. Incidentally, most of the mechanical parts that you see were wind-up devices extracted from toys. It took us over a year to build the devices. We built thirteen of them and every single one of them got stolen at the end of the shoot. I actually like this fact; someone at some point may have opened this case full of these devices and mistaken them for the real thing.

JW: *Cronos* also mediates on the ancient history of Mexico with the device originally being brought to Mexico by an exiled alchemist. Was this an intentional comment on the mixed people that today exist there?

GDT: I was actually more interested in opening the movie like a Hollywood movie. Open it as if you are about to see a super-expensive production but then this production only lasts three minutes. Then you go in to meet the most boring guy on earth. This is what I was attracted to. It's like beginning with a Mexican version of *War of the Worlds* with all of the spaceships arriving and then cutting to a Mexican family working in their fields on their cows and seeing the invasion from their perspective. It's really about the everyday-guy perspective of a Hollywood premise. The image that better represents *Cronos* for me is that of the guy licking the blood from the nosebleed on the toilet floor. There were so many walkouts during this scene. What a waste, it was an extremely beautiful bathroom. There is, however, something about this shot that gets to the very root of revulsion.

JW: Another iconic moment is the police discovery of the body being bled in the alchemist's apartment.

GDT: I also wanted this scene to comment on the rather sad nature of the alchemist's life. During the hundreds of years that he lived he became a recluse, his only company was a hanging corpse.

JW: Did you allow any specific horror films to exert an influence?

GDT: Not really but I do think that *Cronos* and the hanging corpse shot in particular is influenced by Hammer and the sense that you sometimes got from their Dracula movies that it can be very lonely to be immortal. I wish on *Cronos* that I had had a little more experience and a little more budget and then some of the stuff would have had more clarity. That said, I am very happy with some of the images in the film and that one is certainly one of them.

JW: How did you find Ron Perlman who plays the image-obsessed nephew?

GDT: It is with great pride that I say that Jean-Pierre Jeunet and Marc Caro cast Perlman in *La cité des enfants perdus* (*The City of Lost Children*, 1995) after seeing Perlman in *Cronos* whilst they were jurors at a film festival. I wanted to do the opposite of what usually happens in Hollywood movies, such as *Raiders of the Lost Ark* (1981) in which Alfred Molina plays a completely two-dimensional Indian. I really hate it when Hollywood shows Mexicans or Latin Americans as sweaty villains with a big moustache. I wanted to do that to the American characters. I was very conscious that the American characters should be like comic-book villains. Ron Perlman was exactly right to bring a bit of colour and a little bit of a flourish to his character. I told him that his character was a big guy but his nose was his Achilles heel. If you observe the movie carefully you see him constantly smelling everything and paying attention to his nose. I should point out that like most of my films, and this is something that I will do again and again, I did not set *Cronos* in any real world; I don't try to represent reality exactly as it is. I always try to take it a couple of notches above. The Spanish civil war in *The Devil's Backbone* looks like a Sergio Leone western, except at night where it looks like a Mario Bava movie. The New York in *Mimic* does not bear any resemblance to the real New York.

JW: One of the most striking aspects of your films is that you are not afraid of subjecting your child characters to horror. This is rare. American films seldom show child characters undergoing horrifying ordeals. I remember very clearly when I first saw *Mimic* and you actually killed off one of the two kids who breaks into the basement.

GDT: It is something that I really take very seriously when I make the movies. I feel that there is so much more danger in showing kids in a movie about giant dinosaurs and claiming that the dinosaurs won't eat them. In reality, they would. I think it's best to show that should a child ever encounter danger then he or she should act cautiously. Also, most people may remember an altered version of their childhood but for me my childhood was the most brutal and frightening period of my life. I think that children react very naturally to horror, perhaps in a more natural and pure way to adults, and are very much exposed to it. Horror comes from the unknown and you only react with horror to things that you don't know. I want to show that children do not necessarily need to fear what they know, such as the granddaughter in *Cronos* but also that they do need to show caution to what they do not know. If they don't, just like adults, they are apt to pay the consequences. Horror is an extension of the fairytale and in fairytales ogres and wolves ate children and I think that it goes to the roots of storytelling to have children as vulnerable.

With regard to the scene that you mention in *Mimic*, I shot that very slowly over a single day paying very careful attention to pull back and show the final moments from a wide angle. This was for fear of censorship. With every frame I shot I feared that it would never be included in the final movie. Thankfully it is and it remains not only my favourite scene from the film but I think amongst the very best things I have done. I don't like *Mimic* as a whole but that scene and the scene of Mira Sorvino being abducted on the platform are two of the best scenes I have ever shot.

JW: What were the circumstances that led to the invitation to direct *Mimic*?

GDT: Well, four years passed between *Cronos* and *Mimic* and that period passed because I didn't know then what I know now. At the end of *Cronos* I was in incredible personal debt to the tune of a quarter of a million dollars; I may have made a career on *Cronos* but I certainly didn't make any money. I was desperate because I was in no position to have this kind of debt. My father helped me and told me he would take the debt but that he wanted to be paid back in dollars. I watched in horror as the value of the dollar rose. Out of the blue came the offer to meet with Universal Studios to discuss the possibility of a project. On meeting with them it was explained that they would pay me $125,000 for writing a screenplay. I was immediately interested but added that I would only do it if the screenplay were something that I wanted to do. Believing it would be my next movie I wrote *Spanky*, based on the novel by Christopher Fowler. I really think that it was one of the best things I have ever written. Perhaps because of that it was rejected by the studios who said that it was too dark and unlike any other movie in that it sounded like a comedy but then ended up as a tough horror film. I said exactly, that's the whole spirit.

JW: Will *Spanky* no longer happen with you?

GDT: Every year I really try and each time I meet an investor I say 'how about this one?' It has got to the point where it has aged a little bit and I will probably have to re-write it. I lost about a year on this one. Then I started developing a period project and Universal said that they didn't do period movies. Lo and behold *The Mummy* [1999] a few years later. After two years came the chance of doing *Mimic* as a short film. It was actually part of an anthology movie and at the same time I was also developing *The Devil's Backbone* and we were finding very little support in Mexico.

I was never the darling of Mexican cinema because the story of *Cronos* and the Mexican institutions is not a very happy one. When I first presented the film to IMCINE [the Mexican Film Institute] they complained that it was not an art movie; it was a vampire film and that I should go and get some private money. I disagreed. I said that it was an art film and horror can also be art. They invited me to go away and storyboard the movie and come back. I went and storyboarded the movie and then they said that they wanted to see the device in a drawing. After the drawing they wanted to see it physically because they wanted proof that I could create it. In the end it took us almost three years to get the financing secured from IMCINE. When we showed them the finished film they said this is a horror movie and it's not going to go to any festivals, it isn't going to win any prizes. They felt that nobody was ever going to see the movie and that they had wasted their money. Our entire budget for *Cronos* in Cannes was ten posters and a roll of scotch tape. All the producers, my wife and myself slept in a one-bedroom apartment. I thought that IMCINE's attitude would change after *Cronos* won twenty-five international awards and after it became one of the most celebrated films from Mexico in many years. It didn't change.

JW: How did you find the experience of working in the States on bigger budgets and with actors such as Mira Sorvino and Jeremy Northam?

GDT: *Mimic* remains the hardest shooting experience of my life and it is right up there, pricking at my pain threshold. It was a combination of many reasons. Back then it was the most expensive movie Dimension had ever made and it was also by far the most expensive movie I had ever done. I experienced many hardships with that movie. I sustain the belief that you learn through pain and I certainly learned a hell of a lot. One of the main things I learned and which I cherish to this day is that you are always making two movies. You are making the movie that the screenplay is telling and you are making a movie that is pure image, pure cinema. Cinema has a kinship to theatre and other forms of drama in that it needs a narrative, characters and an arc but also in the fact that it may remain full of memorable images in spite of the screenplay not being completely there or screwed with by the powers that be, and that is the most intimate part of the movie and the part that nobody should be able to take away from you. It was a revelation and almost like an out-of-body experience. To this day I can see this being the case with filmmakers such as Dario Argento and Lucio Fulci. Sometimes their films can be completely incoherent but out of this mass of incoherence a beautiful and absolutely powerful image arises.

JW: Did you find yourself subjected to audience preview screenings?

GDT: Yes and much more besides. As well as being hard for me, it was also a hard movie for Miramax to make and I didn't make it any easier on them. At the end of the day with a cold head and a cool heart I see that they wanted to do *Alien* [1979] and I wanted to do *Mimic* and so we ended up with *Alien 3½*.

JW: To jump forward again to *The Devil's Backbone*, how did this eventually come together after the years labouring on the project, and why the decision to have a Spanish Civil War backdrop as opposed to the Mexican Revolution?

GDT: I had been trying to make it fit with the Revolution for many years and for some reason it just wasn't working. I realised that the Mexican Revolution has never ended and secondly was a very complicated mess with factions being sub-divided into other factions. There were a series of internal wars in Mexico that didn't stop until the 1930s or later. It was very dirty metaphorically and I wanted the war to be a war that happened within a family. An intimate war where brothers killed brothers and that was the Spanish Civil War. I wanted a war movie where you could have the war be geographically far away but also have it created within the walls of the orphanage in a very metaphorical way. You have fascism represented by Eduardo Noriega's character and you have the people represented by the children and you have the old Republicans represented by Marisa Paredes and Federico Luppi. All of them felt they were safe from the effects of the war when they were really re-enacting the war bit by bit. I felt that the overwhelming image of the movie was the ghost looking at the bomb. It's a movie that doesn't say that everything ends up happily; it says that the bomb never exploded, the ghost never left the place and the only thing you have as a positive is that the children are going to march.

JW: How did you create the ghost in the film?

GDT: I have a very early drawing that I made when I finished *Cronos* that featured a man drowning in a pool with blood floating from his forehead. It was taken from below and I loved this image. All of a sudden I thought what if a ghost of a guy that his been thrown into a pool with an injury to his head actually walked around with a trail of blood? I found this idea so compelling that I thought this would be the only terrifying thing about the ghost. The rest of it would be like a porcelain doll. It would actually be quite a sad ghost. The idea of showing it very early in the movie was my hope that the movie would eventually clarify for the audience that you shouldn't be afraid of a ghost but that you should be afraid of the living. Never fear the dead, fear the living: they are the real danger.

JW: In terms of the perceived renaissance in Mexican cinema, your Tequila

Gang partner Rosa Bosch spoke of the fact that many Mexican directors working today are no longer working with their back towards the audience. Do you see this as a failing of earlier generations of Mexican directors?

GDT: Well, if you look at the 1970s films they were actually very successful. Arturo Ripstein, Felipe Cazals in their time with movies like *El castillo de la pureza* [*Castle of Purity*, 1972] or *Canoa* [1975]; these were very commercial movies. Now the times have changed and the audiences have changed. Many technical aspects have also changed. Many movies in Mexico remained shipwrecked in the 1970s for almost twenty years. In those twenty years the style of photography, the style of sound design and the style of storytelling completely changed, except in this little time capsule that is the Mexican film industry, and specifically the Mexican art film. All of a sudden things changed abruptly when our generation entered. Some people just very simply didn't like this. Others are very generous and serve as a link for the new generation, in my case Hermosillo and Ripstein were both incredibly generous with me when I was starting but some others really resented it. We almost had a very sad epilogue about the Mexican industry a few weeks ago when they were trying to exterminate IMCINE and the CCC [Centro de Capacitación Cinematográfica] and I said to people that we had to all be united or together we would all go to hell as an industry.

JW: The audiences in Mexico are obviously very sophisticated. The success of something like *Amores perros* [*Love's a Bitch*, 2000] proves that they have moved far away from being content with watching the sex comedies and Hollywood genre rip-offs that were very much in evidence during the 1980s, by all accounts a very dark decade for Mexican cinema.

GDT: I think that audiences are incredibly hungry to see themselves in movies that go beyond what they were previously used to, the dumb comedies, the soaps and the like. They want to see themselves in that car wreck in *Amores perros*. For better or for worse there is a level of excitement that Alejandro [González Iñárritu] gives to his images and there is a level of excitement amongst audiences in saying 'that's the street where I work' or 'there's the street where I live', and there is certainly a level of excitement in recognising yourself in a genre situation. Beyond the social exploration of *Amores perros* the foremost characteristic of that movie is the sheer level of adrenalin. It's a non-stop ride in your hometown that gives such a high. Why do all the chases have to happen in Manhattan? Why do all the exciting things have to happen in America? Why can we not have exciting things happen here in Mexico? What is wrong in doing *Y tu mamá también* [*And Your Mother Too*, 2001], a film described by some Mexican critics as *Beavis and Butthead* as a sex-comedy/road movie in which we recognise our social identity? This film took a proven generic mould and turned it on its head. Where is the sin in that? I really don't understand it. This is what makes it good. The worse and most classist position that a filmmaker can take is to disregard the audience. To disregard the audience is to die and we live in dangerous times because there will come a point where the government will decide to pull the subsidies, to disconnect the patient.

JW: It is tragic that an industry that in so many ways seems so healthy should in reality be ailing. With 3,000 screens, more than any other country in Latin America, a vastly increased market percentage for locally-produced films contributing to a 154 million admissions in Mexico in 2002 – making the country the fifth-largest market anywhere in the world – all should be well. Yet the difficulties of producing films in Mexico, either through private investment or through Fidecine and Foprocine, the two government funds, have reached a critical level.

GDT: The main problem with the industry is the way in which the box-office revenue is distributed. Most of it goes to the exhibitor with very little going back to the producer. This is why we are fighting transnational companies, companies that are very aware that Mexico is an incredibly important market and it is important that legislation changes at a federal level in order for our industry to survive. Mexico has an incredibly rich heritage and history of great movies in all genres and to let our identity in cinema be lost would be a tragedy.

I think also that our government's lack of interest in culture is replicated internationally. There does not seem to be much hope in the world right now. I remember at the time that I felt that NAFTA was so ill-planned as it was passed without getting any consensus from the world of culture as to how to best protect the industry and the local culture. We were raided and invaded by media companies and there was nothing there to protect us. To be honest, our current president is not unlike our other presidents in his disinterest in culture.

JW: How did you find the co-production process on *The Devil's Backbone*? When I spoke to Carlos Carrera [director of *El crimen del Padre Amaro/The Crime of Father Amaro*, 2002] he welcomed the fact that these co-productions enable films to get made but he did bemoan some of the compromises they can enforce.

GDT: I had a very happy experience on the film. Film has shown me over the years that you have to remain malleable when faced with financial proposals.

You have to find the positives under these circumstances. I think that the word 'defect' is a word that we use when we do not correctly observe our characteristics; if you correctly observe your characteristic then it becomes a characteristic and you learn how to deal with it instead of calling it a defect. I think there was a very clear way for me to finance *The Devil's Backbone* and I had already set it during the Spanish Civil War so I didn't have to make changes as financial considerations as I already was creatively engaged before talking to Pedro and Augustin Almodóvar. I also felt that I would benefit from the international cast and I would benefit from the international experience and I was happy to open myself to it. I learned a lot from working in Europe and especially loved the fact that they drink wine at lunch break.

JW: You earlier mentioned some of the visual influences on the film but I wondered if you also paid attention to some of the other films that use the Spanish Civil War in an allegorical sense. I am thinking specifically perhaps of Victor Erice's *El espíritu de la colmena* [*The Spirit of the Beehive*, 1973].

GDT: *The Spirit of the Beehive* is a seminal movie for me. I even modelled the girl in *Cronos* exactly on Ana Torrent. That movie, along with the films of Buñuel and the films of Hitchcock is almost a part of my genetic make-up and is buried deep in my DNA. Visually, however, I tried to make *The Devil's Backbone* completely different to other Spanish Civil War movies. They normally texture it in a different way. I wanted to get the dryness of the landscape and the fact that the orphanage seemed to be almost out of a Mervyn Peake novel, a lonely building in a land of nothing. One of the things that intrigued me about the Spanish Civil War and indeed something that intrigued me about any war, even as a kid, was why don't they go away, why don't they hide in a cave? How can you not see the oppressors coming? All these little musings are because war is not really a purely geographical occurrence. It really permeates our everyday and every act that we do. I remember that the release of *The Devil's Backbone* in America was at a very unfortunate time, shortly after the events of 11th September. Seeing the film in a post-11th September climate made me understand things in the movie that I had not understood before. It became more relevant. I also understood that when the worst possible situation occurs you do not have to be near it, it comes to you.

JW: There are references to Hitchcock and Buñuel in the film. You have the wooden leg worn by the Marisa Paredes character and the very Hitchcockian keyhole shot.

GDT: Both Hitchcock and Buñuel have great keyhole moments. There is a great one in *El* [1952] that involves a knitting needle ready to poke out somebody's eye. In order to get our shot we made an oversized keyhole. I used to call it the Hitchcock keyhole because it was like one of the oversized props that Hitchcock used to get depth of field in films such as *Dial M for Murder* [1953] or the glass of milk that Ingrid Bergman drinks in *Notorious* [1946]. It is certainly a Hitchcock-ian/Buñuelian moment and I dreamt for so long about this sequence and I wanted so much for it to be successful. When I finally made it I was filled with a childish sense of glee at being a little closer to my bastion of heroes.

JW: I read a quote from you where you said that you hate to shoot dialogue but love to shoot cinema.

GDT: Well some people are very good at it like Woody Allen or Quentin Tarantino and I admire them but when I shoot dialogue it is so painful for me. My ideal movie would have no dialogue; it would just be a camera implicating the viewer in the action. I try to use the camera as if it were a curious child, always tiptoe-ing and trying to get a better view but it keeps being pulled away, like when your mother is pulling you away from the scene of an accident but you keep rubber-necking to try to catch the last glimpse of the victim. I love to use the camera in this way to play with perspective. This occurs in *Cronos* where Ron Perlman is beating the crap out of Federico Luppi in front of the billboard. The camera pulls back a mile away so that you see the whole billboard with them very tiny. I like to play hide and seek with the moment and be dragging the camera away just as the worse is about to happen. I have a killing in *Hellboy* that is very much like that. I have the camera in a position and then move it so that you go 'whoa, did I just see that or not?'

JW: What can you say about your regular director of photography Guillermo Navarro? I understand that you are good friends as well as creative partners.

GDT: Guillermo and both trust each other implicitly. I only second-guessed him once and he said 'okay, I am going to do it the way you want it and then we'll see it on the dailies'. We saw his way and then my way and his way was infinitely better. This was very early on during *Cronos*. We both have no ego problems and understand that collaboration is collaboration and so we are free to suggest things to each other. To this day, he understands that I am not territorial but that I do my compositions and my planning of camera moves so far in advance that if you bring another idea it has to be a very well-thought one. In terms of light I can only tell him what I want in terms of how much darkness and how much light and then leave the execution entirely to him. I really trust Guillermo completely.

It has come to the point where it is almost spooky how connected we are; we can complete each other's sentences. Few people know this but Guillermo and I were meeting at my home in Austin to discuss the visuals of *The Devil's Backbone* whilst Guillermo was shooting *Spy Kids* [2001] for Robert Rodriguez. I was showing him some Hammer movies and some Bava movies and he literally arrived to the set of *The Devil's Backbone* with only half a day of prep. He shot *Spy Kids* on a Friday, travelled on Saturday, prepped for half a day on Sunday and then began shooting on Monday. We didn't feel rushed because we know each other so well. After we had tested different kinds of filters for the brown sepia tones we knew exactly what we were doing from that moment on. Guillermo is one of those brothers that you are not given genetically but that you somehow find through life. We bought our house only because Guillermo lives nearby.

JW: How did you originally meet?

GDT: I was doing storyboards for an action sequence in a Mexican movie called *Morir en el golfo* [1990] and Guillermo was the **director of photography**. Guillermo was famous in Mexico for being ill-tempered and when I arrived on the set everybody told me that he was in a really bad mood and not to provoke him. Well, I am famous for being imprudent and stood next to the camera and suggested that he change the lens for this shot. He was looking through the eye-piece but stopped to turn to me and said 'Listen kid, do you even have any fucking idea what the lens is looking at?' I got immediately red-faced and said 'I'll show you what this fucking lens is looking at' and walked right in front of it. Guillermo smiled and said 'I like you.' From that moment on we have rarely had a bad day.

Guillermo also led me to my long-time producer, his sister Bertha Navarro. He suggested that Bertha produce *Cronos*. We met and she hired me to do indigenous make-up and effects for *Cabeza de Vaca*. I said how much work is it and she said on the very worst of days you will be making-up anything up to 200 extras. I said could I hire an assistant? I did the entire movie – a huge enterprise – with one assistant and my wife. Bertha recognised how crazy I was in terms of commitment and loved that and offered to read my screenplay. Just as I say Guillermo is a brother I feel that Bertha is one of those mothers that you also find along the way. I really love Bertha and we are incredibly loyal to one another. I will never forget that Bertha believed in me, a twentysomething kid from Guadalajara who wanted to make this massive vampire project.

JW: Speaking about the differences between your Spanish-language work and your American studio pictures you have said, 'I don't park my car in the dining room and I don't eat dinner in the garage.' The perception is that the Spanish-language films are your more personal works and your American films are where you get to work with big budgets and hopefully have a lot of fun.

GDT: The only movie that blurs this line is *Hellboy*. This is really a combination of both.

JW: And *Blade II*? How does that compare with the experiences of *Mimic* and *Hellboy*?

GDT: It was a very joyful experience. It was the opposite to *Mimic* in that I didn't have any aspirations to making a personal film and just wanted to give a personal touch to a movie that was unequivocally commercial. I was in total agreement with the producers and the studio on the movie we were making. On *Mimic* we were making two different movies. On *Blade II* I was very aware of what I was making and thoroughly enjoyed every minute of it. I was very afraid of fucking around with the screenplay too much because I understood that the franchise had its own rules.

JW: Does the responsibility of a franchise not fill you with fear? There is a reasonably long list of directors who when put in charge of a franchise were hauled over the coals for fucking it up? Look at David Fincher with *Alien 3* [1992].

GDT: The main thing was that I felt that I could exercise some muscles that I was going to need on *Hellboy*. Also, I have all my life made mid-term plans. When I was a kid I decided to study make-up so that I could set up my own make-up company to allow me to do the effects to my own movie. After *Mimic* I said that I am going to do my Spanish movie first and then I will do an American commercial movie and the two together will get my *Hellboy*.

JW: So *Hellboy* is the one that for a long time you have been working towards?

GDT: Yes. Just like *The Devil's Backbone* was sixteen years in the waiting. I can tell you right now that my two favourites of my own films so far are *The Devil's Backbone* and *Hellboy*. I love them both and I could die a happy man just knowing that somewhere there are others who also like these movies too.

JW: How does *Hellboy* fit into the collective works of Guillermo del Toro with its recurring emphasis on horror, religion, insects, machinery and children?

GDT: The way I view movies now is the same way I viewed my Super-8 movies. I think that I did one Super-8 film that was made in many parts and was ultimately good just for the learning. The way I see the movies that I have done is that to me they are all one movie that to me is one big movie that says, 'Hi, I'm Guillermo del Toro and I'm kind of ugly and disfranchised.' *Hellboy* is ultimately what I think an atomic adventure-book movie could be and is very different from the other comic-book franchises and has a huge heart and a lot of beauty in the horror. It also has a lot of beautiful horror and very beautiful creatures and it's a celebration of otherness and being different. It is a beauty and the beast story where at the end they kiss and they both turn to beasts.

I think that a career is a learning curve. Alfonso [Cuarón] and I have discussed this many times. I remember Alfonso being revered as a visionary when *A Little Princess* [1995] came out and maligned as a hack when *Great Expectations* [1997] emerged. I went through similar stuff with *Cronos* and *Mimic* and I said to Alfonso people seem to think that you are making a definitive last statement with every movie. This is not the case; you are searching in the way that a painter may experiment with a blue period or a green period. Goya is one of my favourite painters and I think that Goya didn't really come to be until the last days of his life when he produced his 'Black Paintings'. That is the ultimate expression of him. The same with Alfred Hitchcock. I think that the only real glimpse of the very dark and very complex man that Alfred Hitchcock was comes with watching *Frenzy* [1972]. Sometimes you do not realise who you are until the very last. The opposite to me happened with Buñuel. I think that Buñuel did some of his best work very early on and then went to read what the critics had to say about him and started to make movies that were a little too hermetic. I maintain that his Mexican period is his best period. We are searching but really all our movies at the end of the day are one.

JW: Given this idea that you are searching and that each film is part of a wider work in process, how do you view the criticisms that Mexican directors suffer for choosing to work outside of their country?

GDT: My answer is very simple. I work where I am allowed to, be that Spain, Prague or the US. Wherever I go, however, I am a Mexican filmmaker and that is a fact that gets lost on the people who make these criticisms. They believe – in what is a form of ultimate racism – that if you leave then you are not one of us and you are not going to come back. Well, Alfonso and I came back. Alfonso stayed and did *Y tu mamá también* whilst I was rejected and went to do *The Devil's Backbone*. I was then rejected again because even though *The Devil's Backbone* was half-Mexican in terms of finance the authorities decreed that it was a Spanish film.

JW: We've talked a lot about your contemporaries Alfonso and Alejandro and it is obvious from my talking with you all that you are great friends and form a close-knit circle. Does it help to have these means of support and advice from your co-filmmakers?

GDT: Alfonso was starting *Harry Potter* [*and the Prisoner of Azkaban*, 2004] and asked me if I would recommend some creature designers. I recommended a few that he then proceeded to use. When I was finishing *Cronos* I was really desperate because the first cut was horrible. I showed it to Alfonso and he asked if I had edited the first part. I told him that another editor had done it and he recommended that I do it myself. We tried it right there and took out a lot of hot air in a single afternoon. He literally changed the movie. With Alejandro, I didn't know him back then but Alfonso had told me that I should see *Amores perros*. I saw it and called Alejandro to tell him that he had made a masterpiece but that it was twenty minutes too long. What happened, happened. To this day Alfonso, Alejandro and José Luis García Agraz are the Mexican directors that I keep close contact with. I have lost contact with Arturo Ripstein and Hermosillo but these other guys have become my network.

* * *

Claire Denis

Born in Paris in 1948, Claire Denis was raised in Africa until she was fourteen, her colonial existence later exerting a huge influence on her films. Studying in France, Denis graduated from the Institut des Hautes Études Cinématographiques in 1972, further learning about filmmaking as an assistant to a number of notable directors including Costa-Gavras, Jacques Rivette, Wim Wenders and Jim Jarmusch.

Wenders helped to secure funding for Denis' directorial debut *Chocolat* (1987), an exploration of colonial life and emotional conflicts in 1950s West Africa as viewed through the eyes of a young French girl. Denis would go on to explore outsiderism and themes of racial and sexual conflict and familial dysfunction in films such as *S'en fout la mort* (*No Fear, No Die*, 1989), *J'ai pas sommeil* (*I Can't Sleep*, 1993), TV's *US Go Home* (1994) and *Nenette et Boni* (1996). The latter won the Golden Leopard at the Locarno International Film Festival.

Working with a group of long-time collaborators, including cinematographer Agnès Godard, editor Nelly Quettier and sound designer Jean-Louis Ughetto, Denis has developed a highly individualistic style, replacing the conventional devices of narrative storytelling – dialogue, psychological realism and scenic continuity – by favouring optical and sound elements in order to tell a story in purely visual and aural terms.

Beau Travail (*Good Work*, 1999), in which Herman Melville's *Billy Budd* is relocated to East Africa, has brought Denis her most lasting acclaim. Starring Grégoire Colin, Michel Subor and Dennis Levant, the film follows the obsessive rituals and male-bonding routines of French Legionnaires in Djibouti.

Since this interview took place in 1999, Denis has completed three further uncompromising features, *Trouble Every Day* (2001), *Vendredi Soir* (*Friday Night*, 2002) and *L'Intrus* (*The Intruder*, 2004). Denis also contributed a segment to the portmanteau picture *Ten Minutes Older: The Cello* (2002). Her most recent project is the documentary *Vers Mathilde* (2005), a look at the work of French choreographer Mathilde Monnier.

This interview originally appeared in *Enthusiasm 03* in autumn 2000.

Jason Wood: How did you set about adapting Herman Melville's *Billy Budd* for what would become *Beau Travail*?

Clare Denis: The project didn't start through a desire to adapt *Billy Budd*. It was proposed that I would do some work for the French/German TV station Arte, and the best answer to their proposal was to make a film in Djibouti about the Foreign Legion. The proposal revolved around the question of how it feels to be a stranger, and then I found out that what I knew best about the world of men with its ways, its rules, its organisations are the things I have read in Melville, perhaps without even knowing it. I would never have thought of adapting *Billy Budd*, never for one moment. One reason is because I was not much interested in Billy Budd, but I immensely liked Claggart.

JW: You were also inspired by Melville's poem, *The Night-March*.

CD: I gave Denis Lavant a book of Melville's poetry that I was reading constantly to prepare for the film and I think we shared *that* instead of sharing a lot of psychological talk about the part, which I hate.

JW: The film is very sensuous, with a perfect synthesis between man and nature. This synthesis is largely achieved through the choreography.

CD: I knew Bernard Montet and I had wanted to work with him before but had never had the opportunity. We agreed that this was the right moment for us to work together. Two years ago I took Denis to a ballet choreographed by Bernardo. We didn't even have a script then. I didn't have dance in mind. I asked Bernardo to help me to create a group that would be of today and believable. We never mentioned the words 'dance' or 'ballet'. We spent hours together in a place in Paris performing physical exercises that any soldier would do. Slowly, little by little, we had the music, we added this to the exercises. We used the same music whilst shooting. We had playback on set, in the middle of the desert.

JW: Let's talk about the astonishing dance that Denis Lavant performs to the Corona record at the very end of the film.

CD: When I saw Denis with the gun, it was then I thought that the dance should be at the end. We all felt like Denis, we knew Galoup's dance was going to be the answer to everything, because of the construction of the film, the soldiers exercising during the day and the girls dancing in the club during the night, the pattern of day/night, day/night. In fact, the only reason we did two takes of the dance was because we could not see dailies and to be safe in case something went wrong in the first take. But in that first take, in just one take everything was said, for Denis, for the crew, for all the actors. That one take was the end of Djibouti. It was finished. Everything was expressed in that dance.

JW: How did you settle upon Djibouti as the location for the film?

CD: I knew Djibouti since I was a child and when I was preparing the film I made five trips there for location scouting and took a lot of pictures. Certain locations like the nightclub I wanted – the Las Vegas – and parts of the country were not available for our film. There was a small town I wanted for a scene, Djoura, but there was the war with Eritrea and the army didn't want us to go there. The owner of the Las Vegas nightclub did not want us there because he thought we were anti-legionnaire.

JW: Did that become a problem throughout the shoot? Or was it the homo-sexual aspect of the film that troubled the authorities?

CD: No. The Djiboutian Republic almost immediately accepted the project before they saw the script – even though they would rather have had a documentary, but OK, they would accept fiction – but right away the French Foreign Legion people were not at all happy about me doing a film about them. It is also true that the French Foreign Legion do not like the subject of homosexuality and no not like the homosexual image.

JW: You described homosexuality as being like 'an invisible enemy' to the Legion.

CD: That's exactly so. The rumour had also started in Djibouti that because the film was made with so little money it could only be some kind of porno. A rumour in a small town is something you cannot stop.

JW: Was the small budget and lack of co-operation from the authorities a contributing factor to the final look of the film?

CD: If I had had a big budget and not having the co-operation of the army, I could have gone elsewhere. But we realised that the most important part was to be in this place, in this part of the world, with this group of men, and that we would manage.

JW: In all your films you deal with issues relating to minorities and the dispossessed. Do you feel that this is part of your responsibility as a filmmaker or is this something that just comes naturally?

CD: It has to be natural. A political gesture would not last long enough to sustain a film. When you start feeling out actors or people you have to have some solidarity or comradeship. I have tried sometimes to decide that one character will be the bad guy, and another the good guy, and then immediately find out, after writing, that both are equal: just two characters that conflict.

JW: Another theme that runs through your work is a sense of rootlessness and a focus on characters struggling to belong. Given your colonial childhood, do you see this as an autobiographical element?

CD: I had a great childhood and was very happy to grow up in such beautiful countries. You are lucky when you get to know other cultures. On the other hand, one has to cope with the world as it is. Cities are now full with people looking for a place to live, a place to work; cinema has to deal with what is going on while you are alive. I like reading science fiction, but I don't imagine myself doing a science fiction movie because there are so many things that I do not understand in my own times.

JW: You have made documentaries as well as fiction. Can you see yourself returning to the format?

CD: At the moment I have a documentary project that might happen. But sometimes it happens that one film or a project becomes more important or more urgent than another. *Beau Travail* for instance was not originated by me, but by

Arte. A year later I would not have done anything other than *Beau Travail*. I would have refused every other project. That's because my interest grew and I found the film in my mind. A project is only a project.

JW: You seem very proud of *Beau Travail* and it is your first film to secure UK distribution since your feature debut *Chocolat*. Are you disappointed that so few of your films have been released here?

CD: It's too hard to be disappointed. It is too difficult a life to figure out how to get into the production of projects, and on top of that to suffer from not being distributed. Life is too short! I was sad, of course. Also, I am not proud of *Beau Travail*. It is the result of a lot of energies from all over. To be proud would be very naïve. It was very lucky we could do this film because we were so close to not doing it and it is this that makes me very happy.

[At this moment, Denis Lavant appears.]

JW: Denis, your part must have been very tough to train for.

Denis Lavant: Strangely enough, I was already in shape before we started filming, before I arrived in Djibouti. I was slightly apprehensive of what lay ahead, but I was prepared.

JW: Claire, you have collaborated with Abdullah Ibrahim and your films are marked by your work with Tindersticks. Similarly, *Beau Travail* has an eclectic soundtrack featuring the Corona's *The Rhythm of the Night* and Neil Young. Is it a conscious decision to incorporate music so fully in your work?

CD: To me music is not some kind of decoration you add in the editing room. It has to be part of the work; otherwise I would rather not use it. A film can work without music but when it is part of the space, you have to work it in. Music for me, even while writing a script, is to open a new space for the film. Abdullah really gave me the space I needed to recreate a part of Cameroon – he was also a musician in exile in New York – so it was like a key to re-enter. With Benjamin Britten it is different, because I think Britten has been the source of most musicians who have written for cinema. He has been looted. When you listen to Britten you recognise a lot of music that has been used in films. I think it is music that – especially *Billy Budd* – has the space of the ocean and that the voice of the sailor and the voice of Claggart are creating a complete world in themselves. It was not easy to obtain the rights to use Britten but I refused to give in because it was a harmony and it had so much to do with the film. It took a year to be certain we could use it. On the set we had the music playing. It gave us the dimension of the ocean within the desert.

JW: Melville once again seems popular for directors to adapt. Why do you think that is?

DL: Distance. The distance between when the books were written and the here and now.

CD: Also, Melville has always been a popular author with artists, obviously with Britten, with painters and filmmakers. *Moby Dick* has been made into a film, and now *Billy Budd* for the second time. Last year Leos Carax made *Pola X* [1999], which was also based on a work by Melville, *Pierre or The Ambiguities*, which was different because it was a work that had not been explored before. If Arte had not asked me I would never have done it, not another adaptation of Melville because I feel that Genet's adaptation – *Querelle* – was the natural end to it. I think Melville's reputation will simply grow and grow.

JW: You have worked with important filmmakers: Rivette – and you collaborated with Serge Daney to make the documentary *Jacques Rivette, le Veilleur* [1990] about him – Costa-Gavras, Jarmusch, Wenders. How important was it working with these people?

CD: Working on *Paris, Texas* [1984] was especially important, if only because of the work with landscapes which has affected how I have worked with landscapes in my own work. I never use the landscape separately from the characters. However, I do think that you can learn more or just as much about how to make films from simply watching them rather than from continually working with filmmakers, unless of course you are an actor or a technician.

JW: *Beau Travail* is enjoying some fantastic reviews. Some have even gone so far as to call it one of the greatest films of the last decade.

CD: If I were to be very honest, it is difficult to understand what happened. What I mean is, what makes a film that film and not another one? It is not a question of being humble, it is purely that sometimes you put a lot of energy and, yet, something is missing, and sometimes you put a lot of energy and something comes out of it. It is the mystery of sharing.

* * *

Atom Egoyan

One of contemporary cinema's most distinctive voices, working also in tele-vision, opera and installation pieces, Atom Egoyan's work blends detachment and compassion to explore themes centring around identity and alienation, familial and personal dysfunction and sexuality.

Born in 1960 to Armenian refugees in Cairo, but relocated at an early age to Victoria, British Columbia, Egoyan initially grew up consciously rejecting his own ethnicity in favour of assimilation into his adopted culture. It was this experience that would later come to exert a profound influence over his work and thinking. His work is also marked, both visually and thematically, by a consistent exploration of the manner in which personal experience is mediated and manipulated by digital or video technology. A final key facet to the director's work is the key collaborative relationships he has formed from his first feature, *Next of Kin* (1984) to *Where the Truth Lies* (2005). Key personnel include Egoyan's wife and muse Arsinée Khanjian, producer Camelia Friedberg, editor Susan Shipton, cinematographer Paul Sarossy, and composer Mychael Danna. Egoyan's most recent work is the fascinating √ *Citadel* (2006), a video-diary exercise in which he charts his wife's emotional return to Lebanon. As one would expect with Egoyan, in the film nothing is what it seems.

He has also ventured into more mainstream territory with the Academy Award-nominated *The Sweet Hereafter* (1997), from Russell Banks's novel, wherein he utilises a fragmented narrative to convey a sensitive and poetic treatment of grief; *Felicia's Journey* (1999), another adaptation (this time from the novel by William Trevor) also effectively exploits the landscapes of the Midlands of the UK as *The Sweet Hereafter* does those of parts of western Canada.

I have had the pleasure of interviewing Egoyan numerous times throughout the years. The following exchange took place in London whilst the director was combining post-production work on *Felicia's Journey* with his directing of an opera, *Doctor Ox's Experiment*. The interview formed the basis for my film, *Formulas For Seduction: The Cinema of Atom Egoyan* (co-directed with Eileen Anipare, 1999).

Jason Wood: I wondered if we could begin by talking about *Calendar* [1993]. It's a hugely personal work that also seems to encapsulate the search for identity that punctuates your films.

Atom Egoyan: It is a really personal work and it is, along with *Family Viewing* [1987], the most autobiographical piece. It was so liberating to go to those church sites and to shoot those scenes and to realise a fantasy. As a young child in the diaspora your only contact with your culture is with those church images that are sent out every year and it was fascinating to actually tell the story behind those images and to situate myself behind some of the things that my character is saying. Specifically, I really thought that I was from here but being here has made me realise that I'm from somewhere else. That's so true.

As an Armenian born in Egypt, so much of what I thought was Armenian was actually Middle Eastern, but that's the culture I was raised in and that my parents were raised in and certainly that my wife has been raised in. Arsinée Khanjian was raised in Lebanon and what we share as what we think are Armenian are actually Middle Eastern traditions and when you go back to Armenia you realise that it's not a Middle Eastern culture at all, it's a Caucasian culture and their habits and their social manners are really different to what constitutes Armenian; and that was a shock.

When we went to shoot that film in Armenia, one of the reasons I designed it so that I was behind the camera the whole time was that we'd be able to come back and find another actor who could then dub over my questions and dialogue and then put those in those other scenes, but for technical reasons it was not possible. There was so much dialogue that was overlapping, and that meant that I had to play the part. It was such a low-budget film that we couldn't think of re-dubbing the whole thing and I was put in the situation where I play a character who I think was involved in my own worst nightmare of who I might be.

JW: And did you find acting that part to be in some way therapeutic?

AE: I don't find acting anywhere near as therapeutic as making a film. It was a character that I could almost see myself falling into should, heaven forbid, something like that ever happen to me.

JW: And what about some of your primary filmmaking influences?

AE: Well, next weekend I'm going to Belgium where they're presenting my imaginary cinematheque. I had to choose a hundred films and they're all over the map. There's certainly the great Italian masters like Antonioni, Pasolini and Bellocchio and Fellini of course. There's also certainly Bergman, Buñuel – a huge influence – and, of course, David Cronenberg. I'd also say a lot of the American cinema of the 1970s.

JW: I know that you're an admirer of Coppola's *The Conversation* [1974].

AE: *The Conversation* to me is a magnificent work and a moment of pure adulation was when I was on the jury in Cannes and Francis Ford Coppola was president of the jury and I actually took him the jacket of my video cassette of *The Conversation* to sign. All you have to do is remember what that work meant to you. I also had a close contact over the last year with Michelangelo Antonioni because I was supposed to be back-up director on his new project. No matter who that person is one can't forget the enduring effect that their work has had on us, and how it inspires us to be who we are. It's important to do things that keep that excitement alive.

JW: An incident that continues to reverberate is Wim Wenders gifting prize money he had won for *Wings of Desire* [1987] to your own *Family Viewing* at the 1987 Montreal Festival of New Cinema and Video.

AE: Truth be told, Wim hadn't seen the film at that point and he liked the idea of giving away his prize money to a film to which the jury had given an honourable mention. The great myth that I was circulating for a long time, and certainly didn't put an end to, was that he had seen the film and was so moved by it that he gave it the money. He did see it subsequently and thank God he liked it. I mean, he didn't ask for the money back, which would have been embarrassing.

That gesture of Wim's in 1987 in Montreal has had enduring ripple effects. For example, we're still talking about it. It was just so unexpected. I really do believe that one of the things that one is indebted to do is to help introduce new talent.

If you have some sort of status as a filmmaker and you are able to use that to support projects that you believe in, such as first features, then it is incumbent upon you to do that. I was lucky to start making my first films before *sex, lies and videotape* [1989] came out; that was the film of course that changed everything, the whole independent scene.

To me the incredible heroes of the independent scene are people like Hal Hartley, Jim Jarmusch and certainly Alan Rudolph and John Cassavetes before them. These people were somehow able to make their films in a system that was hostile to subsidies. There is also someone like Jon Jost who is one of the forgotten heroes of the American independent scene. Jost was a huge inspiration to me, making feature films for under $10,000. I think I'm in a really privileged situation because I'm able to make films that look and sound the way I would want them to be even if they had millions more. I'm working with a really dedicated crew and I'm working in a system that is able to cherish and support the films as a cultural product.

I have to also say that the films that I have loved have come out of similar situations. Bergman was working in a similar situation with the Swedish Film Institute and certainly a lot of the French cinema of the 1970s. There was subsidisation. It's very much like opera; people expect it to be subsidised in Europe. In America they don't and it's very much based on what the public wants, but that can be so inhibiting. One of the reasons that I really love working in Canada is that it's very difficult to be caught up in this momentum that has happened around first features coming out of the States, where there is a whole mythology about what that means and it has become the trademark of capitalism. You make something from your own ideas and you make it cheaply and suddenly it brings back tons of money; well, that's such a terrible pressure to put on someone at the beginning of their career.

JW: Do you try and deal equally throughout your work with issues of a national consciousness? *Gross Misconduct* [1992], which you made for Canadian television, deals very specifically with these issues, no doubt as a consideration for the audience who you were making it for.

AE: I felt that was a great Canadian gothic tale. That's why I was so excited about that project and it's still one of those projects that lingers in my mind. I always think should I remake it as a film. It is a great story and it actually did happen; it really is death by time zone. It is about this father who dreams that one day his little boy would become a hockey star and that he would watch him on television and on the night that all this happens the country decides not to show the game in his part of the country but to play another game, and this father just went crazy. He walked into his TV station, held it hostage, demanded that they play his son's game and took a pistol to the TV programmer's head and said 'there's something wrong with CBC programming and something's got to change'.

JW: And how do you react to a charge frequently levelled at you that your work is purely cerebral, structurally complex and thus somehow lacking in emotion?

AE: My reason for making films has always been emotional and I have never understood the claim that the work is cold, because it's really about people who are holding back emotion, but what they are holding back is torrential in a lot of situations. I look at *Speaking Parts* [1989] or *Family Viewing* and the experiences that these people have endured and are trying to cope with are operatic, but they have arrived at a point where they cannot afford to express those feelings. So I was confused by that accusation because I thought that there was something that wasn't getting across. Also, the films do use humour and there is an irony, which if you don't perceive the films that way then I don't think that you are getting the full experience. I do think that my strength is in setting up formulas for seduction based on structure, more so than on the image itself.

JW: How did you come to Russell Banks' *The Sweet Hereafter*?

AE: From the moment that I read that book I was aware that Banks has the ability to inhabit the voices of people other than himself and to find patterns to their speech and their mannerisms which means surrendering yourself completely to somebody else. I can't do that with my writing. I think I'm very good with strategies and structures and I can represent characters to a certain degree but after that I really want the actor to inhabit them. But here was this great material about a town – which I didn't know as I wasn't raised in a town like that – but Russell made me believe that I could create that town. I saw that novel as a gift.

JW: You've always worked closely with composer Mychael Danna but I think his contribution to *The Sweet Hereafter* is especially impressive.

AE: Mychael's contribution has been huge because in many of the films where you are not quite sure what the emotional life is, Mychael's music always tells you that there are emotions that are beneath the surface and there are times – and I think this is really powerful – where the music gives you more of an emotional feeling than the images do. And the shift and the movement of the film is to reconcile what you feel should be happening, through what the music is telling you, with what the images are saying, as opposed to film music, which just tries to elaborate what you're already seeing. That's something we're both keenly aware of and try to explore with every film.

If you look at *The Sweet Hereafter*, the use of early music is not what you'd expect. It has very specific associations, but to hear those medieval instruments suddenly paints the whole film as a Brothers Grimm fairytale. There are associations of a crusade, but you have a sense of it being of another time which gives it a timelessness when, in fact, it's very, very reality-based.

One of the fears that we had about the film was that it wouldn't be a TV film about an accident, because we can get all that by watching one of those incredible parades of emotion that you see on a Jerry Springer or a Phil Donahue show where people just let emotion out. Here, when you tell people what the story's about, it's as if they can see something that they can see on television but through the music you are able to heighten and give different direction and surprise people and disturb people as well. It's not what you'd expect to hear.

JW: Your work is also marked by your collaborations with cinematographer Paul Sarossy, editor Susan Shipton and Arsinée Khanjian. Would you be able to comment on the creative import of these relationships?

AE: Paul and Susan are essential to what I do. I trust Paul completely with light, Susan to find the internal rhythm of a scene. Arsinée is the source of so much of my creative energy, and her face is an object of complete fascination.

JW: You have our own repertory cast of actors such as David Hemblen, Gabrielle Rose, Maury Chaykin. How did you come to work with Ian Holm and how did you find the experience of working with a 'star'?

AE: Ian is an extraordinary actor and somebody who I think is greatly undervalued. He's also a wonderful person to work with. He's so generous. When I announced the cast, that it was going to be Ian Holm, there was a stunned silence because they are all from theatre and what he means to theatre actors is very similar to what I feel about Pinter or Antonioni.

Ian, from the moment that he came into the unofficial repertory company, was so impressed by the actors and let them know that and felt that he wasn't up to their standards and was quite genuine about that and he just made himself vulnerable. So much about this system, this star system, is about making people as detached and as invulnerable as possible.

I've always done my own casting and it's always been through theatre. I watch a lot of theatre and a lot of them are actors that I've seen in theatre or I've seen as character parts in other people's films and they are people that I have a really strong attachment to. When you respect an actor from what they've done on stage, I think that means something to them because that's when an actor is most in control, much more than in a film when it's the director who orchestrates things. On stage, you really see that is the actor's medium. So when you're taking them from stage and when you're not even subjecting them to the process of auditioning, because that can be disastrous when you're asking actors to audition and come back, because they should feel from the moment that they read a script and when you offer that role to them that they are the people who should play those parts. That's the best way to start off a relationship with an actor, to say 'this role is for you, you don't have to audition for it, it's yours'. I think that allows the actor to feel a tremendous sense of confidence.

Unfortunately, what happens a lot of the time is that because an actor has to go through so many hoops and so many executives approving them that there is this lingering sense that maybe they shouldn't be playing this role. This can find its way into what you see on screen ultimately.

JW: After *The Sweet Hereafter* and many years of writing your own material you tackled another adaptation, William Trevor's *Felicia's Journey*.

AE: I again fell in love with the book. I think Trevor is a writer that I can learn a lot from. I've met with him and I think that he is a master storyteller. Again, he's one of these writers that has this superhuman gift of being able to inhabit people other than himself. I find this story so compelling.

The film is about two people who are timeless and yet very much of this time: one being this monster of a character who is completely influenced by modern technologies and media and yet doesn't seem to be, who actually seems to be a relic of a previous time and that is fascinating; and this young woman who comes to England and is a relic of a time when people still write letters. It's just about people finding a consciousness. I've always been attracted to the thriller as a form as well and this allows me to explore something that I don't think I would have been able to come up with myself and make it my own.

JW: As you work with bigger budgets and larger production companies with rafters of executives, do you fear your films having to be subjected to test screenings and market research? I can imagine there being resistance to your somewhat elliptical narratives.

AE: If you were to show *Exotica* [1994] or *The Sweet Hereafter* to a test audience and ask them what would they change, you would come back with a list too heavy to carry. Everyone would like to see these films follow a cohesive, narrative, linear pattern, but I just can't make them that way and I just don't think that way. The relationship we have to a finished film is very different to something we think we can change, so I'm really frightened of that process and I just don't know how I could cope with it. It's this idea of surprise, of not knowing what the result will be, and of trying to find a way to keep the process alive for yourself.

Sometimes I can read a really linear, well-written script and go yes, this is a movie that I would really love to see but I could not for the life of me spend a year laying out what's already there. There has to be an element of surprise. I have to feel that I don't quite know how pieces are going to fit and manipulating the question of time seems to me to be so seductive – that we can drift and actually address thematic issues through people's relationship to time. Film is a medium that first and foremost records time and gives the illusion that it is projecting time. It's an extraordinary book – Tarkovsky's *Sculpting in Time* – but that is your material and to not question the natural impulse to linear and narrative consequence and sequence is I think really limiting. It's just not the way I think. I like to remain excited by the process and one of those ways of remaining excited is by not knowing, even as I'm writing sometimes, where something will lead. That's why I can't write a treatment.

JW: Very much to the forefront in *Family Viewing* but a recurring motif in your films is the recording and manipulation of memories and experience. This strikes me as quite a sinister concept.

AE: It's sinister and yet it's also so touching. When someone tries to destroy or enhance their experience by a natural manipulation of the recording of it it's such a frail and vulnerable thing to do because it's not dealing with a real issue. It's like a cry of despair or pain, it's like saying this is what I'd like to be able to do; I'd actually like to go back and change the course that events have taken but we can't. But to think that we can somehow deal with that through a secondary source is very much a part of the specific moment in our cultural evolution and it's something that I find fascinating and sad and quite funny sometimes: that we can actually think that we have control over our fate by exercising control over the most obvious representation of our fate.

JW: To quote from *Family Viewing*, the people in your films 'love to record' and commit to tape. For many of the characters in your films it offers both a form of frequently sexualised therapy.

AE: I think that this has become so persuasive, we all have systems where feelings and ideas can be transcribed to pieces of tape and through various types of technologies. There's something almost casual about it. The way in which we surrender our process of organic memory and our sense of how we can subjectively block out ideas or retain certain images. Now that has become quite suspicious to us because we give everything to an undiscriminating technology which just records and we have to deny those processes because we don't know what we are keeping or throwing away because everything is stored and that has changed the way we behave, I think.

I'm interested in seeing how human beings react under pressure and I'm interested in people who think they have systems that deal with neuroses, and I'm really fascinated by this notion of therapy. I'm attached to this idea of creativity and there are people who can be very creative about things in their own lives and that might include finding a sexual practice that can help them release certain things or it might mean actually finding a pattern which others might see as being diverse or deviant, but it allows them to cope with something. Sometimes that pattern may not be the best thing that person can do, but they are almost aware of that and you want to applaud them for the effort and there's something very human about their desire to come to terms or find a way of dealing with their pain.

JW: Do you have a defined Atom Egoyan audience in mind when conceiving and constructing your films?

AE: No, but I also have the highest expectation of my audience. I have to. For the type of films I make your point of departure is the belief that your audience is infinitely curious, exploratory and trustful, that they are able to trust what you are doing. For instance, I love films that start off and set a tone of mystery; that start off and say you have to be prepared to go on a journey and you cannot expect that it's going to follow a formula. I'm attracted to that type of film. The criticism I've always received for all the films is that they start off slowly. What people mean is that they don't necessarily tell you who it is that you are supposed to identify with or why.

You have to be able to understand that very often a reviewer or even a jury – having been on a jury myself – what they extend to is the result of an immediate impression and what endures is something that you won't even know until weeks, months or maybe even years later. I have to believe that people are going to the films prepared to be there for the hour and a half that the experience will take and if they drift at certain moments, that's fine. It's something that I find quite pleasurable. I love to drift. There's no better place for me to just let go than in a dark room that's projecting images at twenty-four frames a second. It's one of the essential powers of cinema: images that suggest that what is happening is real and to not question that seems a great shame.

JW: You like to diversify. You have worked on art installations; written librettos [for a chamber piece called *Elsewhereless*] and have directed operas such as *Doctor Ox's Experiment.*

AE: Directing *Doctor Ox's Experiment* and working with Gavin Bryars' music was a thrill and a huge honour but I can't help but feel that it is a sideline to what is my vocation ultimately. The more I work in other media the more I understand what I'm attracted to in film. With cinema you're given an instrument which can actually reflect a point of view and which can situate the viewer in a really dynamic way which any other medium, including opera, well there's just something antiquated about the theatrical experience. When it works and when you have a genuine sense of transformation and transfiguration it's really spell binding and yet those moments are really rare. It's something that I'm drawn to because it was my initial passion and love. With the camera, from the moment I started playing with the camera, well you are able to reflect one's way of seeing the world in a really literal manner. The issues it provokes, the issue of why we need to record images, why we need to transmit images, what we expect to get back from those images, those are all so crucial to our society. It's impossible to feel irrelevant when you are working in the film medium while all these other professions somehow risk a sense of being outside what are our most crucial and pressing issues. That is, what do we expect to see or how has technology changed our sense of what experience is and what constitutes experience.

* * *

Stephen Frears

One of Britain's most respected and eclectic filmmakers, Frears made a tentative start in film, rising to prominence on British television with a series of well-observed state-of-the-nation dramas. More concerned with character and narrative than visual flourishes, Frears gives due credit to writers, enjoying fruitful collaborations with Hanif Kureishi, Alan Bennett and Christopher Hampton. His most notable films deal with outsiders on the margins of society, exhibiting insight and compassion rather than easy sentiment. Since the American-financed *Dangerous Liaisons* (1988), Frears has alternated personal projects, usually shot in Britain, with bigger-budget studio assignments.

Born in Leicester in 1941, Frears first entered the theatre after studying law at Cambridge, working with directors Lindsay Anderson and Karel Reisz and actor Albert Finney at the Royal Court Theatre. Reisz employed Frears as an assistant director on *Morgan: A Suitable Case for Treatment* (1966), as did Finney on *Charlie Bubbles* (1968) and Anderson on *If...* (1968). Through his Memorial Enterprises Production Company, Finney also part-financed Frears' directorial debut, *The Burning* (1967), a short political fable shot in Morocco. Thereafter Frears worked regularly in British television, directing *St Ann's* (1969), a documentary about a slum district of Nottingham, and episodes of *Parkin's Patch* (ITV, 1969–70) and *Tom Grattan's War* (ITV, 1968–70).

After making his feature debut with *Gumshoe* (1971), Frears returned to television for many years, working on the BBC's *Play for Today* and London

Weekend Television's play slots, collaborating with Alan Bennett on works such as *A Day Out* (1972) and *Me! I'm Afraid of Virginia Woolf* (1978). Three bigger-budget television films at the start of the 1980s, specifically *Walter* (1982), were significant successes and convinced Frears to return to features for the hitman/road movie hybrid, *The Hit* (1984).

Continuing to work with first-rate writers, Frears' subsequent filmography is indeed impressive, with films such as *My Beautiful Laundrette* (1985), *Prick Up Your Ears* (1987), *The Grifters* (1990) (produced by Martin Scorsese) and *High Fidelity* (2000) standing out on his CV.

This interview took place in 2000 when Frears was promoting *Liam* (2000), his collaboration with respected television writer Jimmy McGovern. Set in Depression-era Liverpool, the film deals with poverty, racism and religious bigotry, as seen through the eyes of a small boy. Since the completion of *Liam* Frears has directed *Dirty Pretty Things* (2002), *Mrs Henderson Presents* (2005) and the enthusiastically-received *The Queen* (2006), for which Helen Mirren won Best Actress in at Venice Film Festival.

The interview appeared originally in *Enthusiasm 04* in summer 2001.

Jason Wood: How did *Liam* come to fruition.

Stephen Frears: Well, it looked at one point as if *Hi-Lo Country* [1998] had collapsed and Tim Bevan and my agent took me out for a compensatory lunch. Alan Yentob came over and introduced Jimmy McGovern and Jimmy – whom I'd never previously met – said 'I'm writing a script for you.' It turned out to be *Liam* and he sent it to me and I thought it was great. It also reminded me of my childhood, even though there was no poverty and my upbringing was very middle class.

JW: How familiar were you with McGovern's work?

SF: I certainly knew he was a good writer. I also thought that the project should get made and in a kind of very old-fashioned way I thought that the BBC should make it because he is a writer they should support.

JW: Was he an easy man to work with?

SF: Talented people are always easy to work with.

JW: You've got' a reputation for working closely with writers and seem to show a respect for them. Do you feel the writer is often under-valued in cinema?

SF: In many cases the writing is the gold dust and once you've invented a device to get back to the book – as was the case with *High Fidelity* – or back to the text you can then simply raid the riches. To me it seems like common sense to give the writer his due accord. On *Liam* Jimmy knows full well what he did and I know full well what I did. To pretend otherwise would be quite simply dishonest. I think writing is very dynamic, good dialogue can be very sexy and can get people very excited. Look at people like Lubitsch, Billy Wilder and Preston Sturges, that's what really works. I like Hanif Kureishi's writing; it's very provocative and immediately put people on edge to be in the presence of something that was that funny, that cheeky, that paradoxical and that lively.

JW: That's certainly true of the writing in *Gumshoe*, perhaps my favourite of your films.

SF: Good for you. A man of taste.

JW: For all the important issues with which *Liam* deals there are certainly some very humorous moments.

SF: The problem was stopping Jimmy going for the jokes. He so loves the jokes. He has a tremendous sense of humour and would always shamelessly go for the jokes each and every time. He's a complete whore; cheap laugh, go for it!

JW: Perhaps the most important part of the film is the way it depicts fascism creeping into the consciousness of the working classes following the closing of industrial-based employment.

SF: Fascism was always offered as a solution to any plan.

JW: It reminded me of another British film, Pawel Pawlikowski's *Last Resort* [2000]. *Liam* looks at the seeds of fascism but still feels contemporary despite its 1930s setting.

SF: Do you think so?

JW: I do. People always look for scapegoats.

SF: I suppose they do but the world has changed so violently. I'd draw a parallel with Arthur Scargill and the closing of the mines. Scargill said this is what's going to happen and he was exactly right. I mean he completely fucked up but everything that he said was going to happen did. The peculiar thing about Mrs Thatcher was that instead of saying to the working classes 'look, the world is changing and we'd better work out how to deal with you', she chose to make matters worse. Because of her own prejudices she made matters worse for people confronted by the problem of history. Her reaction was so downright unpleasant and nonsensical.

JW: Did you actually film in Liverpool? The street looked very authentic.

SF: We did, but the houses were in Wigan. It was a half-heritage area, the streets were cobbled because the new residents wanted them to be but it was a wonderful place to film. Stephen Fineren was also a very good production designer and I had a very good director of photography in Andrew Dunn .

JW: Another important aspect of the film is the devout Catholicism, which obviously informed McGovern's childhood. Did you have a similarly religious up-bringing?

SF: No. I was brought up in the Church of England in a conventional middle-class family. In later life I turned out to be Jewish.

JW: The film catches the vehemence and the cruelty of religion as well as the more positive aspects.

SF: They would say, of course, that it was very humane. Ann Reid, who was brilliant in the film, was especially of this opinion. One of my children for a time went to a school on an estate which was run by a Protestant woman and her only concern was to get the kids out of the estate. She said that if I'm very tough then perhaps they'll get out. Also, if there is little opportunity or little future religion can be an opiate. The priest in the film – who was actually very funny and let us film in his church – was a Jesuit and I remember saying to him, blimey, I thought you lot would be the worst. It is all a very complicated issue and I hope the film reflects an ambiguity about religion. I originally talked to Brendan Gleason about playing the priest and he said, 'look, the priests I know do good as well.'

JW: Ian Hart's character is the one who most publicly questions religion and his punishment at the end of the film, which is of course also a punishment suffered by his innocent daughter, would seem to reinforce the coda of Catholicism.

SF: Jimmy would say it was because he was the victim of fascism.

JW: Others could see it as a pro-religious argument.

SF: That's a good point and I have to say I hadn't thought of that.

JW: You work with a very good cast.

SF: Ian Hart is a wonderful actor. Talented and very dedicated and very serious about his work; he was a real treat to work with. Claire Hackett as the mother was a stroke of luck, she'd just come back from New Zealand and it meant that she hadn't been over-exposed. I also think the cast avoided many of the clichés that they could have fallen into.

JW: How did you find working with the younger actors.

SF: Anthony Borrows, the young boy who played Liam, was very good wasn't he. But I really thought that Megan Burns as the daughter was very talented. I kept telling everybody that she's coming up on the inside. She was initially very shy but then you could see the steel in her. She was very impressive. The boy was much more physically expressive.

JW: Was it difficult for him to get the stuttering right?

SF: Jimmy used to stand over him and get him to do that. Jimmy suffered very badly in his childhood from a stutter so that part of the film was very personal and very autobiographical.

JW: Numerous scenes are through Liam's eyes. I love the sequence where Liam witnesses his mother and father's pre-coital fumbling.

SF: Strangely enough, Jimmy thought that he had written a film that was entirely through a child's eyes but I kept saying no, there are many scenes where the child is not even present and to that end I think the title of the film is slightly misleading. It's just as much the girl's story for example. But you're right, that scene is a wonderful scene. I went back and re-shot it. Everybody said why are you re-shooting it until they saw the rushes and said, 'You were right, it's absolutely wonderful.'

JW: What did you change about it?

SF: The new scene, the one that exists in the film, is more elegiac; it has more grace and more passion. It is like something out of a John Ford film, for example *The Quiet Man* [1952]. The light was also perfect when we re-shot. I'm very proud of that scene.

JW: Speaking of John Ford, how overt a reference to *The Searchers* [1956] was the final shot.

SF: It was very conscious. I would also hope that the viewing of *Liam* would not depend upon a knowledge of *The Searchers*.

JW: As a director with a long career, does experience become more beneficial with each film?

SF: Well, you are often trying to make complicated ideas very clear. In as much as I can see my development I recognise that I can say many things in a shot and yet crystallise it down to one single moment. It's simply a recognition of the place of experience. It's one of the pleasures of developing.

JW: Ostensibly a melodrama, *Liam* is also a highly political film yet it avoids being didactic. You often succeed in dealing with politics in human terms.

SF: I was really politicised by Hanif Kureishi so much of what I do I learned from him. He was sort of describing his own family and what was going on around him so it always was very human. It's also in this instance another strength of Jimmy's writing.

JW: I get the sense that *Liam* is a film that you're rather proud of.

SF: I perhaps need more distance from it but I recognise that you have good days and bad days and I had a lot of good days on *Liam*.

JW: How important to you is the approbation of critics? You've done pretty well.

SF: I could tell you about critics I'd happily line up against the wall and shoot. They're often just journalists who write about themselves. Don't forget also that a lot of my films have been slated. *Mary Reilly* [1996] for example, which I can't pretend entirely worked but it certainly had good things about it. It's also as foolish to listen to the good reviews as it is to listen to the bad ones. That said, it's always nice when people like your work.

JW: You seem keen on taking risks and as such have managed a balance between personal projects and studio fare. How have you retained your autonomy?

SF: I take risks every time, I would hope. I like to set off into the unknown. I also often make films that I don't know anything about such as the working class or the Irish or cowboys. I've also made a lot of mistakes with my films. I should never have moved *Sammy and Rosie Get Laid* [1987] out of Brixton. And I misread *The Van* [1996]. You can't lose your independence of mind and to be fair the Americans give me an easy ride. They take one look and think 'give him whatever he wants – but not too much money, because he's never going to do exactly what he's told'. They somehow know how to deal with me. When I was spending a lot of money I got into a mess but when Joe Roth hired me to make *High Fidelity* he said to make it as if I was making an independent film, which was a very sensible thing to say. I'm jolly lucky.

JW: Finally, much has been made of the fact that you're taking a sabbatical from directing to concentrate on your teaching. Why choose this moment when so many things seem to be going right?

SF: That's easy: I'm knackered. It's that simple. I got *Liam* three or four years ago and I remember fifteen months ago thinking that if I didn't make it this year then it would never get made and after almost blackmailing the BBC into doing it I thought I'd better do it after *High Fidelity*. Then George Clooney rang up and asked me to do *Fail Safe* [2000] so I did all three back to back. You also just get bored with the inside of your head. It's hard to find new things and you become more aware of the struggle. To come out with a film that's interesting after struggling is to be admired. The teaching is also a selfish thing because it opens your mind up.

JW: Will there, however, be more films from you?

SF: I bloody hope so. For my sake as much as anyone else's.

* * *

Alejandro González Iñárritu

Born in Mexico City in 1963, former DJ and commercials director, Alejandro González Iñárritu's first feature film, *Amores perros* (*Love's a Bitch*), world-premiered at the 2000 Cannes Film Festival and went on to win the Grand Prix in the Critics' Week. The film would go on to win numerous other international prizes, including a BAFTA for Best Foreign-Language Film; the New York Film Critics Circle award for Best Foreign-Language Film and awards from the Bogota, Chicago, Cuba, Edinburgh, Flanders, Moscow, San Sebastian, São Paulo, Toronto and Tokyo international film festivals. In addition, the film swept the Mexican Academy of Cinematographic Arts and Sciences' Silver Ariel awards with 13 wins. *Amores perros*, with its intersecting narrative structure and fast editing, is widely credited with kick-starting a critical and commercial renaissance in Mexican cinema.

A contributor to the post-September 11 portmanteau film *11'09"01 – September 11* (co-directors included Sean Penn, Youssef Chahine, Amos Gitai, Shohei Imamura, Claude Lelouch, Ken Loach and Samira Makhmalbaf, 2002), González Iñárritu's second feature was *21 Grams* (2003). Set in Memphis, the film retained the director's key technical collaborators, most prominently cinematographer Rodrigo Prieto, for a piercing tale revolving around grief, tragedy and atonement, themes being developed in his work.

Also scripted by Guillermo Arriaga, *Babel* (2006), the director's third feature premiered at the 2006 Cannes Film Festival and brought him a Best Director prize. The film sees González Iñárritu and Arriaga pursuing again the themes of *Amores perros* but on a bigger scale. Again adopting what has become a tripartite narrative structure, the film undoubtedly confirms González Iñárritu as one of the pre-eminent filmmakers at work anywhere in the world today.

Extracts of this interview, which took place in 2003, appear in *The Faber Book of Mexican Cinema* (Faber, 2006).

Jason Wood: I'm interested by in the way in which your films, and perhaps *Amores perros* specifically, have managed to connect so explicitly with audiences. Do you think your background as a DJ has been a contributing factor in this?

Alejandro González Iñárritu: I think it goes back further than this. First of all, I am an autodidact and a kid from the streets. I grew up with parents who taught me love and education as my main tools, but with three sisters and one brother it was a very, very limited economic situation. I lived in a neighbourhood very similar to that of Octavio and Susana in *Amores perros*. The green mosaic on the front of Octavio's house is a homage to my house in the Narvarte neighbourhood. Because we were a family of five I did not get that much attention; therefore I was very free-spirited, growing up and learning about life on the streets from the time I was eight years old. At the age of 16 I escaped, hitchhiking, with my girlfriend in search of myself, selling jewellery on Mexican beaches. Secondly – and I think I have only just realised this while trying to understand what it is that I do – it was also important to me that I boarded a cargo ship crossing the Atlantic. I took the ship once from Vera Cruz and another time from Coatzacoalcos. I crossed the Atlantic twice and went along the Mississippi too. I worked washing the floors. I spent three or four months on each trip, mainly with cargo, but often with the strangest of people. I took the first trip aged seventeen and the second aged nineteen. On this occasion I remained in Europe, surviving for one year on a thousand dollars. I did every kind of job, including picking grapes with the gypsies in Spain and dancing in a swimsuit in the pool of a discotheque to survive. I think these two experiences crossing the Atlantic taught me more than any university.

Then I returned to create a rock band, to be a serious musician and a filmmaker after seeing the film *Yol* [1982]. I started to study communications to have a general understanding of everything, when suddenly a friend of mine, Mariana Garcia Barcena, offered me an opportunity to be a DJ because she liked my voice. I had a three-hour show where I could play, say and create anything that

I wanted. I learned to entertain people with my favourite music, my characters and ideas and my bizarre imagination. I then became the director of the station at 22 years of age and was listened to by millions of people in the biggest city in the world.

JW: Do you also feel that your background in commercials forged an ability to connect with people and convince them that what you had to say and the stories that you wanted to tell were worth paying attention to?

AGI: After five years, I thought that I had completely cracked radio and considered myself a master of the medium so I suddenly felt poor. I quit when WFM was the most important and influential radio station in the country because I realised that I wanted to make films and to communicate through a visual medium. To do this I had to learn how to work with images. I was lucky. After the huge success of the radio station, I received the opportunity and support from Miguel Aleman – my former WFM boss – to create the corporate image of a huge TV corporation. With my partner, Raul Olvera, I started to write, produce, direct, edit, post-produce and sell approximately eighty commercials a year for the next five years. It was crazy but the first time that I went on a set as a director, my only experiences had been with a Super-8 camera when I was 11-years-old and to have been the assistant director and composer for a short film taken from a story by Julio Cortazar directed by Pelayo Gutiérrez during university.

I have learned skills by doing them. I was born this way because I believe that beyond where you come from, as Kafka was an insurance salesman, or García Márquez was a writer of advertisements, or Visconti a noble aristocrat, for an artist born as an artist, maybe it doesn't matter if you study. I learned on the sets, doing horrible things, experiments, failing and spending more time on them than in my own house. Also important to my development was my theatre studies with Ludwig Margulles, a great teacher who strengthened and expanded my concept of directing. But it was the commercials that gave me the opportunity to play with all the tools, to understand the mechanics, to create and explore in 30 or 60 seconds, different genres, tones, beats, rhythms and most importantly, to have a camera, a couple of actors and tell a story and say something through images and sounds. All of the things that I have directed were written and produced from the beginning to end by me so that gave me the best education in the world, the freedom and the tools to make anything happen. Most of these commercials were more about emotion than product and you could discuss them with people because they were transmitted via television but the problem with the commercials was that they filled your pocket but emptied your brain and soul. It was not a wise interchange so I decided to quit after five years again and

I wrote and produced with Pelayo a 30-minute pilot for TV with Miguel Bose as the star. It was a great exercise to confirm to myself, before making a feature film, that I could direct something larger than 30 seconds. My goal was to have at least one good scene, just one would have been enough for me. There is one scene that I still like today. With the next step, *Amores perros*, I thought should I? Can I? Now today I know that I can.

JW: *Amores perros* **was funded entirely privately. Was this and the fact that you didn't come through the more traditional film school route a source of resentment from people within the Mexican industry?**

AGI: There was some resentment, yes, and I think that sadly this a basic emotion of human nature. It is a very destructive and terrible feeling. However, I think that there was more of a feeling of surprise because, as well as coming from the wrong side of the tracks, I also lacked academic credentials. As you point out, the government did not help me and that really surprised a lot of people. People thought 'who is this guy and who does he think he is to make a film like this without an educational institution like the Centro de Capacitación Cinematográfica behind him? This guy comes from the world of commercials. Oh my god! Let's put a cross on him!' I was breaking the rules and *Amores perros* raised a lot of questions about the system. A lot of institutions and ways of thinking were shaken. This was a very positive after-effect of the film. The film that perhaps initiated this was *Sexo, pudor y lágrimas* [*Sex, Shame and Tears*, 1999] by Antonio Serrano, which also proved that there was an audience for Mexican cinema and middle-class Mexican stories that could be told for Mexicans.

JW: **How did your relationship with the writer Guillermo Arriaga begin?**

AGI: I was connected with Arriaga through Pelayo Gutiérrez, who is now my Executive Producer at Z Film, the production company that I have in Mexico. Pelayo helped me produce *Behind the Money* [c.1988] but I was desperate because they loved the pilot, but it was never accepted as a TV series because it was too expensive to shoot. I was developing an idea about a family from Guerrero and their two young sons who began to involve themselves in the guerrillas of Chiapas with Marcos and the consequences of that, and I wanted a writer to help me so I wanted to read scripts and Pelayo sent me a very good one that was fluid and extremely well written. I said 'who is this guy?' It was Guillermo Arriaga. We were introduced and went to dinner.

Guillermo has been a teacher all his life and I had previously made some declarations about how bad my teachers were and expressed my belief that cinema could not be taught in classrooms, that cinema was outside, in real life. Guillermo was initially so mad at me, asking, 'who do you think you are?' but I think that deep down he thought that I was right. I told him that I was developing a project and I would love for him to write it. We started to work, but ten days later he called me back and said that for personal reasons he could not continue with it so we decided to work on something else. This something else was a short film for the Mexican Film Institute [IMCINE] that was eleven stories connected by the tiniest of details. We had a great time working together and we were flowing with ideas. IMCINE never gave us money and we never made it, but it was a good multi-story exercise. He then told me that he had an idea that he really wanted to develop and he revealed to me the plot of *Amores perros*. We started working together based on that idea and it all fell into place from there.

JW: How did you begin to develop the film together? In terms of narrative and visual strategy the film was, especially for a debut, quite unique and has certainly subsequently been much imitated both within Mexico and internationally. Did the ambitious undertaking not awe you?

AGI: I always knew we were crazy, but if I am going to make a film and invest so much in it then it has to be a personal one and I have to be challenged. *Amores perros* was certainly personal and definitely a challenge. I have involved myself in every detail and every line of both scripts, and even sometimes I discussed the blocking of the actors that I had in my mind with Guillermo so that he could translate that in the script. As he was writing the film, I was already directing it in my mind, three years in advance from when it was to be shot. Every book, every song, every smell and everything that I absorbed within those three years helped me to know and reveal the characters, and then to be able to share that with Guillermo. Knowing that I would be the captain and would navigate that boat for the next three years of my life, I participated very closely in the idea, concept and design and involved myself in such a way that I was more aware of the advantages and disadvantages of the project. But it was Guillermo who wrote, solved and conceived the thing and who I consider one of the best screenwriters in the world. I think that during the script development we argued a lot in favour of the project, but after we were able to agree on that, he visited me during the shoot with his family for a week or so and then saw the final cut. Fortunately, even with some of the changes and scenes that I had to take out or move around, he froze for a couple of hours, but then he seemed to like it.

With regards to the visual style, it was something that I was experimenting with long before *Amores perros* through some exercises that I did in some internationally-awarded commercials. Rodrigo Prieto, Brigitte Broch and Martin

Hernandez have been working with me as a team and developing different explorations together for several years so we understand each other almost telepathically. They know exactly what I like or don't like and what I'm interested in.

JW: **From speaking to people such as Guillermo del Toro and Alfonso Cuarón it is obvious that you all form a very close-knit community. Did you seek the advice of such people when making the film?**

AGI: Completely. I tried to involve them from the very moment that I began developing the script. Del Toro and Alfonso have had great input into *Amores perros*. Antonio Urrutia, Carlos Cuarón, José Luis García Agraz, Eliseo Alberto and Ernesto Bolio are people that I respect a lot and it is great that I can count on them and they can count on me. I love to read or participate in what they are doing and to help in anything that I can, even with bad ideas or just raising little questions that will possibly bring answers.

JW: **I understand that del Toro was especially helpful and generous with his time during the editing stages.**

AGI: He was, as were all the people I mentioned above. Del Toro called me without even knowing me after seeing a rough cut of the film that was passed on to him by his close friend Antonio Urrutia. Guillermo said to me 'what the fuck and who are you?' He told me that he loved the film but he thought that I should cut it as it was a little long. We began a series of intense telephone conversations, with him calling me every day at 7am! He had a lot of very radical ideas, including taking out the majority of the second story, to which I replied, 'fuck you, who do you think you are?' At this time del Toro was in Spain during the production of *The Devil's Backbone* [*El espinazo del diablo*, 2001]. He flew to Mexico and knocked on my door. I opened it and he said, 'Hi, I'm Guillermo del Toro' and then he spent three days with me working on the film and sleeping on my floor. He also ate everything that he found in my house.

By that time, I had already spent seven months editing the film alone in my house and even when I was really happy and very, very close I knew that I should cut it a little bit more but didn't know how. During this time we had a lot of discussions as, at the time, the film was almost 2 hours and 40 minutes long. He really helped me to pare it down another seven minutes and encouraged me and told me not to be afraid. I really appreciated this, as there are times when as the director you can begin to lose your perspective. Guillermo has the mind of a producer too and I really believe in him. I don't always believe producers and tend to always produce my own things but the fact that he is also a director meant that I was able to trust him. He and Carlos Bolado helped me at the end to reduce the fat that is so often simply left in films.

JW: We've very briefly touched upon the complex narrative of *Amores perros* with its tripartite plot structure and use of multi-characters but I'd like you to talk a little about the visual aesthetic of the film and your relationship with cinematographer Rodrigo Prieto.

AGI: I have been working with Rodrigo for many years now. We made a commercial together for a bank in which we really explored the potentials of hand-held camera and the skip bleach process. We love this commercial. The skip bleach really captured the light of Mexico City, especially given that we shot the commercial on a very grey and overcast day. Commercials for me were always exercises, a way of exploring methods and approaches that I could use in a feature film later. People say that *Amores perros* is very stylish but I do not think that this is true. You and I and every human being sees the world in hand-held. In other words, we look and move our heads. My head and eyes have never been mounted on a crane, a dolly or a tripod. Those things are stylish and unnatural to our relationship with the world. The approach is both more intimate and more real. The skip bleach process I find has a spiritual quality that I relate to and really love.

JW: What do you consider to be the main themes of the film? Obviously love, hate, violence and revenge are prominent.

AGI: It deals with so many universal things, including those that you rightly mention. I think that *Amores perros* and *21 Grams* are universal because globalisation is not about the market and the money, but about the human emotions and dramas and it doesn't matter which country you are from or what your needs, religion, culture, government, tradition or market position are. We feel the same for the same kind of primitive and basic human problems that we deal with. We all are broken. The thing that I really wanted to explore and I sincerely hope I did so was the whole question of the father figure and the symmetry between Cain and Abel. I really only discovered this symmetry while I was making the film, but then it became present all the time. This subtle undercurrent and the marked absence of father figures is something that I really enjoyed exploring. At the same time I always find myself in a difficult position explaining my films because I will need a lot of therapy to begin to understand and clarify, not only what the films are about, but also why I make them. I love discovering things while I'm doing them or things people discover when they see them but I don't think painters are thinking about what it means with each brush stroke. I think that after they finish, in a very subconscious process, they discover it or people reveal it to them.

JW: The car crash is very kinetic and bone-crunching, but as Arriaga has pointed out it is also a very effective device through which to bring together disparate characters from a wide variety of social and political backgrounds. Logistically, however, the crash sequence must have been a nightmare to complete.

AGI: It was very hard. We didn't have much money so I had to shoot the car chase in just one day and the car crash in half of a day. We were pulling the car using electric power and the people were furious in the streets. The police were there to help, but were not really helping us. The day we shot the crash we had nine cameras and the sun was beginning to go down and the whole situation was becoming very dangerous. The video assist projecting the nine cameras was off because of a technical problem. Rodrigo Prieto and I were running from one angle to another like crazy. That same day in the morning we shot the scene of the bank robbery and we were exhausted. The car that was hit travelled a hundred metres without control and people were desperate to see what was happening despite our pleas for them to stay clear and keep out of the way. The car was travelling at one hundred kilometres per hour and ended up accidentally hitting a taxi that was parked nearby and nearly killing a hundred people that were two meters from that taxi without security. It was insane. I will never forget the sound of that crash and the braveness of Emilio Echevarría who knew the danger he was running being in front of that car where nobody knew exactly what would happen after the other car hit it at forty miles per hour. You would never see this kind of car crash on film in the United States. The shot and the whole set-up were very risky which also makes it feel so real.

JW: Gael García Bernal is magnetic as Octavio. Is this the first time you had worked with him?

AGI: No, I had worked with him a couple of years ago on a commercial and I have nothing but praise for him. As I told you I started to direct *Amores perros* years prior to when the film began and this is the case when one of the first and most crucial decisions that a director makes in a film was in my advantage because of that. At that point Gael didn't have any film experience but he was studying theatre in London and had participated in some TV soap operas when he was a child because he's the son of two talented actors. I knew that he was the one for the part but I was initially worried because when we first started rehearsing he did not seem to have much idea about who his character was. I remember that when he arrived on location he asked me if I thought that his character would play tennis in the afternoons and I remember saying 'what are you thinking? This guy is from the lower class!'

Gael was a little lost because we had been communicating mainly by telephone and because of school commitments he arrived on location later than many of the other actors. I was worried. But then, he went out for one or two nights with a few guys and then he got it just like that. He began to talk with the right kind of slightly vulgar accent and underwent something of a surprise and almost instant metamorphosis. He was and is a natural and I was fascinated since the first day by the supernatural relation between him and the camera.

JW: Were you surprised at all by the success of the film in Mexico? It has become celebrated and yet by highlighting poverty and social deprivation shows the country in a very realistic if unflattering light.

AGI: I was completely surprised. That said, when I was editing the film during seven months in my house I knew I had something that had the capacity to touch the hearts of people and I knew that it captured life. But I never imagined how people would react to it. I also was surprised by the reaction to the film outside of Mexico because at this time I had no idea of the bigger picture of cinema. I had not been to festivals and was not a cineaste; I was just a guy who happened to like films. I had no perception of the film within the world so it was overwhelming for me when *Amores perros* took the place that it did within the cinema world.

JW: What was it that convinced you to follow up *Amores perros* with *21 Grams*, and was it a natural decision to again work with Arriaga?

AGI: We have such a good experience and results working together that it was a natural decision for both of us to work again on the next script. However, this script was very difficult and much more ambitious and this time the process of development with Guillermo was more complex. We were more conscious of the things that can go wrong and aware of how easy it is to fail and also how difficult it is to get things right. This script was three years of going back and forth and I involved as many people as I could to ensure that we approached it from all possible angles.

At one point I reached a crisis and thought that I would not make the film. I wasn't happy with the interior life of the characters and the way the structure and many others things were coming out of it. *21 Grams* was a radioactive material in which any false note, any little thing less or more than needed, could be fatal.

The tone and the performances that I needed in order to make this film feel real and not over the top because of the nature of it was a very tough thing to achieve so the process in the script was very stressful and very delicate from my side. Fortunately, Guillermo's talent, nobility and wisdom were able to solve things so much better than I thought were ever possible. There was a magic moment where things fell into place and we suddenly were in total agreement.

JW: It was originally written in Spanish and to be shot in Mexico. Why did you decide to relocate the story to the States and why to Memphis?

AGI: The main reason I relocated was that I wanted another challenge and this gave me the opportunity to go to new territories. This really excited me and got me focused. I always focus more clearly when my adrenalin is running high. I think that you can know your idiosyncrasies much better and your *Mexicanidad* from the outside rather than just by living in the inside in your own little ranch of fear and prejudice. On a more personal note, the level of insecurity is very high in Mexico and to live in Mexico with two children was becoming very hard for me. Some people incorrectly thought that *Amores perros* had made me a millionaire and it was a little bit frightening dealing with the possibility of being kidnapped. Also, it is hard enough to make films in Mexico. It is equally hard to survive on the salaries directors are paid. The normal fee is about $40,000. When, as I do, you invest three years of your life in a project, this is not so much money. The main reason, however, is that for this particular film, I wanted and needed to work with the very best actors in the world and English was the universal language that would allow me this opportunity. I am not only talking about Americans, but French, Australian and Puerto-Rican actors.

I decided that I did not want to shoot either in Los Angeles or New York because these cities have become like a set for me; I have seen them so many times on film that it is predictable. I needed a city that is not a movie city. I also needed a city that I liked, that has a certain smell, a distinct personality and a unique quality. Thirdly, I needed a city far from LA and New York to get all these actors out of their houses and away from their wives and kids and friends. I wanted them to have no distractions from their work. I found all these things in Memphis. It also has a real history; a sadness that I guess is intrinsically linked with it being the birthplace of the blues.

JW: What did you want the film to achieve visually? For example, you retain the use of hand-held camera and play with the colour of the film stock.

AGI: I wanted to make a film that is even more intimate and raw. I wanted it to be as direct as possible and not at all stylised. Rodrigo and I wanted to disappear so that the people felt that there was no lighting from a source or a photographer. I wanted the people to feel like they were looking at some images from a documentary, things that were captured in real time in a real way. I think that with this film Rodrigo touches your heart with every frame. He also really helped me to narrate the tale by pointing out details that proved to be extremely important. This is deliberately a very quiet and subtle film compared to the neurosis of *Amores perros*.

JW: The structure is again complex, especially in terms of the timeframes in which the narrative unfolds. You also again incorporate highly contradictory characters. Is this part of your need to challenge yourself and your audience?

AGI: I think that one of the problems with cinema and also with cinema writers – and this is where Guillermo really excels – is that they ask you to judge the characters. I never judge the characters; I always feel tenderness for them, always. No matter what they do or no matter who they are I personally feel emotionally attached. This is one of the things that I really work on in the script. In *Amores perros* El Chivo is a killer, but one of my goals was to make people understand this guy as a human being. This is imperative for me. This is also true of *21 Grams*. You are emotionally drawn to the characters and want to follow them no matter who or what they are. I wasn't worried about the chronological order of the facts, but rather the emotional order of the events. I like that this film obligates you to judge again the same fact that you already saw before and revise your prejudice. The editing phase was a very experimental and psychological time.

JW: With *21 Grams* you retain your core technical crew including director of photography Rodrigo Prieto and production designer Brigitte Broch. Was it important to have this harmony between first and second features?

AGI: They are my family and my partners. It's an organic work and I hope that I can work forever with these people. That way you develop continuity and are able to grow together. I have been working with Rodrigo and Brigitte for the last ten years and with Martin Hernandez for twenty years. Memphis was like a Mexican invasion. Fortunately, after *Amores perros* all of us continued to grow and learn more about our craft by working with others. Brigitte worked on various projects and Rodrigo worked with Spike Lee and Curtis Hanson on *The 25th Hour* [2002] and *8 Mile* [2002] respectively. Martin did the sound design for *City of God* [2002] and Gustavo Santolalla and Anibal Kerpel completed the music for Walter Salles' *The Motorcycle Diaries* [2004]. When we all got together again they were able to bring me the things they had learned and we returned to our roots.

JW: I was struck by the way in which in *21 Grams* you saturate the film stock to assign a specific tone or colour to the three central characters.

AGI: We did this with *Amores perros* too, to capture their emotion and psychology. In the case of *21 Grams* it was very subtle. Paul was blue, Benicio was yellow, and Naomi was white, with a little yellow too. It gave mood and feeling to their characters.

JW: Do you find strong parallels between the themes of 21 Grams and *Amores perros*? Loss and redemption strike me as paramount to both.

AGI: I was very interested in these subjects and also in how these people can survive. The basic things that human beings suffer are the same. Yeah, I think that in the end I have an obsession and probably I will be repeating myself in different ways and times, but I definitely have a shadow that I project and I can't escape from it. The main difference between *Amores perros* and *21 Grams* was that *Amores perros* was three stories that intersected in an accident and *21 Grams* is only one story told from three different points of view. All these people reach a point where they stop living and merely begin to survive. How can you return to your life after such a moment? I think that redemption is not the end or an infinite state once you reach it as many people believe. I think that it is just a temporary state to begin again the strange cycle of life. I was interested in hope and I sincerely wish that I were able to convey this, as it is, I admit, a very intense and heavy film. I did struggle a lot in the editing and could see the film getting heavier and heavier. It was as if I were the pilot of a jumbo jet that was in danger of never taking off. I really tried to make the point that despite the intensity the characters were brave enough to confront their amazing losses.

JW: You accord Paul a voice-over. He is the only character who has one.

AGI: I felt that it was necessary to have a point of view. I pay a great amount of attention when I am blocking a film and at various moments I found myself asking whose point of view is this? Is it Paul, is it Cristina? I felt that it was important at the end of the film to present very clearly one point of view. At the end the film it is like a memory for Paul and how he remember events. I needed one leader, the one who redeemed the other two.

JW: I was struck by an earlier quote from you where you said that 'to understand the light, you have to know the darkness'. The sense of loss in this film is so profound that I can only surmise that you have known this darkness.

AGI: Completely. My wife and I lost a baby two days after he was born. I dedicated *Amores perros* to Luciano, the son that we lost. *21 Grams* I dedicate to my wife. The presence of the absence is heavy.

JW: You deal with loss in the film in a very direct and almost brutally honest way.

AGI: I can tell you that there is no bigger loss than the one that Naomi's character suffers in the film. Some people have said that this is too much but I say to them that life is like that. A friend of mine just recently lost his father and his sister to cancer. They died just two days apart. To put this in a film would feel as if you were making some terrible soap opera but life is sometimes like that. There was a critic in Mexico who didn't like *21 Grams* and I told him that the reason he didn't like it was because he has nothing to lose. He has no wife, he has no children, not even a photograph of a dog or a plant. I love this comment and I feel that anybody who has something to lose or has already lost something can connect with this film.

JW: Did you feel a lot of pressure when making it?

AGI: I left my country, my house, my company and all the things that I had achieved up until that moment, including my commodities and success with *Amores perros* to accept a self-imposed challenge. The stress of the move and the development and all of the possible things that can go wrong to make a film happen were very stressful. We arrived four days before 11th September and the vibe with Bush changed radically, not only in the US but also throughout the world. My kids felt alienated and it took my wife and I a lot of time to get used to the city and to know who was who. It was like starting all over again and consequently it was tough and stressful, as is anything that is really worth doing. Once I was fully immersed in it I did not worry so much.

JW: And how did people within Mexico greet your decision to set your follow-up project outside of the country.

AGI: First of all I am not a diplomat and I am not an ambassador and I am not paid by the government to represent my country. I am a very proud Mexican and I feel even more Mexican the further I go from my country. I feel more Mexican than a lot of corrupt politicians or bureaucrats. It is a great thing for an artist to be travelling because it gives an even greater perspective of oneself and of one's country. In order to know yourself you have to explore other cultures. The people who do feel this are suffering from a very reductive patriotism. Why is it that painters and writers can go and live and work in other countries but filmmakers cannot? I think that a country is not a piece of land or a flag. A country is an idea that can be expressed through images, words and many other forms of expression. I feel very proud to be part of the community of world cinema and to tell whatever story I want to tell in whatever country.

JW: *21 Grams* is obviously still a very personal work. Your close friends and contemporaries Guillermo del Toro and Alfonso Cuarón have tended to make less personal, bigger-budget projects in America, reserving their more personal projects for Mexico or their mother tongue. Is this a pattern that you can one day see yourself following?

AGI: Well, I would love to shoot in Mexico again and I think that the pattern that they have invented is beautiful as it affords them so much freedom.

JW: I find it hard to imagine you ever making the kind of compromises that may be necessary for a studio project.

AGI: Yes, I admit, this would be very hard for me. What has always helped me in my life is that I don't always know what I am going to do but I have always known what I am definitely not going to do. I can't imagine myself working to orders or the authority of another voice. In fact, I have a problem with authority full stop. When somebody tries to interfere even a little bit in my process it is very hard for me, so to submit to this machinery is not in my character. But you should never say never because there could be some great novel's rights in the hands of the studio.

JW: Did you make it clear that you would not compromise on *21 Grams*?

AGI: I did a very positive thing. I didn't show my project until it was completely finished, and when I say finished I'm not talking about the script but all the other main decisions. I didn't want to show it to anybody because as in *Amores perros* I didn't want anybody involved in the creative process more than Guillermo and myself. I financed the scouting locations in several US territories, I started the casting process eight months in advance with Francine Maisler and I got the three main actors attached to the project before any studio read a line from the script. This meant a lot to me as it meant that the actors were supporting me because they loved the script. They trusted me as a director and I considered them partners of the project. Ted Hope budgeted the film so when I presented the project to the five main studios I said to them this is the script, these are the actors, these are the cities and this is the budget. I want complete creative control and final cut.

Four of them were really interested in it and I just received support, respect and enthusiasm from all of them. In the end I went with Focus Features because some very good filmmakers told me good things about David Linde and James Schamus. I was in total control of the creative process so I was as independent as on *Amores perros* where I had a great experience with Altavista Films with Alejandro Soberon and Martha Sosa producing their first feature. I regard myself as an independent film-maker and when I work with a company I like to work with, not for, them because in that way the only beneficiary is the film itself.

JW: You worked with Steven Soderbergh's editor Stephen Mirrione on *21 Grams*. How did you find working with him? I would imagine, given his work on *Traffic* [2000] that he was very in tune with your creative process.

AGI: He really saved me a lot of time; on *Amores perros* I spent seven months editing. Stephen is amazingly clear and creates amazing clarity. He is not just a 'cutter'; he really understands characters and takes care of them and of the actors. He allows scenes to breathe through his understanding of subtext and created a lot of tenderness with the characters. I would say that he is a sculptor more than an editor. He submits his work to the will of the story and to the characters, which is rare for an editor; many of them just want to impress you. The editing on *21 Grams* is very subtle; you hardly feel it. He was great.

JW: Earlier you spoke of your satisfaction with one minute of *Behind the Money*. Is there a particular scene that pleases you from *21 Grams*?

AGI: Fortunately there's more than one minute that I like in this film, especially in the performances. I think that one of them is the moment where Sean is asking the doctor if he is going to die after his new heart fails because his performance is remarkable. He expresses such fragility. Paradoxically I was really afraid of shooting the doctor scenes – and there are quite a few of them – because they are always so hard to get right and are frankly mostly unbelievable. Another moment is when Naomi Watts throws Sean Penn out of her house after discovering the truth. Every time that I watched this scene I was moved by it. Naomi's range and honesty is unbelievable. I also like Benicio's simplest moments, such as his arriving home from jail and kissing his little boy or at the end of the film when he's in the rural clinic asking Naomi for forgiveness just by looking at her.

JW: Though you deny being an ambassador for your country you have nonetheless been thrust into something of a diplomatic role for contemporary Mexican cinema. There are many exciting talents coming through but the industry and the structure that supports it seems to be shot to pieces. Just a few days ago plans were announced to end the Mexican government's decades-long involvement with the industry by dissolving both IMCINE and the Centro de Capacitación Cinematográfica and to sell off the Churubusco Azteca studios. Is it difficult to be optimistic about the future?

AGI: When it was suggested to Churchill that he should close the museums and the cultural funds for every cultural project because the country needed money for the war, his response was that if we sell and close that, then what we are fighting for? Mexico is a country of miracles. In fact, it is a miracle that we are even still alive because there are so many things that have to be solved. Everybody is talking about the hot things that are happening in Latin American cinema and in Mexican cinema in particular and I feel ashamed about this because I know that nothing is happening. This is the problem. All these films by people such as myself, Alfonso Cuarón, Carlos Bolado or Carlos Reygadas that have come are quite simply miracles that have exploded.

In poor countries such as mine, art is a secondary need; people should come first and I agree with that, but if the money that we pay in taxes will go towards food, education, medicine and all of the things that they say the money is going towards, everything will be alright. But the problem is that our politicians are the shame of the nation. They spend millions of dollars in costly presidential campaigns in which they fight between one party and the other without any result, solution, ideas or straight planning for the country. By so clearly favouring the television industry over the cinema industry these self-same politicians forget that the cinema industry can create a lot of employment, exportation and very positive cultural and economic consequences. With just with 2% of what they stole or 1% of what they spend to promote themselves, we could have a powerful industry.

***

David Gordon Green

Born in Arkansas in 1975, raised in Texas and schooled in North Carolina, the young writer/director David Gordon Green built a solid understanding of the South before making his debut feature film *George Washington* in 2000. The slow-moving and thoughtful film was cast almost entirely with non-professional actors and offered a naturalistic glimpse into another world. Beautifully shot by Tim Orr, the film evoked the work of Terrence Malick, with whom Gordon Green would later collaborate, in its subtle favouring of tone and emotion over narrative urgency. The film was also remarkable for its sensitive rendering of the world of young adults.

If *George Washington* offered a tantalising glimpse of an extraordinary talent, *All the Real Girls* (2003), winner of the Sundance Special Jury Award, confirmed Gordon Green as one of the most lyrical and distinguished voices in contemporary American cinema. This time working with actors of the calibre of Patricia Clarkson and Zooey Deschanel, the film was every bit as charming and unassuming as the director's debut. Again instilling himself in the community in which he filmed so as to better understand its mechanics and so as to not unbalance its equilibrium, Gordon Green crafted a superlative if resolutely low-key account of the onset of young love. The tagline for the film's poster summarised it beautifully: 'Love is a puzzle. These are the pieces.'

With its echoes of Charles Laughton's *Night of the Hunter* (1955), Gordon Green's more recent *Undertow* (2004) is an ostensibly more straightforward genre piece filtered through Green's extraordinary sense of composition. A dramatic thriller about two brothers who run away from home when their lives are disrupted by a violent uncle, the film remains powered by character, emotions and moments of truth. Sadly, Gordon Green's filming of *A Confederacy of Dunces* remains unrealised.

The following interview took place at the 2003 Cambridge Film Festival to mark the UK premiere of *All the Real Girls.* The interview originally appeared in *Projections 13* (Faber and Faber, 2004).

Jason Wood: I understand that you and Paul Schneider began writing *All the Real Girls* before your first feature, *George Washington*. Why did you wait until after *George Washington* to re-visit it?

David Gordon Green: I wrote it with Paul when we were right in the heat of relationships and, like the characters in the film going through a lot of 'stuff'. I was getting a little aggressive with the writing and being a little too self-indulgent with the material. I needed to step away from the absolute moment of it. At the same time my goal was to make it at a point in my life where I could do it pretty quick so that it wasn't a guy looking back on a series of events or a point in his life without nostalgia or sentiment. I didn't want it to be an *American Graffiti* [1973] type of movie. I wanted it to be something that felt immediate. It was important to let the wounds scab over a little bit to be able to take more of a technical approach to it and more of an honest approach to the actors. Also, for a first film I needed to make a movie on which I could get away with a little bit more and make a little less narratively and so we designed *George Washington* as a vehicle that if a reel got lost in the mail then a reel got lost in the mail; we really didn't need it. In my head, *All the Real Girls* was something that was so performance-based that I needed to be able to burn a lot of film to let the actors loosen up and improvise and let it feel real. They had to feel they could mess up whereas in *George Washington* they couldn't as we had to keep going, we couldn't do it twice as we couldn't afford another take.

JW: I understand that the collaborative process with Paul Schneider – who also appears in *George Washington* – was very important to you. However, was there resistance from the producers to having a relative unknown in the lead role?

DGD: We had several opportunities to make it beforehand if I wanted to look at other marquee-value actors. Paul was a guy I went to school with, where he was an editor, and was the right man for the role. When the money was offered to make the movie, it was also suggested that I should look at X and Y actor and Paul commented that this might be the only opportunity to make the movie. We talked about it and Paul suggested that perhaps I should do it but it just wasn't an issue. It never came up again as I made it clear that if you want to do this, and you are interested in the script great, but it is with Paul. The second that Sony and Jean Doumanian, one of the film's other producers, got in the room with him they recognised that Paul had a charisma, a voice and an approach to acting that isn't traditional and so decided to take the risk that nobody was going to lose their lunch if the film flopped.

JW: Again you cast a mixture of professional and non-professional actors, with the non-professional actors coming from the community in which you film. This is obviously very important to you.

DDG: Absolutely. To bring an authenticity to the texture it's always important to me to bring people with dialects and accents so that the words that come out of their mouths are what they would say. A perfect example is the scene between Noel [Zooey Deschanel] and her friend sitting on a porch; one shot, two girls talking with Noel's back to the camera. It was two actors talking in a scene that was not scripted. I knew the other girl, Amanda, a lovely 21-year-old with four kids, and wanted her to speak and tell her stories. I know that she comes from an amazing place and has an interesting background and so we all sat down together to talk about what we wanted to do which involved Zooey keeping within her professional understanding of what the scene needed to achieve and Amanda bringing a real natural life to the dialogue and the improvisation.

JW: It's unfair to pick out performances, but once again Patricia Clarkson really impresses. Was she someone you had wanted to work with for some time?

DGD: I wanted to work with her since I had a real father/son bonding moment when my dad and I went to see De Palma's *The Untouchables* [1987] and she walked on the screen and we looked at each other and went 'Damn!' I was about seven but to have that 'hey, you're my son', that was cool. I finally brought my dad to the set fifteen years later. Also, I work with every actor in a different way but my approach is the same: to find out what they're willing to give and where they are willing to open themselves up and invest in the character. I then try to give them as much freedom as possible. Patricia and I came up with a lot of the characteristics that her character has and I had a vague outline of what I want the character to achieve and how I want them to relate with certain people and then we come up with her background and the specifics together.

JW: Again with this film you ensured that your crew were fully integrated into the community where you shoot. Why is this so important to you?

DGD: It was particularly important on *All the Real Girls* because Paul lives there [Marshall, North Carolina] and my director of photography Tim Orr is from there so I didn't want to appear rude. We had a lot of ties with the community and that is always important to me. For me being the outsider, I went there a year in advance and started working jobs and meeting people and understanding the place and discovering things such as the richness that's in the back alleys of that town that a normal film crew with its location scout just misses. A lot of the characteristics, the mannerisms and some of the dialogue that's in the movie I got from working in a factory and talking to people.

JW: Are you from those parts yourself?

DGD: No, I'm originally from Texas.

JW: You display a very good nuance for life in these Carolina towns.

DGD: Well I went to school there and it's cheap to make movies there. The picture of the American South in my opinion is often caricatured and simplistic. Everybody is named Billy Bob, has missing teeth and rapes each other's cousins. Sure, that goes on, but we don't all do it. It was important for me to step away from the Southern clichés of traditional Hollywood movies and show what I'm more familiar with and what is more interesting to me. The mission statement is to offer something that is a little less stereotypical and a little more authentic.

JW: You also deal with the subject of youth and the travails of love without resorting to cliché. The first shot of the film opens on Paul and Noel having already met. You avoid the preamble. Was this an early decision in terms of approach?

DGD: In a way but it's also kind of frustrating. A lot of people come up to me and said, 'what a weird little love story, what a weird movie you've made'. Now to me, what's weird is when you see a movie when people look great and have the perfect comeback when they've messed up their relationship and instantly know how to fix it all; the music swells and then they love each other. That's weirder, isn't it? I've had love at first sight certainly but never do the heavens open up and bathe me in light. Also, when people make out and they hook up and they stay up late, their stomachs growl and they fart to make situations awkward, funny and vulnerable. If I'm going to show people my work I want to show them something that they're not seeing everyday and in some situations they can fill in the blanks themselves. They met somewhere, that's cool, the exposition and the obvious notes you can fill in for yourself. We even shot a lot of clichés, some terrible stuff just to see what we really needed and what the bones of the structure needed to be. Our first cut of the movie was three and a half hours long and it was really about filing it down to the essential elements. We wanted to try something different; you can see people stumble into romantic situations in any video shop.

JW: Was there pressure from the producers and the distributor to make the film more conventional? I understand that you shot a lot of sex scenes?

DGD: From any financial entity there is a hunger to make a movie as marketable as possible but that's understandable as it's their business and how they make their livelihood. At the same time they do present you with creative ways to accommodate that. We did shoot a lot of sex scenes and nudity but it took me out of the moment and replicated things I'd already seen before. It wasn't in any way interesting to me. I think of this film as being the scraps that the traditional romantic movie would leave on the cutting room floor.

JW: *All the Real Girls* has a timeless quality to it, making it very hard to date it.

DGD: A film like this that doesn't have an immediate life. It's not *Terminator 3* [2003] opening on one day around the world and makes $200 million at the box office. In the States *All the Real Girls* opened in February and it's still playing, slowly travelling from place to place and it will then open in Europe and other countries for the next couple of years. I don't want it to go out of style, I want it to go ahead and just be out of style. The other thing that frustrates me with many movies is that everything is so contemporary due to product placement. Sure I'm somewhat manipulating the environment because everyone obviously goes to Starbucks and Wal-mart. I want it to be a movie in it's own little capsule so that twenty years from now people can say, 'when and where the hell was this made?'

JW: Both *George Washington* and *All the Real Girls* are distinguished by their cinematography. How did you originally meet Tim Orr?

DGD: Myself, Tim and Erin [the film's costume designer who recently married Tim] all went to school together. In fact, 65% of the crew were at school together. Paul and I also worked at a film archive were Tim was the projectionist so we all bonded over films whilst cleaning 35mm prints and enjoying illicit late night screenings of *Deliverance* [1972], a real love story! Tim and I have always worked together and share a similar sense of composition. I completely trust Tim and the economic situation of the movies I make is that I don't have time to be running around doing all the stuff. I also want my friends to do what their jobs are because they have a lot of fun doing them.

JW: You pay a lot of attention to sound on the film, both the soundtrack and general sound design.

DGD: As much as the pictures, images and lighting are details that people absorb and make the movie something to look at, so sound, and indeed sometimes the lack of it is also a huge part. Where we choose to have silence, where we choose to have music and where we choose to just have the ambience of the surrounding area, all that is very important to me. There is also experimentation within that. In the middle of a dialogue the sound will drop out and you won't hear the words the characters speak.

JW: I understand that the title is taken from a David Wingo composition that wasn't used in the film. What other titles did you consider?

DGD: I considered a lot of titles actually. *South of the Heart* was one but people that didn't get the end thought that it was a TV movie title.

JW: What future projects are you working on?

DGD: Well, as soon as I wrap *Undertow* starring Jamie Bell I'm going to be going down to New Orleans to tackle *A Confederacy of Dunces*. This will give a chance for me to do some comedic stuff. Steven Soderbergh is executive producing.

JW: Finally, people seem unable to mention your work without making comparisons to Terrence Malick. Are there other figures that you would cite as influential?

DGD: Well, I like movies a lot and admittedly I do find the American cinema of the 1970s to be a rich source of inspiration but equally I find the *Dukes of Hazard* TV series has had an influence on me. Frederick Wiseman, 1970s Coppola and Robert Altman are all ballsy, brilliant filmmakers. I like a lot of more obscure stuff too; Michael Ritchie is I think a very under-appreciated filmmaker, equally Charles Burnett's *The Killer of Sheep* [1977], *Billy Jack* [1971] and James William Guercio's *Electra-Glide in Blue* [1973]. I think there was a period between *The Graduate* [1967] and *Ordinary People* [1980] where things started to rock. People were taking chances on the narratives and the cinematography and actors were throwing their careers on the line and doing very complicated work. Things weren't so on the nose and manufactured which was inspiring for me as an audience member and so I try to replicate that kind of enthusiasm through the films that I make.

***

Robert Guédiguian

Born in the mixed neighbourhood of L'Estaque, Marseilles, in 1953 to an Armenian dockworker father and a German mother, an interest in ethnicity, heritage and cultural diversity have remained consistent preoccupations throughout the work of Robert Guédiguian.

Contemporary Marseilles is a landscape Guédiguian knows intimately – its geographic and physical contours as well as its denizens who inhabit the docks, streets, apartments and bars that feature so prominently in his films. The L'Estaque area is communal and Communist, and Guédiguian was a militant from a young age, leading the Young Communists. Politically engaged, socially involved and absolutely contemporary in his concerns, he has quietly carved out a cinema of great dignity marked by a complete love and understanding of both the strengths and weaknesses of his characters.

Guédiguian studied at l'Université d'Aix-en-Provence, where he met his wife, the actress Ariane Ascaride and another actor, Gerard Meylan, also a former Young Communists leader. The creative trio are joined by a third cast member, Jean-Pierre Darroussin. Filling out Guédiguian's regular production team are Jean-Louis Milesi, with whom he has co-written his last eight films, and Bernard Cavalie, who shot many of them. The idea of community, reflected in his habit of working with a recurring cast and crew, is central to Guédiguian's oeuvre as he elucidates the realities denied so vigorously by opportunistic politicians – Marseilles, with its immigrant experience, is a microcosm of the new, multi-ethnic France.

Guédiguian is very much grounded in the politics of 1968 when France was highly politicised and he was deeply involved in political organisation between 1968 and 1980. When the Communist Party signed a joint manifesto with the Socialist Party at the end of the 1970s, Guédiguian ended his political militancy and took up working in the cinema. After co-writing one screenplay in 1978, he collaborated on another which became his first film, *Dernier été* (*Last Summer*, 1980). Subsequent acclaimed features include *Marius et Jeannette* (1997), *Á la place du Coeur* (*A Place in the Heart*, 1998) and *Á l'attaque!* (*Charge*, 2000).

Despite his political background, Guédiguian's films rarely centre on political activity. He is a social realist with a strong humanitarian bent. The following interview took place to coincide with the release of Guédiguian's ninth feature, *La Ville est tranquille* (*The Town is Quiet*, 2000), a characteristically intelligent, and of course Marseilles-set, drama that won the FIPRESCI prize at the 2001 European Film Awards. Guediguian's most recent film is *Le Promeneur du champ de Mars* (*The Last Mitterand*, 2005).

This interview originally appeared in *Enthusiasm 05* in winter 2002.

Jason Wood: It felt refreshing to watch something that was honest and imbued with integrity. These are qualities for which your work is renowned.

Robert Guédiguian: I try to be honest and I do what I can, as I feel that I am fully responsible for my work. I try at all times to show both honesty and integrity.

JW: You work regularly with many of your actors, Ariane Ascaride and Jean-Pierre Darroussin especially. Is it a question of trust?

RG: Ariane and I have worked together on something like eleven films and so to explain the attraction of working with her is difficult. I do work very regularly with my actors and could advance numerous hypotheses as to why this happens but it would become a bit introspective. It's quite personal to me and connected to the age that I am now and the fact that we've been making films together for twenty years. Jean-Pierre and Ariane can speak directly for me, often of very intimate things. Sometimes it can be quite subtle, a gesture or a look for instance.

JW: The characters in *La vie est tranquille* are typically ambiguous.

RG: Yes, particularly because they are such confused characters. I wanted to capture the confusion of their past and present thoughts. This was something at the script level, to combine very mixed and contradictory character traits and political, religious and philosophical beliefs.

JW: This ambiguity is perhaps most evident in the tense relationship between Ariane and her drug-addicted daughter.

RG: I would not want to bring judgement on her acts, but I feel that there is a strong argument that she brings life to her little girl by what she does.

JW: You show kindness but avoid sentimentality. I found the scene where Sarkis plays the piano before you pan to the hand-written sign explaining both his background and his dreams incredibly moving without being manipulative.

RG: This I suppose goes back to the point about honesty and integrity. The camera has to retain certain objectivity in moments such as this. There is a point you find whilst you work that allows you not to get too close to your subject but also not to remain too distanced. I believe this point can only be found during the working process.

JW: The film's title has a universal quality but also gives the work the sense of being a fable.

RG: The title is actually a very old idea. The title came to me many years ago and I wrote the script later with that title in mind. Proof that sometimes you can start from a title!

JW: The narrative structure is ambitious: characters and concerns, initially disparate, slowly come together. Was it difficult to translate this from script to screen?

RG: It's never easy to tell a story during an hour and a half, even if there is only one character, not even with all the worldwide rules and guides of cinema. The film I have just finished shooting [*Marie-Jo et ses 2 amours*/*Marie-Jo and Her Two Lovers*, 2002] should in effect be simpler because there are only three characters, but *La vie est tranquille* just kind of 'happened' and was actually quite easy.

JW: You manage to give equal weight to each character and situation.

RG: That could come from a certain conception I have because I feel that every character is of equal importance, from the one that has three words to say to the one that has three hundred. This is very much *people's cinema*. I often think of Jean Renoir in this regard.

JW: The film treats your native Marseilles like a character; in some ways it is the most important character, often dominating the landscapes and the people's lives.

RG: It is true. Marseilles is a character in the film. We worked on each locale of each specific character to heighten this feeling. For example, the area where Paul's parents live was filmed in a working-class area, whereas the area where Paul lives is more modern.

JW: You tackle universal and pressing themes in your films: race, intolerance, addiction and politics. You manage, however, to avoid being didactic when depicting contemporary society.

RG: I am not a man of spectacle or show and with my films I try to do the best I can. I feel that there is a huge responsibility when making something that is exposed to a lot of people. On every shot I question what does this shot tell, what does it impart, what meaning is conveyed by the way we frame the action. Film is also very contradictory, you might have to say or depict something that may seem mean but if it is also true then you have to go with it.

JW: The film opens and closes with beautiful tracking shots, both set to profoundly beautiful music.

RG: I felt that a film with such a long inventory of arduousness and misery really needed some light, some gravity, especially with the closing image. The image is also a metaphor; the beautiful music that the young prodigy plays is on a piano delivered by racists who are themselves transfixed by what the child plays. Music is important in other ways too; the three most positive characters – the black rapper, the music teacher and the child pianist – are all musicians. Beyond the actual film, I also wanted to show that people in ghettoised areas, forced to live on estates and in impoverished areas, can use music or some other form to create something beautiful. We should all have access to beauty.

***

Lucile Hadzihalilovic

Shown to great acclaim at the 48th Times London Film Festival, *Innocence* (2004) is the astonishing debut feature of Lucile Hadzihalilovic. Born in Lyon in 1961, she is a graduate of the prestigious l'IDHEC.

Previously best known for her association with Gaspar Noé, Hadzihalilovic edited *Seul contre tous* (*I Stand Alone*, 1998) whilst Noé shot her arresting black comedy filmella (running 52 mins, it doesn't qualify as a short or a feature) *La bouche de Jean Pierre* (*The Mouth of Jean-Pierre*, 1996). With *Innocence* the director and screenwriter has created a strange, haunting and strikingly original self-enclosed world.

A dark yet beautiful fable, *Innocence* contrasts the atmosphere of the gothic horror writings of both Shelley and Poe, with the light of youthful purity. Based on a story by Frank Wedekind, the film is set in a girls' school situated deep in a forest, where new pupils arrive in boxes and are raised in a strict but benign old-world atmosphere. The girls live in small groups, each age allotted a different coloured hair ribbon, but the sweetly idyllic atmosphere has a sinister undertow. What happens in the main building, where the older girls go at night, and where do the mysterious underground tunnels lead?

Exploring themes of maturity, friendship, loss and happiness as the young girls prepare for their ascent into womanhood, Hadzihalilovic creates a strange, subterranean environment that fetishises images of childhood and femininity. Part Angela Carter and part Walerian Borowczyk, the film marks Hadzihalilovic out as one of the most distinctive talents in recent European cinema and it won her the best new director award at the San Sebastian International Film Festival.

The interview took place at the 2004 London Film Festival.

Jason Wood: Can you tell me about the genesis of *Innocence* and how important script development is to you?

Lucile Hadzihalilovic: When I read Frank Wedekind's story, I was sure I had found a real subject, something strong to play with. And this is more important to me than the script itself, which is, in a way, only a work of condensations, connections, declinations of motives. To me, a script is, above all, a basic structure on which you can lean to build a visual and aural world. Then, scouting and casting break this structure because you don't find what you are looking for, but other things. So you have to re-organise the puzzle. Then, shooting breaks the puzzle again and then editing … At the end, what's left from the original script is probably what makes the heart of it – at least this is what I hope.

The original story was atmospheric and psychological, following one girl from the moment she arrives in the school, until she leaves, seven years later. For practical reasons, I've split the main character in three: Iris, Alice and Bianca. Also, I have invented two other characters: the two girls who want to escape from the school. I tried to make the story more synthetic and more abstract. And in a way, more dramatic.

JW: You mentioned Wedekind's short story. How did this initially come to your attention and what were the primary aspects of the story that you wished to explore?

LH: A friend gave me the story to read, telling me that it was definitely for me. I hadn't read anything from Wedekind at that time but I like very much German literature. Nevertheless, I've never previously found a text that presented everything I wanted to recount on screen in quite such an incredible and visual way. What I liked the most in the story was the way the school was set up: an enclosed space where young girls live in a self-sufficient community, the importance of dance and physical exercises, and the essential relationship with nature. I was also very intrigued by this utopia (to educate children by liberating their bodies) and all the negative totalitarian affects that can have. The school is a paradise and a prison at the same time. And above all, I loved the way the mystery remained at the end of the story. This lack of explanation obliges the reader to make his own interpretation.

JW: It's always tempting to believe a filmmaker's work contains something autobiographical. Did you refer to anything from your personal history in the creation of an eerie, self-enclosed world where fetishistic images of childhood and femininity are pushed to their limits?

LH: The film is totally autobiographical. Under the fairytale aspect, all the emotions and feelings are the ones from my own childhood. But, of course, I was in a very normal school, not even a boarding school, not even a school with dance lessons or white uniforms and I had an open education. I didn't have more problems with my femininity than the majority of most of the girls. I never was a graceful doll, or a 'garçon manqué', but these fetisihistic and archetypal images of childhood and femininity were certainly present in the background in the 1960s, as well as today.

JW: Your visual style is unique; especially in the way it creates its own sense of logic and time. Were there any filmmakers, writers or artists that shaped your sense of construction and aesthetic style? I certainly detected Angela Carter.

LH: The films that make the strongest impression on me and therefore influenced me a lot are: Kubrick's *2001* [1968]; *Night of the Hunter* [1955]; *Eraserhead* [1976] and the films of Robert Bresson and Dario Argento. In literature, I love tales. But more than Angela Carter, I prefer Andersen and his marvellous and cruel stories, and also Hoffman. Kafka and Bruno Schultz and all this literature of the 'inquietante étrangeté' have also made a deep impression on me.

For *Innocence*, the main visual reference was the Belgian and English Symbolist painters. And also Magritte.

JW: Equally impressive were the textured performances from a young cast. Could you say a little about your casting process and perhaps also talk about how you found the experience of directing actors.

LH: My idea was to find girls who had never worked in front of the camera but who had practised a bit of dance. We didn't do any standard screen tests. After an initial selection we organised mini dance workshops plus a short interview. Then, I set up groups of children, trying to get a microcosm with different types of girls. We did almost no rehearsals and not too many takes, especially with the youngest girls, as it was hard to keep their interest and attention. We were constantly coming up with new ways of maintaining this attention.

I tried to have as few lines as possible, so the children could learn their dialogue just five minutes before the take. I wanted them to be as fresh as possible but asking the girls to be 'natural' in front of the camera was difficult because we gave them a lot of constraints; most of the time the camera was still and we asked the girls to keep certain positions inside the frame. The costumes and the ribbons were also a constraint. The result was that sometimes the children were a bit stiff or cold but at the end I liked it. It corresponded well to the world of the school and it was also touching. It's the opposite of how children are often seen playing in public, falsely at ease and coquettish.

Regarding Marion Cotillard and Hélène de Fougerolles who played the two teachers, the challenge was to not let the children throw them off, to manage to act out their scenes despite the girls' sometimes unpredictable reactions.

JW: There seems to be a strong link between the young girls' physical and emotional development and that of nature. This is a subject that is relatively rarely explored in contemporary cinema.

LH: I liked a lot the pantheism of the original story and I tried to stress this aspect as much as possible. That's why I invented also this biology class. In the original story there were only dance and music lessons.

Maybe it's personal, but when you are a child, before you become a teenager and prefer to lock yourself in your room with friends to listen to music and chat, being in contact with nature is something very important and very pleasure-giving: swimming in a river, rolling in the grass, running in a forest ... Also, nature is a place where adults give you more freedom when you are a child. So you can have wonderful territories for games, experiences and explorations.

JW: Though there is little use of music in the film the use of sound is exemplary. What function did you wish the use of sound to fulfill?

LH: The soundtrack is essential of course, even if it's minimalist. It is based on the sounds of the park and the sounds inside the houses. Each of these elements can be reassuring or harrowing in turn. We tried to compose a kind of musical and dramatic score containing a number of leitmotifs: the clocks, the water, the train, the lamps, the insects...

The only music heard in the film comes almost only from a few classical pieces, which the girls dance to. I didn't want music the rest of the time because I wanted to highlight the other sounds and avoid any outside commentary. Like with the lighting, I wanted each sound to have an intrinsic justification, a source within the film's own universe. It gives the décor weight, its own existence. It makes this world look richer but also, after a while it gives you a feeling of claustrophobia. No sounds filter into the park from outside, as through it was a 'vacuum-packed' world.

JW: An inevitable question I'm afraid, but you obviously have a close association with Gaspar Noé, having worked with him on a number of occasions. How would you describe the working relationship and the affect that your association has on each other's work?

LH: Gaspar is my first audience. We have a different perception of life, but many references, tastes and enemies in common. When we did *Carne* (*Flesh*, 1991), *Seul Contre Tous and La bouche de Jean-Pierre*, we produced these films ourselves, with almost no money at all. So it was very natural and simple to help each other on these films. But with *Innocence*, as with Gaspar's *Irreversible* (*2002*), there were producers and enough money to pay a crew, so we weren't forced to work on each other's films. But, of course, all along the making of *Innocence* and specially during the editing, Gaspar gave me advice.

* * *

Hal Hartley

Undoubtedly one of the most distinctive voices in contemporary American cinema, Hal Hartley has continued to plough his own independent furrow, paying scant regard to cinematic fads and fashions or the dictates of dominant mainstream cinema, and imposing his own idiosyncratic style and sensibility on established genres and conventions to give the impression that his films exist in a world almost entirely of their own. As director, writer, producer, editor and composer, in the latter category often under the Ned Rifle moniker, Hartley has amassed a diverse and distinguished body of work that to-date includes ten features (excluding the hour-long *The Book of Life* (1998) but including the recently completed *Fay Grimm* (2006), a follow-up to *Henry Fool* (1997) and numerous experimental shorter pieces. Teasing out the potentials of the medium to their fullest, there is the overriding impression that each of his films is part of a longer, continual work in progress in which his own capabilities as a director and his relationship to his spectators is constantly being challenged and redefined.

Born in 1959 in Islip, New York, Hartley grew up in Lindenhurst, a working-class commuter belt of Long Island. The environment in which Hartley spent his formative years acted as a setting for his early output and also had a lasting effect on his depiction of blue-collar lives and the struggle with the class and culture dichotomy. It also informed Hartley's own astute understanding of the dynamics between aesthetics and economy, instilling in the director a low-budget mindset that was to serve him well in a career founded on being very creative on limited means. He studied painting at the Massachusetts College of Art in Boston between 1977–78, a subject that was to exert a profound and lasting influence in terms of favouring tableaux-like arrangements of figures and landscapes. Then Hartley began to develop an interest in film, making a number of Super-8 shorts. In 1980 he enrolled at the State University of New York Purchase film school. *Kid* (1984), Hartley's graduation film contained numerous stylistic and thematic motifs that would later develop into an authorial signature, most notably perhaps a frustration with suburban small-town life, tersely spoken dialogue, a minimalist approach to *mise-en-scène* and a distinct, almost fastidious approach to framing and composition.

Early features *The Unbelievable Truth* (1989), *Trust* (1990) and *Simple Men* (1992) defined the director's visual acuity and trademark use of witty, aphoristic dialogue and formed part of a playfully self-referential Long Island trilogy in which long-lasting associations with cast (Martin Donovan, Robert John Burke, Adrienne Shelly) and crew (director of photography Martin Spiller) were forged. A move into bigger-budget fare followed with *Amateur* (1994), a project written for Isabelle Huppert dealing with politics, pornography, violence towards women, and floppy discs. Described as a 'thriller with one flat tyre', the experience of making the film was not an altogether happy one and Hartley recharged his batteries by returning to the experimental, non-narrative bent of shorter pieces such as *Theory of Achievement*, *Ambition*, *Surviving Desire* (all 1991) and the wildly ambitious New York, Berlin, Tokyo love-triangle drama, *Flirt* (1995).

One of the first directors to embrace the possibilities of shooting on hi-definition digital cameras, Hartley seemed to retreat further into more radical film texts with pieces such as *The New Maths* and *Kimono* (both 2000) as his determination to refuse to compromise his work or bend to convention saw him pour his energies into teaching and establishing his Possible Films production company. Hartley has recently returned to features and though *No Such Thing* (2001) and *The Girl From Monday* (2005) may have lacked the impact of his first features, they certainly demonstrate that Hartley is a director still unafraid to take apart and reassemble the medium. At the time of writing, *Fay Grimm* is beginning to generate some of the strongest reviews of Hartley's career. An ambitious and political work, it should see the director return to our screens with some force.

The following interview took place at Hartley's True Fiction offices in New York in May 1997 whilst Hartley was in post-production on *Henry Fool*.

The interview later formed part of the documentary *Trouble and Desire: An Interview with Hal Hartley* (co-directed with Eileen Anipare, 1997).

Jason Wood: *The Unbelievable Truth*, your first feature, was made for around $200,000. You've stated on occasion your admiration for films that display inventiveness in recompense for the lack of finance for which they were produced. To that extent, do you feel that your first film has acted as a blueprint for what was to follow?

Hal Hartley: Well, I don't think that the first one set any sort of standard way of working that I followed, because the next film had considerably more money and although it was still low-budget, I'd have to say that having a low-budget mind-set from well before I made my first feature film is a good creative discipline. It sets certain challenges. It's exciting for me to think that I have to make something with nothing or with limited means. I don't think that that's a creative urge one needs to apologise for.

JW: I remember you saying that you take a lot of your inspiration from small companies.

HH: Even more so as I get a little bit older, have more experience and meet more people who have small companies, and now I understand the problems and the joys of running a small company. Probably more so than when I started making movies, because I have a small company myself that I have to run. I appreciate having conversations with people who have, maybe, a small design firm or people who build radios or something. Actually, it's much more fun to talk to people like that than filmmakers or theorists.

This film that I've just finished shooting [*Henry Fool*], I made for so little money. It's comparatively the smallest money I've had to make a film since *The Unbelievable Truth*. It's just that on *The Unbelievable Truth* people didn't get paid until we made money on the film and there was only a crew of around fifty people, so I felt like I was really working under the same confines and I felt myself sometimes solving a creative problem by really reaching back and saying like, oh, you know, I used to do this a lot, didn't I. I used to do real close-ups like this and I haven't done that in a while. It would be fun to do it again with ten years of extra added experience and skill on the part of the crew. To do even a small insert shot of a hand holding a pen, ten years ago we might have done it a certain way and might have felt terribly inspired and attentive, hard working, but there's no accounting for how much you gain in ten years. Frank Stubblefield, my gaffer, he now has an interest in lighting a hand holding a pen, which is ten times more powerful.

JW: You're not afraid to recycle images. The beginning of *Amateur* was virtually the final shot of *Surviving Desire*.

HH: It's more just process. I'm not afraid of letting process show, and process for me extends over the course of any number of films. In that period of time, from 1991 to 1993, I made a lot of films actually, a lot of smaller video pieces. There were certain kinds of graphic motifs that I found quite powerful, like I didn't think I really did it well at the end of *Surviving Desire*, although on a certain level it worked perfectly. It was funny, ironic, but it really wasn't what I was after, and so you have another opportunity to do it.

JW: You talk about the fact that *Henry Fool* was made for less money but do you find that as each successive film takes more money, especially in the UK, your reputation grows? Do you find that bigger companies to make bigger films with bigger budgets approach you?

HH: Not really. There isn't that much logic to it anymore. I mean, it was really, really hard, almost impossible to raise money for my new film unless I wanted to make it for about $400,000, which would have been cheaper than *Trust*. As it turned out I raised a little bit more than that so now I'm making a film for about the same amount of money I made my second feature film with, seven or eight years ago. The climate changes and it changes all the dynamics of the assumed value of an artist's work. You know, I'm not complaining, it's just that's the truth and I knew I would be just the work – kind of product in a sense – and that I would find the money somewhere and I did. By and large it's been a great experience.

JW: The producer Nick Weschler said that it's very soul destroying, it's like re-inventing the wheel. Every time the producer or independent filmmaker wants to raise money he has to go out and re-invent the wheel; the reputation counts for nothing.

HH: It could be. I don't feel it is ultimately because I just refuse to let it mean anything or change my assumptions about my work.

JW: At least you stay in control. Exploitation is a theme covered a lot in your work, especially in regards to women. At least it means that you are able to exploit your own talent rather than have someone exploit it for you.

HH: You can have control and be not working. You know, being a producer is this balancing act, constantly doing exactly what you want to do but being realistic enough to know that you're going to have to make some compromises. I guess that if there's an art to producing, then that is exactly what it is. I compromise every single time, I adjust my expectations of the work and the way I want to work usually. I would like to work very slowly and without a set schedule but that's impossible – never happens. So I say okay, I'll work that way and I'll make this film with a real tight schedule, with less money, and I'll make sure it's no longer than 110 minutes.

JW: In one of the first interviews I read with you, you talked about the idea of the work being the work. You said that the work is the work but seeing as you write, produce, direct and score the movies yourself, you must know that your stamp is pretty undeniable.

HH: As a producer, and going back to this finance thing, the only thing I have is my reputation, and that will duck and weave. After making a film like *Flirt*, which did pretty good for me here in the United States and England, but not in France or Germany where my films usually do well. You know, it kind of shook out in a different way. I couldn't find sources of finance in the regular places; I had to adjust. So, you really are only as good as your last movie. Business is business and that's how it is. I just try not to take it personally. But when I said the work is the work – I don't remember saying it, but it sounds very much like something I would have said – I think that what I refer to is that I may have all these ideas about what a great film is and then I go out and I make a bunch of footage and I start editing it and my ideas take a back seat to the reality of the images I have made. If there isn't an authority to the pictures, to the performances and to the creative gestures, you can't lie about it to yourself. You have to say, well okay, now I'm going to make a different sort of movie to the sort I thought I was making. I think that's probably true for any creative person working in any medium.

JW: *Flirt* is one of your more experimental films. Is this true of *Henry Fool*?

HH: I was going to shoot the entire film on video, with this digital video camera, but it just became impractical – I just couldn't do it. No, in a lot of ways *Henry Fool* is much more conventional. I think it's got a very strong story; that maybe its subject matter might be a little unconventional, but that's what people say about my movies all the time. In a way I feel that it's more conventional in a fun way than *Flirt* definitely, but even more than *Amateur* and *Simple Men*.

JW: To remain with *Flirt*, there's an interesting scene where the German builders discuss the possibility of the filmmaker succeeding or failing. One of them says 'Well, to be honest, I think he's already failed but at least this time the failure has been interesting.' The whole sequence acts as quite an interesting summation of your career so far. When you look back, in what ways do you feel that you've either failed or succeeded?

HH: Well, I always feel I'm failing in not owning up to what I really like about movies. That moment in *Flirt*, and probably one of the reasons why I like *Flirt* so much, is that it really did not disguise its process at all and something is really happening when you're watching that movie. You know, you're watching me make a movie but you're also watching yourself assess the success or failure of that movie at the same time. So I like that, and I don't do that very often; I needed an experimental format to do that. But I also like a well-made, well-crafted story and the way it's told. On the other hand, I have things that I guess you'd call more experimental and more formal. And that ambivalence that tugs back and forth between these two poles, that makes the kind of film that I make as a result of these things. If there's a Hartley stylistic it can't be anything but the result of how I deal with what I feel are my failures and how I struggle with them.

JW: It's interesting that you made a straight genre film. *Amateur* was really a thriller, which is a bit of a departure for you. It was obviously still a Hal Hartley film but in the thriller genre. I know that you described your early films – *Trust* and *The Unbelievable Truth* – as melodramas. But you also said that, for better or for worse, they are in the Hal Hartley genre, which in the UK especially coined a phrase. A lot of people think that your films are not like anything else. What would you say are the vital constituents of the Hal Hartley genre?

HH: I guess this particular indifference I was talking about, this not feeling entirely at home with telling the story, is what I consider a healthy disregard for the convention of storytelling. I don't really want you to lose yourself in the story. But I have a really high regard for storytelling in fiction and I realise that part of this fictive dream is essential. If I keep talking about it I'll sound psychotic and I guess it is. It's a kind of psychosis. You want to do two totally, radically different things and the way you happen to rope and tape them together somehow constitutes your style.

JW: All your films have very beautiful narratives – you could write them as short stories. A lot of people mention your dialogue. You write very funny dialogue with tropes and repetitions that run through the work. The transactions between the characters are often pure poetry. Is your ear for dialogue a facet of your work that you're particularly pleased with or pay a lot of attention to?

HH: I do pay a lot of attention to it. I pay attention to the rhythm or the melody, in a way that anybody who's writing a play or a poem would. In the early films it was really all I had.

JW: Whit Stillman said talk is cheap, something that you had access to...

HH: Yeah, I depended on it a lot. I think it's something I'd like to try and move away from; I don't want to lean on it quite as heavily as I have. *Henry Fool* I wrote with probably unequalled fervour but when I was shooting the film I found myself finding all sorts of opportunities for letting the actors' own cadence and understanding of things come into play. I often wrote large pieces of it and then took out all the punctuation, so that way an actor would really have to find their own way into the block of dialogue and discover new things there.

JW: Is this something that you are doing more and more? You once said that you didn't find improvisation to be very successful yet mentioned that for *Flirt* you cast Parker Posey and Dwight Ewell for their idiosyncratic qualities, for their abilities to bring something to their characters not in the script. So are you gradually revising your thoughts on improvisations?

HH: No, I think that you have to distinguish between improvisation and spontaneity. I think that Parker is a very spontaneous actress. In my experience there's always a period of improvisation in the rehearsal, but actors really bring very little from it. Maybe there are these brilliant little moments but they don't remember them and they don't really give them any particular insights. What I find much more effective is in the actual moment of shooting, in the place, the weather might be different than expected, and the weather itself might affect how an actor responds to the text, to the limitations that I've imposed by the shot, and I want that to bleed into it. That's the breath.

JW: To return briefly to the dialogue. I know it's something you said you're keen to get away from but have you any literary aspirations of your own?

HH: Well, I've written the first draft of a play [*Soon*], which will be produced at the Salzburg Opera Festival next year. That's the first time I've really put my hand to writing something outside a movie. Beyond that, I keep my diaries, journals and notebooks all the time. I'm pretty strict about that. I never wrote seriously, conscientiously, until I began to write screenplays. I used to just make lists of pictures and at a certain point people started saying things. I thought, maybe I should write down what they say and describe things. I got quite involved with it because I was also learning to edit films at the time. And editing and writing for me are things which frame the directing. If there's some poetic precision to the way I write, it comes from editing, and my directing benefited from both.

JW: Assisted by Jeffrey Taylor you score your own films under the pseudonym of Ned Rifle. Is it something that you do because you can or do you enjoy the notion of putting a little full stop at the end of the film?

HH: It comes from the fact that I think very musically about the pictures. It's usually been quite simple – it gets more elaborate, more sophisticated as time goes on. I took a music sight-reading in notation class last semester and I've benefited enormously from it. Twelve weeks of careful analysis of chord structures, and stuff like that, gave me the confidence to say, 'I'm going there and I can do that. There's no law that says I can't do this.'

JW: The music, especially in *Amateur*, is very sophisticated.

HH: Yeah, that was kind of a breakthrough. It was really the music we made for *Flirt* that opened the doors to what we did in *Amateur*. Jeffrey Taylor and I worked in this one room for a week and made the music for *Amateur*. I would come in with rough sketches of most of the pieces and we would elaborate on them. It was a great week. We felt really excited and have decided that when *Amateur* comes along we are going to use real instruments: violins and cellos and stuff like that. We had to learn a lot about recording – live players – it was really good. And compositionally I really benefited from working with Jeffrey. With his experience in wider compositions he was able to take fairly simplistic forms that I had come up with and elaborate on them.

JW: I know you've got a big interest in the American music scene. Bands such as Yo La Tengo appear on your soundtracks quite often. You seem to be musically inclined.

HH: It's just like anything else, I listen to what I like and draw from it. I am probably badly influenced by the various things I like.

JW: A lot of filmmakers form a working team they come back to again and again. You work with Martin Donovan, Michael Spiller and Jeffrey Taylor. What benefits do you find from working with a regular crew?

HH: I think you can move a lot quicker. They know a lot of the things I don't care about on the movie set, like continuity, bad continuity. Continuity doesn't fit into the kind of pictures I'm making. It helps, I guess, sometimes but it doesn't have to be an overriding concern. That and sound-recording discrepancies. If I had to explain my aesthetic approach to a sound or continuity person every time I went out to make a movie it would be exhausting! These people know what to pay attention to.

JW: Michael Spiller particularly complements your work with his crisp photography. It must be great to work with someone who is tuned in to your visual aesthetic.

HH: We go way back. The first time he shot anybody's film he shot mine. We were at school together. At the beginning of our third year we began to specialise. I knew I wanted to spend more time with the actors and Michael was clearly becoming a cameraman, so we had our first experience together. We were drawn to each other for certain things we saw in each other's work. It's push and pull – a nice dynamic. I benefited a lot from Mike's experience. I don't work with anyone else but Mike shoots for many, many people and he'll often come back from working with somebody with something he's learned: 'Let's put this on the lens here, or look at this, or I'll tilt up just as she's going out left.' It's a good dynamic.

JW: How important a role would you say politics plays in your work?

HH: I think I try to give evidence that I recognise it as part of our shared human experience. I deal with politics in human terms rather than dealing with humans in political terms. I think in *Trust* that was much more up front about it. In *Simple Men* it was more outrageous, meant to just underline the relationships of fathers and sons and brothers and brothers.

JW: Your ability to write strong female roles is often commented upon.

HH: I think I'm just ultimately more interested in women. I think the characters that I made in the beginning, particularly in *Trust*, was something I wanted to see. I imagined this woman into existence; just the kind of woman I would fall in love with. Then when you get that out of your system you move onto different types. I think I have fun with the childish side of men and with being a man. You know, like flouncing around in the mud, being childish and stupid. But at the same time truthful. I think like Martin's characters, or Bob's [Robert Burke]. That was probably the kernel of *Simple Men*: silly men who are perfectly correct in certain things. And also I think that women, the opposite sex, will always be just that much more mysterious to you than your own sex and therein lies the attraction.

JW: Do you feel that it is a thin line between exploitation and objectification? There are women that took exception to the female characters in *Amateur*.

HH: It is a thin line. There is something that film does. It tries to disentangle this fine thread of what is an exploitative watching from a respectful representation. I don't really have any answers. I think I try to work it out in the film. I enjoy watching. I enjoy creating women who attract me to them. People talk about it especially with *Trust*. I mean, that girl is just as created by a male attraction as the women in *Amateur*; it's just that I needed to look for different things at different times and they were separated by three or four years. I looked into one basket pretty thoroughly with *Trust* and wanted to explore more things about myself and my desire to watch.

JW: You've talked about your films as being attempts to make some philosophical sense of your own existence. How successful are they in achieving this?

HH: They help. I think because they're active. It's hard when you're making a movie, creating something, to just be theoretical. I think work is great for that because it saves you from just getting lost in theory.

JW: How closely do you associate with the characters you write?

HH: I identify pretty strongly with all the characters. I couldn't write them if I couldn't understand them on some level. Mystery leads to attraction but you can't really get anywhere in shaping a character unless you make certain assumptions based on your understanding of being a human being. You start to formulate possibilities for these people. You know, there are plenty of instances of things that you know are just funny that anybody could relate to. A lot of the time I try to reach for things that I find genuinely archetypal, not that they feel really close to me but because I recognise them easily without having to struggle, without having to intellectualise. It just feels right, the shape of the character, the consequences of an action, and the type of action.

JW: Ned Rifle crops up again and again: he's the author of 'The End of the World' which Audry reads at the end of *The Unbelievable Truth*. He's another author in *Trust*, of 'The Man and the Universe'. And he's the character, Ned Rifle. Also he's the moniker under which you compose. Where does the name Ned Rifle come from?

HH: When I was a fourth-year student in film school, I was making my thesis film, *Kid*, and the leading character was called Ned Rifle. Mostly because, all the scripts I produced at film school, we wrote in class. To keep things interesting I would give characters sort of funny names, ironic names, anything. We used to crack each other up that way and Ned Rifle was one of those recurring boobs who would show up in my screenplays. He was in *Kid* but I cut out any reference to his name because I shot those scenes so badly. Also, during that year I was studying the western film and I had a tutorial to get extra credits by watching all the western films, writing papers on them so I was flooded with these western sounding names.

JW: In terms of relationships, your films seem to deny the characters a happy ending. It's like you're suggesting that love and harmony are impossible.

HH: Well, I try to avoid happy and sad endings and reach for true and false endings. I think my endings strive to be true and not forced. It's a complicated thing. I think the endings of *Trust* and *Simple Men* are not bad endings. Things have worked out the way they probably should work out, and there's possibility, which is very important. I want that the film should end with a gesture of possibility rather than with complete closure. I think the same, but in a much more complex way, with *Amateur*.

JW: I think the men do what's right, which is quite brave of them. The choice Robert Burke makes at the end of *Simple Men* is the right choice. But you also seem to deny consummation of the sexual act.

HH: *Henry Fool* has consummation. Raw, ugly, consummation. But fun, raw, ugly, fun consummation!

JW: You display a tremendous acumen for movement and music in film. The choreography sequence at the start of *Flirt*, the whole of *Ambition* is meticulously choreographed; the dance sequence in *Surviving Desire* and *Simple Men*. Are there any plans for a musical?

HH: For years I thought it would be fun. If I make a musical I really want to make a musical where I also have an interest in making the soundtrack of the movie first. Not just the music, I mean everything. Record all the dialogue, the sound effects and create an aural landscape, a 90-minute track and then shoot the whole movie like a rock video. Everybody's got to mime things, or not mime them. I think that would be a good way to make a musical. I'd like to make a musical that somehow really incorporates the characteristics of the medium. Not that illusion, certainly not making it look like people are really singing.

JW: It's obvious to see in your work associations with Bresson, Godard, Wenders. On British Television last week you talked about Hitchcock. How important are filmmakers of that era to you? *The Unbelievable Truth* was almost like a Preston Sturges or a Frank Capra.

HH: Very much. Preston Sturges and Howard Hawks – I really drew a lot from those guys, their movies and their scripts. I think every filmmaker is really important.

JW: You've become something of a figurehead to the independent scene. You yourself would have probably looked to John Cassavetes or John Sayles. A lot of younger filmmakers, Richard Linklater and Kevin Smith, now are citing you. Do you feel comfortable with this or would you rather be distanced from any scene or clique?

HH: I wouldn't want to be associated necessarily with a clique for the wrong reasons. I think if a person's experience and output encourages somebody else to do good work, or attempt to do good work, that's great and I'm happy to be used as an example. But it's hard, I'd be careful to isolate or indicate a clique that I think I'm representative of or anyone else for that matter. When I started making films everybody would say 'in the mould of a Jim Jarmusch'.

JW: Did you find that annoying?

HH: Well, it wasn't that annoying to me. Being mentioned in the same breath as Jim Jarmusch was kind of swell, but I always thought that he must be so embarrassed to tug not only the weight of his own reputation and work, but of other people as well.

JW: There seems to be an interest in your work in blue-collar workers. I know that you worked yourself for a while in the construction industry. I also read that you wanted to be a carpenter when you were a kid.

HH: Well, that's just it. I come from a blue-collar world and appreciate a lot of it while feeling at the same time I had to get out of there because little by little you discover who you are and what your desires are. It's stuff that you understand. I try to break things down, to distil situations, characters and gestures down to something really concrete. Blue-collar people deal with things. I'm sure white-collar people deal with things too but there's something about the imagery of a carpenter who takes objects and nails them together and makes another thing. It's very much like filmmaking.

JW: There is running through your films a sense of religion. There's also this idea of salvation, retribution and suffering in order to gain salvation and retribution. Is this religious aspect something to which you pay particular attention in your work?

HH: I think so. I don't consider myself Christian, mostly because the definition is pretty tight, but there's a lot that I respond to. I read a lot about different kinds of religions.

JW: Finally, in hindsight, which of your films has given you the most pleasure and which has come closest to achieving what you set out to achieve?

HH: Probably *Flirt*. Up until *Flirt* it was *Ambition* or *Theory of Achievement*, one of those. They had the right balance because they were shorter films. The right balance between the plastics of the medium and the pleasures of telling the story.

JW: I'd probably pick *Surviving Desire*.

HH: That's probably my least favourite.

JW: I'd probably pick *Ambition* or *Theory of Achievement*...

* * *

John Hillcoat and Nick Cave

The third collaborative feature between director John Hillcoat (born 1961) and writer-musician Nick Cave (born in 1957), *The Proposition* (2005) is a powerful and intelligent Australian western set in a savage corner of the bushranger outback. Bloody and uncompromising, Hillcoat pictures the outback as a place of extreme cruelty and beauty, whilst strong performances from all the cast do justice to the elegance of Cave's script. The Nick Cave/Warren Ellis score further heightens the film's astonishing existential force.

Having initially met after Hillcoat directed a number of arresting music promos for Nick Cave and the Bad Seeds, the Australian duo first collaborated for the big screen on Hillcoat's feature debut, *Ghosts... of the Civil Dead* (1988). A brutal prison drama set in a high-security jail, this brutal work was co-written by Cave and featured his first character performance as the psychopathic Maynard. Unfolding in flashback to detail the events that necessitated a lockdown, the film makes few concessions to commercial considerations and refuses, like *The Proposition*, to establish a fully sympathetic character. The stark cinematography by Paul Goldman and Graham Wood further enhances the film's urgent, nihilistic streak.

Emerging almost ten years later, *To Have and To Hold* (1996) addressed similar issues of isolation, following two ill-fated lovers (Tchéky Karyo and

Rachel Griffiths) in a jungle town in Papua New Guinea. Though neither performing nor contributing to the writing, Cave was responsible for the enveloping soundtrack, which was also notable for coaxing Scott Walker from self-imposed exile to perform.

The critical and commercial approbation generated by *The Proposition* has led to Hillcoat and Cave announcing another project together. Described at its earliest inception as a romantic comedy set in Hove, *Death of a Ladies' Man* is set to go into production in 2007.

The following interview took place on stage at the premiere of *The Proposition* during the 2005 Cine City Festival in Brighton.

Jason Wood: Was it always your ambition to make a western?

John Hillcoat: I've always been into the anti-westerns of the 1970s. I've always been amazed at the history in Australia and I wanted to embrace that genre, given that our bushranging films actually pre-date the western. I thought the ingredients of struggling with the climate, the clash of cultures, that kind of lyrical, mythical quality of the power of the landscape hadn't been fully explored.

JW: Did that interest you too, Nick?

Nick Cave: Not really. Basically, John has been talking about doing an Australian western ever since I've known him, which is about twenty years, and that I would do the music. But it was taking an enormously long time to get a script together, and eventually John asked me to write the script. I wrote the script in order to do the music really, which is what I was mostly interested in. He gave it the theme of 'an Australian western' and a bit of research, but I was more interested in writing a script per se, than this particular one. I grew up in Kelly country, where Ned Kelly died, so I knew a fair amount about these kind of characters.

JW: You've said that you found the narrative parts pretty easy to write, because you're a narrative songwriter, but you found the dialogue hard – how did you get over that?

NC: Initially I didn't know whether I could do it or not.

JW: The two of you have worked together before on *Ghosts... of the Civil Dead* and *To Have and To Hold*. How does your relationship work?

NC: I didn't really do any research, but Johnny did an enormous amount. I would just email my pages to him and we'd talk about it in the evening, and it just continued that way.

JW: You can see the heat and the flies in the film. Were the crew and cast surprised by how arduous filming was?

JH: Yeah, particularly the British actors who had never worked in Australia. Ray Winstone stopped off in Dubai to try to acclimatise, but he had no idea. I had a dialogue with Emily Watson before she came out, and she was explaining that when the temperature is in the twenties, it's okay, but in the thirties she really starts to struggle, and we were shooting in the high fifties. And she had to wear a corset and all the fabrics were original and thick wool. It was extremely difficult. It actually changed how they moved and even how they spoke. The scene where John Hurt first appears, it was 57 Celsius and the medics were getting very worried about John, and the camera eventually got so hot that it couldn't be touched, so we had to go to night shoots.

That scene with John Hurt, when we came to do the reverse-shot on Guy, there was just a little tip of John's shoulder in the frame. I asked Guy if he wouldn't mind letting John step out and cool down a bit, which he was fine about, but John insisted on being there for Guy, and he performed as if we were doing a close-up on him. That was the feeling amongst the cast – they were incredibly loyal and generous.

NC: I wasn't there for the shoot, but I went for a week before to rehearse with the actors. It was very moving for me to see this pile of words that I'd written being brought to life by these brilliant actors. Guy was incredibly pernickety about every detail – why does he get off this side of the horse instead of that side – there was this endless stream of nonsense that came out of Guy's mouth. But that's the way he works. Ray was the complete opposite of that. I really enjoyed that process.

JW: Location becomes another character in *The Proposition* and in your films in general.

JH: It was quite a weird experience. For anyone who knows Australia, it was a three-hour flight and a three-hour drive to this tiny town [Winton in Queensland]. The location featured lots of sacred Aboriginal sites and massacre sites. The place has an amazing history, and the Aboriginal people lent their support because they really want to get this side of their history out there. The people in the town were extraordinarily supportive, and a lot of the extras were from the town. There were all these weird connections – like my sister conceived her first child in Winton, and her son is half-Aboriginal, so his ancestral lands were there. But we ended up at that location by pure coincidence, for pure financial reasons. Then I discovered during post-production that my grandfather and his father both lived and worked at the same station where we filmed.

JW: The violence in the film is pronounced and yet it is often followed by mom-ents of sadness and longing.

JH: For us, the film was about the physical and psychological effects of violence and we didn't want to shy away from how brutal those times were. I deliberately didn't use any slow-motion, so everything is deliberately fast and chaotic and slightly confusing. What we wanted to linger on was not the violence, but how people are affected by it. In our history, I believe very strongly that everyone involved was morally compromised, whether you had righteous ideals like Ray Winstone or whatever perspective you were coming from – no one came out unscathed. We wanted to show all the kinds of violence from that time, including the black-on-black violence. It was actor Tom E. Lewis's idea to kill the tracker, because he said that was the first person he would attack. We have this notion that Aboriginal people were a very nomadic and peaceful group that were then annihilated, but actually they put up a fierce battle, and they were also fighting each other.

JW: What were the emotional effects of being out in the landscape?

NC: I grew up in a very small country town, so I was horrified to be there, because my entire childhood all I wanted to do was get out. But coming back as a grown-up, it was very beautiful.

JH: Most Australians haven't been to the outback. They've been everywhere in the world except the interior. The power of it is amazing, and like John Hurt said to me, it's like eternity, like another planet. I got a strong, strong feeling – that Nick also picked up – that we don't belong there.

JW: What kind of human traits inspired you to come up with the psycho-pathic brother, Arthur?

NC: I was increasingly tired of watching films where in every scene the villain was as bad as he could possibly be – it's like this arm-wrestle between filmmak-ers to see who can make the most despicable villain. I really wanted to create someone who had a great love of things as well as having an amoral side.

JH: Andlikealotofpsychopaths,whenthesunsetcomes,hegetsverysentimental.

NC: There is that mixture of sentimentality with people. I've found that quite common in people.

JW: Who is the hero in the movie – is it Captain Stanley or is it Charlie Burns?

NC: We were trying to make an Australian western, and the difference is that America sees its history in terms of black and white, the good guys and the bad guys. We wanted to create something where morality is blurred and where your allegiance to the characters swings back and forth, the way it does in real life. I don't particularly believe in the concept of good guys and bad guys.

JH: It's also an Australian thing – our whole history is inspired and based on failure.

NC: Fervent incompetence … It seemed important and poignant in some way that the boy who hangs out in the hills was a really nasty piece of work, but at the same time had a really nice singing voice. There's an innocence about him.

*** *

Tranh Anh Hung

Born in 1962 in My Tho, Vietnam, Tranh Anh Hung relocated with his parents to Paris aged twelve following the fall of Saigon. After two well-received short films, *La femme mariee de Nam Xuong* (1988) and *La Pierre de l'attente* (1990), his career exploded onto the international scene with his first feature production, *Mùi du du xanh* (*l'odeur de la papaya/The Scent of Green Papaya*, 1993). A placid but visually intoxicating tone poem told through the eyes of a young peasant girl forced to work as a maid to a family in Saigon, the film's subtle yet incredibly detailed glimpse into the interior life of a Vietnamese household in the 1950s is made all the more remarkable by the fact that the film was shot in the Boulogne studios. The film won a César for best first feature and the Cannes Camera d'Or.

    Xich lo (*Cyclo*, 1995), Tranh's second feature, continued the director's interest in Vietnamese culture but offered a differing perspective on the themes of family values, bonding and commitment. Abandoning the gentle minimalism of his debut, Tranh returns to Vietnam for a brutal, if brilliantly rendered, portrait of modernisation, as experienced by an 18-year-old cyclo driver. Set in the tumult of Ho Chi Minh City, the film deftly sets up the grinding poverty and mind-numbing routine endured by the protagonist, his older sister (Tranh Nu Yen-Khe, the director's wife), his younger sister and his grandfather and their spiralling descent into poverty and desperation. Set in motion by the theft of the young protagonist's rickshaw, *Cyclo* boasts a dark visual power, its urgent, hand-held camera feverishly evoking social and spiritual turmoil. The film continued Tranh's habit of securing major awards, carrying off the Golden Lion at the 1995 Venice Film Festival.

The somewhat Chekhovian tale of three sisters who live in close proximity in present day Hanoi, Tranh's third film, *Mua he chieu thang dung* (*At the Height of Summer*, 2000) was a return to the more gentle and restrained aesthetic of *The Scent of Green Papaya*. On the anniversary of their mother's death, three sisters meet up to honour her memory. Intensely close, they seem to tell each other everything and seek each other's advice on every subject. And yet each of them has a secret. One month later, following a turbulent period of temptations, disappointments, suspicions, separations and mis-understandings, each of them has revealed what the tact and discretion of familial relationship has always kept hidden.

Exquisitely acted and beautifully photographed by Mark Lee, Tranh's expertly crafted, sensuous film is an elegant and resonant combination of mood, ravishing visuals and Ton That-Tiet's beguiling music.

Sadly Tranh has remained quite of late, the Jimi Hendrix project referred to in this 2001 interview as yet unrealised. This interview originally appeared in *Enthusiasm 05* in winter 2002.

Jason Wood: You've previously described *At the Height of Summer* as having a comic element. This to me seems misleading description.

Tran Anh Hung: To tell the truth, that statement is very old and was written towards the end of writing the script. It was actually just something for the pro-ducer to show to help the film in terms of international sales.

JW: It certainly confused me. It is a departure for you in many ways but I certainly didn't see a comic element to the film.

TAH: It has nothing to do with the film as it exists today. There is a slight mis-chievous nature to it but you're right, it couldn't be described as a comedy. In a way, because I had a child at the time, my little girl may have loosened my tongue because I certainly set out to make a film with more dialogue because my first two features were almost totally silent. I wanted to have long moments of silence followed by scenes that were in terms of narrative very rich and laden with dialogue. And as I was writing them I discovered that what you need to do is make the characters say something simple which seems to hint at something, a truth for instance that actually may be quite deep. I also wanted the dialogue to be very sincere and without local colour; I rejected all local colloquialisms to arrive at a dialogue that had a certain naivety and innocence.

JW: Continuing the theme of dialogue, there seems to be a distinct sense of rhythm to the way the actors speak.

TAH: I wanted the actors to reach a certain musicality and sense of melody when they spoke and we worked very hard together to achieve this. We made sentences longer to enable the melody to naturally blossom.

JW: You are primarily known for the visual splendour of your work, which is again very much in evidence. Did you enjoy this process of playing around with the dialogue?

TAH: Oh yes, very much. Of all my films, *At the Height of Summer* was the most pleasure to make. To really search for a character's breath and to find a way to make a character come to life on screen was very thrilling for me.

JW: I think you were aided in this regard by your cast, many of whom you'd worked with previously. Was your previous relationship with them a defining factor in your decision to cast them again?

TAH: It was a big factor yes. Absolutely. They inspire me and even when working on the other films together, they would perhaps do something that would cause me to think 'that is not right for this film, but for the next one...'

JW: You have always used contemporary music in an interesting way. In *Cyclo* you used the anthemic 'Creep' by Radiohead, *At the Height of Summer* uses work by the Velvet Underground to commentate on both character and narrative. You also make use of more indigenous music. It's fair to say that music is important to you.

TAH: There are always three types of music in my work: American, which is something that touches me personally in my own life and which we cannot escape from, there's Vietnamese music, and then there's the music composed for the film. I always know all the pieces of music I wish to use before the film even starts shooting. For example, I am currently working on an English-language project in the States, which uses the music of Jimi Hendrix. This film will uses twelve pieces by Hendrix and hopefully they will make people listen to Hendrix in a way they have never listened to him before. I always think musically. What I desire most for a film is that there should be a certain rhythm; I can only begin to write a script if I feel the rhythm of the film within me. I may not even know the story or the theme; the theme must give a physical sensation to the spectator and nourish the spectator. The image must of course make sense and it must also be tactile which is why many of my scenes are rather long and possessing of a certain fluidity, in terms of the camera movement, to give a sense of presence to the spectator. This is the hardest thing to create in cinema; I want to conjure a feeling of anticipation with my images.

JW: The images in your film certainly stand alone. You are also very good at capturing texture and sensuality. Everything seems so striking. This is certainly true of the scene in which the sisters prepare the ritualistic meal.

TAH: In the scene you mention I think that this is also down to the actresses who have a natural grace, the grace is there and so it is not too hard to capture it. They are also extremely expressive which complements the images I use.

JW: *At the Height of Summer* hints at the complexity of relationships.

TAH: It certainly focuses on the partial revelation of secrets. For the couples in the film it has to do with desire and infidelity. What interested me was to look at the idea of the couple in the context of Confucius, for example how to communicate to the spectator a difference without too clearly explaining it. In the film, where the photographer tells the truth to his wife, she cries because it is painful to her. It is at this moment that I choose to cut. I go back to them only when she is proposing a solution, what I cut is actually very precious in Western cinema, that's to say the confrontation. In the West confrontation is dynamic, in Asia it is not necessarily so, it is the moment when each character asks, which part of this pain shall I keep within myself.

JW: Talking of the West, is it pleasing that your films have accrued for you such a mighty reputation. In Europe especially your work is extremely well received and respected.

TAH: Of course, it pleases me a lot. I personally don't fully understand why. What is really important is that it enables me to make other films; I would love to be able to view my films through these Western eyes.

JW: What also struck me were the strong female characters you create with your latest film.

TAH: This is interesting. In many countries, *The Scent of Green Papaya* was attacked by feminists because I talk about solitude without attacking it; this is because I feel that the aim of art is to move people and in the best possible scenario to create a chaos of feelings within the spectator, causing him or her to later re-arrange personal feelings accordingly. What I love is to show things that move me and what moves me is that in Vietnam there are men who do nothing and women who do everything. But in Vietnam the women do everything with pleasure; it's the opportunity to talk and discuss sex and men so that's what I show with this film. It was not necessarily a conscious decision.

JW: You mentioned that your next project was to be set in America. Is this something that particularly excites you or do you fear that your work, which is visually very poetic, could in some way be diluted?

TAH: I'm looking to go beyond cultures and work on the specific materials of film art. There is still so much for me to explore. What worries me with my next film is how an image will appear, that is how to prepare the actual image and how it will work with the music of Jimi Hendrix. That's what really excites me.

JW: I didn't realise you were such a Hendrix fan.

TAH: Actually I'm not. My interest is really only for this film. For this film, he is the greatest composer on earth.

* * *

Cédric Kahn

Born in France in 1966, writer-director Cédric Kahn has, over the last ten years or so, established himself as one of France's most talented and versatile filmmakers. Following one well-received short, *Les dernières heures du millénaire* (1990), and one little-seen feature, *Bar des rails* (*Railway Bar*, 1991), Kahn first came to attention with *Trop de bonheur* (*Too Much Happiness*, 1994), a slice-of-life coming-of-age tale concerning a group of high school students who are on the verge of graduating. Widely regarded as one of the most honest and perceptive films about teenage life, the film established Kahn's ability to tap into the nuances of mundane, everyday life. The film won the Prix Jean Vigo and the Prix de la Jeunesse at the Cannes Film Festival.

Also collaborating with other directors on their scripts, including Brigitte Rouan's *Outremer* (*Overseas*, 1990), Laurence Ferreira Barbosa's *Les Gens normaux n'ont rien d'exceptionnel* (*Normal People are Nothing Exceptional*, 1993) and the upcoming *Les Ambitieux* (*The Ambitious*, due for release in 2007) by Catherine Corsini, Kahn, who has also made pieces for French TV, gave a further glimpse of his confidence behind the camera with *L'Ennui* (*Boredom*, 1998). Engrossing, erotic and sometimes comic, *L'Ennui* tells the story of a restless philosophy professor tired of teaching and troubled by the happiness of his ex-wife. His mid-life crisis takes a turn when he meets the young, enigmatic and far from intellectual Cecilia, with whom he embarks upon a sexually-charged affair. Enlisting his ex-wife as a reluctant confidante, Martin claims that he is bored by Cecilia, yet continues to see her, fascinated by her uncomplicated attitude towards love, life and sex. But, upon learning that Cecilia is also seeing a much younger man, Martin's desire becomes tainted with jealousy and eventually becomes an uncontrollable obsession that threatens to consume him. Adapted from the novel *La Noia* by Alberto Moravia, the film brilliantly traces a slow and steady descent into paranoia.

Kahn would again touch upon this subject in *Roberto Succo* (2001), in which newcomer Stefano Cassetti gives a riveting, extraordinarily intense performance as the psychopathic Italian killer Roberto Succo, who was declared France's public enemy number one in the late 1980s after escaping from the mental institution where he was being held for the brutal murder of his parents. Travelling between the Mediterranean and the mountains of Savoy, Succo left a trail of inexplicable murders, rapes and abductions which police investigators struggled to connect. Kahn offers a gripping dramatisation of true events and gives a terrifying but resolutely non-sensationalist insight into the disturbed mind of a serial killer.

Kahn's most recent work is *Feux Rouges* (*Red Lights*, 2003), another work taken from a literary source, this time from Georges Simenon. Another restrained yet utterly compelling journey into the unknown, the film follows a bickering couple on their way from Paris to collect their children from summer camp. Annoyed by her husband's drinking, the wife leaves him in a desolate bar to make her own way to their children, unaware of a radio announcement revealing that a dangerous killer has escaped from prison. Relocating the novel from the United States, Kahn and his co-screenwriter Laurence Ferreira Barbosa also stripped down the book to the core, concentrating all the action on the two leads. As in his previous films, Kahn prefers to tell a gripping story: in the confines of the car the couple are forced to contend with each other's presence and the tension slowly builds, reinforced by the dark tones of the music ('Nocturnes' by Debussy). The human side of the tragedy is central to this story: as the night progresses a primitive fear colours the film. The ride becomes a nightmare in a world of anonymous roads, cars and neon lights where nothing is what it seems. Kahn deliberately created a sense of unreality through the film, shooting all the night car scenes in a studio.

The following interview took place in 2002 and originally appeared in *Enthusiasm 06* in spring 2003.

Jason Wood: On the surface at least, *Roberto Succo* seems to be a very different film to *L'Ennui*.

Cédric Kahn: I do like to do different things but I am not so very sure that the film is so different.

JW: How then did the figure of Roberto Succo first come to your attention and what was it about him that suggested that his story would be suitable for a film treatment?

CK: The most important thing about Succo is that he is a very unusual character. He is very multi-faceted and has many different aspects. He is hard to both define and understand. What's fascinating about all the statements from people who had actual contact with him is that he was different in each and every case; he is like a chameleon.

JW: The film goes to great lengths to present this multi-faceted character. You avoid stereotypical serial killer/sociopath clichés.

CK: When I wrote the script, I was determined to present as many different aspects to the character as possible. For me, this was the best way to get away from the fantasy of a killer and at least try to get somewhere near the truth.

JW: I understand that Pascale Froment's book *Je te tue. Histoire vraie de Roberto Succo* was important to you. How did you decide what elements of Froment's book to discard and did you deny yourself extrapolation?

CK: I certainly didn't want to add anything to the actual facts because I felt that would actually weaken the power of the facts and the events themselves, which were so rich. It returns to my earlier point and my fascination with Succo's multi-faceted personality. I wanted to show the facts that would most readily signify this personality. The only thing I did do was take out a lot of the repetitiveness of Succo's behaviour and I also highlighted the cruelty of his acts.

JW: Is Succo a powerful figure in the French consciousness? Did he not perversely become something of a political figure?

CK: The real story was not so well known but about a year after the events a play was written about Succo by Bernard-Marie Koltès, a very fashionable playwright. The play presented Succo as what can only be described as a *black angel*, an anarchist hero. The image created of Succo by the play replaced that of Roberto

Succo as public enemy no.1. The play has created a good deal of confusion.

JW: In popular culture in general, however, there is a tradition of creating heroes out of criminals. We have done it in Britain with people like the Krays but I think your film assiduously avoids this. Were there works that you looked at and thought, well I certainly want to distance my film from this approach?

CK: *Natural Born Killers* [1994]. I absolutely wished to avoid making this kind of film. Films that did positively influence my approach include *Badlands* [1974] and *The Honeymoon Killers* [1969]. Also, I would cite Truman Capote's book *In Cold Blood*, which was a huge influence on Froment's book.

JW: I understand that James Ellroy was also a reference point for you.

CK: Very much so. I was more influenced in my making of the film by reading James Ellroy than by any other film I might have seen. What I like in Ellroy's work is his sympathy for the victims; he shows little interest in the actual criminals. This is an approach that can obviously be attributed to the fact that Ellroy's own mother was a crime victim.

JW: You show a great interest in forensics.

CK: Clearly. This I would again partly trace back to Ellroy. Also, and to finish on Ellroy, I wanted to adopt the narrative device of the investigator falling in love with the victims; it is because of this love that an obsession with the investigation develops.

JW: I enjoyed the way in which you use the photography of the victims in *Roberto Succo*. Are there other scenes of which you are particularly proud?

CK: They are important sequences for sure but to be honest as sequences they were not so hard to do. It was a kind of cinematic short hand; a photograph can carry as much emotion as a carefully-staged scene. I am not a director interested in brio and showing off; I care about this revealing of emotion. Also, I am never fully satisfied with my films.

JW: You're like Woody Allen.

CK: Yes, perhaps. However, the Swiss scenes I am very happy with and I think that the scene where Succo is in the nightclub works well.

JW: The nightclub scene certainly shows Succo's failed attempt to blend into social situations.

CK: Whenever he is in a social situation he simply cannot function or find his place. This is also true of the scene where he goes to meet Léa from school.

JW: It's certainly in these social situations that he often finds himself reduced to shouting 'I'll kill you' to everyone he meets, which is not the best way of trying to fit in.

CK: He becomes like a child.

JW: The film exists as a hybrid of genres; it has some of the aesthetics of a documentary, it has elements of the thriller, it is part biography and in some scenes it feels like a romance.

CK: I am certainly interested in all genres and thought I could again use these genres to tell each particular story, each attack, depict each victim differently.

JW: Did you enjoy working in cinemascope?

CK: Very much. It is of course more expensive and people tried to tell me to do it differently. It is a great pleasure to film in this format, which of course dictates certain things with regard to the *mise-en-scène*; on a very simple level, for example, you can show more things in a single shot, which can make each image more complicated to construct.

JW: You've talked about Succo's multi-faceted personality; it interested me the way in which you also chose to show his capacity for love.

CK: This aspect of the film was based on the statements of the Léa character and so is factual. I also do not believe that there people who are completely incapable of affection, even killers. Just like us, killers are human, which is true, even if difficult to accept. Conversely, it is difficult for many of us to accept any human carrying out terrible, almost incomprehensible acts.

JW: Stefano Cassetti gives an amazing performance as Roberto Succo. He was a real find, especially given that he is not a professional actor.

CK: He was found purely by chance. Casting was open to both professional and non-professional actors. I don't believe that the distinction between the two is useful, for me the only question is whether the actor has talent or not. The actor on screen is always a combination of his own personality and his ability to portray somebody who is not himself. Any actor, whatever his training brings something specific to the character. Stefano, of course, did bring something very specific and particular. There were many professionals who wanted the role; it is after all an attractive role, especially for actors in France who do not often get the chance to play the part of a character like this. Having said that, the casting was not open to French actors, as I wanted an Italian for the role.

JW: How did Patrick dell' Isola come to be involved?

CK: We did lots of tests, but what was crucial were the tests between Patrick and the actress who plays Léa, Islid Le Besco, as they had to really complement each other. If you like, these two actors were chosen as a pair, as in some way were Islid and Stefano. I also saw Patrick in Marion Vernoux's *Rien à faire* [*Empty Days*, 1999] and I thought that he would be very believable as a gendarme and not in any way a caricature.

JW: We began talking about *L'Ennui* and the inherent similarities between your films. You deal very often with characters in crisis, specifically men, raging against some kind of inner turmoil.

CK: I think that films are always made about such people. Cinema is all about people in crisis because they make such good subjects. Truly interesting cinema, if not all cinema, is about someone who is looking for something.

* * *

Asif Kapadia

Having won a Cannes Grand Jury Prize and the Grand Prix at the European Short Festival with *The Sheep Thief* (1997), his graduation film from the Royal College of Art, Asif Kapadia (born in Hackney, London, in 1972) made an immediate impact with his debut feature *The Warrior* (2001).

An understated parable about a warrior's quest for redemption after renouncing violence, the film shows the warrior and his ruthless band of thuggish soldiers going to make an example – with flame and sword – of a village that had failed to pay its taxes. During the raid, the Warrior has a vision that momentarily finds him in the mountain village of his youth, then coming out of his dream to find snow still on his feet. It's a magical moment, and just one of many in this contemplative movie. In response to this mystical experience, the Warrior flees his desert home with his son in tow. The other soldiers are sent in pursuit, with the Warrior's son being the first of many sacrifices. Devastated, the Warrior drifts towards the mountains, falling in with an escaped slave and an old blind pilgrim. A showdown between the Warrior and those pursuing him is, however, inevitable.

Originating from a Japanese folk tale (there are also hints of Kurosawa), *The Warrior* is a timeless tale stunningly filmed in the deserts of Rajasthan and the mountains of northern India and a moral parable with biblical overtones. Kapadia, who co-scripted with Tim Miller, crafts the film with maturity, drawing a brooding, emotive performance from his lead and astonishingly naturalistic support from a supporting cast of largely non-professional performers. The film won the Alexander Korda Award for Best British Film and the Carl Foreman Award for the Most Promising Newcomer at the 2002 BAFTAs. Kapadia also won the Evening Standard British Film Award for Most Promising Newcomer and the London Film Festival's Sutherland Trophy.

After a prolonged absence during which a number of projects failed to come to fruition, Kapadia is currently working on *The Return*, a psychological horror starring Sarah Michelle Gellar and Sam Shepard.

This interview took place in 2001 and originally appeared on www.kamera.co.uk.

Jason Wood: Having admired your earlier shorts I was pleased to see *The Sheep Thief* appear on the DVD of *The Warrior*. Could you speak a little about the processes involved in making this film and how, if at all, it influenced the approach that you took to *The Warrior*.

Asif Kapadia: *The Sheep Thief* was my graduation film from the Royal College of Art Film School. When making it I had no idea what I was getting myself into, but I knew that it would be my last short film and I wanted to push my crew and myself to the limit. If I screwed it up, at least I had done it whilst a student.

The idea came from a story told to me by a teacher when I was about 7 years old. It was an old Bible story of a thief who becomes a saint. I love classical tales. I didn't believe the concept would work if I set the story in Ireland or the Lake District. It needed to take place in a timeless landscape. I had only previously been to India for a week or so, and the idea came up of shooting the movie there, on location, with non-professional actors, in Hindi, with a minimal crew. We hooked up with the students from the Indian Film School in Pune, raised the finance – £25,000 – and seven of us went off to Rajasthan with a 16mm, to find a location, cast the movie and shoot the film. The process of making the movie was the toughest thing any of us had ever been through. We all went a little crazy.

JW: For a first feature *The Warrior* was an extremely ambitious undertaking. What kind of elements led to your decision to embark on the project and how much depended on your sustaining the confidence to pull it off?

AK: I felt the central idea to *The Warrior* was very strong, I loved the story and was desperate to make it. There was never a doubt in my head that it would make a great film. Whenever I pitched the tale to people, they seemed to love it too so I really thought Tim Miller [co-writer] and I had something good. I was also excited by the idea of shooting something on a bigger scale, with a bigger cast, horses and burning villages. The entire project was a huge leap into the unknown but it was the challenge that excited me. I was going to learn the hard way but I felt confident as I had confidence in my script. The producer was totally supportive; I had my crew from *The Sheep Thief* around me, and was able to cast the film as I wanted. FilmFour, the financiers, were brilliant all the way through. So I felt confident together we would make it work.

JW: The film has a very distinct and distinguished visual style. Was your approach and your aesthetic set in place before you began filming and how much did you allow yourself to respond to the challenging yet picturesque filming conditions?

AK: I had been developing my style with my shorts whilst at the RCA and continued it with my first feature. The script is written so that the story is told with pictures and with minimal dialogue. I love to use the frame, spend time on the composition, and be confident enough to hold a shot. I don't like to cut or move the camera unless it is motivated. The idea is for me to tell the story with the camera and not to load the non-professional actors with pages of dialogue.

Of course when you're shooting, anything that can go wrong will, so you have to be prepared to compromise. In the case of *The Warrior*, we began running behind schedule, it was so hot, and things were running slow. So we ended up shooting with two cameras on simple scenes and on bigger sequences we had three cameras. That was an education, we had no video assist, the rushes were sent back to the UK and there was a two-week turnaround. So I had to learn to explain in great detail what I wanted from the second operator who was often far away on the other side of the mountain shooting on a long lens. I had to trust my instincts to decide if we had enough to make the scene work or to do the sequence again, which could have involved setting fire to a village all over again.

JW: What cultural and technical challenges did shooting in the blazing deserts of Rajasthan and the snow-capped foothills of the Himalayas present?

AK: There were about thirty crew from the UK, France and Canada, the other 200 crew were from India, so there was an interesting balance of learning to collaborate together. There were also the language issues whilst shooting off the beaten track in rural locations. The European crew had to learn to work with translators.

In the heat the video assists kept blowing up, we went through about four of them, so we were shooting blind. We were in pre-production and casting during the monsoon. When we started shooting the temperature was about 47 degrees in the desert. We finished shooting in the Himalayas in December and were on certain sequences at 10,000ft under about six feet of snow.

The biggest compromise came with the end of the film in the mountains. I had written a big climax to the film in a holy lake with a cast of thousands. In this scene the Blind Woman was supposed to in a sense 'see' the Warrior washing away his sins in the lake. Unfortunately at 12,000ft in December it was too cold for anyone to go in the water. The location was on top of a mountain, a four-hour drive up a narrow track; there was no electricity, hot water or anything up there and we ending up spending the night as it was not safe to return down the track after dark. So from a cast of thousands the scenes became a cast of one with only the Blind Woman in it.

JW: When the film was released, critics who universally praised the film were quick to offer comparisons with Kurosawa. Flattering I'm sure, but was he in any way an influence? Also, knowing how cine-literate you are would you be prepared to divulge directors who have in any way informed your work?

AK: It's an amazing feeling to see people mentioning *The Warrior* in the same sentence as a cinematic god, but generally the comparison was used as a short-hand to explain to the audience the type of film it was. To be honest before we wrote the film I had not really seen any Kurosawa films on the big screen, they have only recently been re-released in the UK. I love Kurosawa's films but I would say the movies and directors that really inspired me were Tranh Anh Hung's *Cyclo* [*Xich lo*, 1995], Zhang Yimou's *The Story of Qiu Ju* [*Qiu Ju da guan si*, 1992], Bresson's *A Man Escaped* [*Un condamné à mort s'est échappé*, 1956], Hitchcock's *Vertigo* [1958] and *Psycho* [1960], Kenji Mizoguchi's *Ugetsu Monogatari* [1953] and Sergio Leone's *Once Upon a Time in the West* [1968].

When I first saw *Cyclo* at film school, it was like a light bulb going off; the director was Vietnamese, he had studied at film school in Paris and it was a European film by someone who understood the Vietnamese culture. It was his second movie, he shot it with a mixture of professional and non-professional actors on location. The movie was a huge motivation for me to shoot *The Sheep Thief* in the same way. In the end I met my producer Bertrand Faivre, who worked for the French company that made *Cyclo* and *La Haine* [*Hate*, 1995].

JW: Apart from directorial influences, I believe that a Japanese folk-tale given to you by your writer was also a foundation for the film. How closely did you stick to this tale and what particular elements inspired you?

AK: My co-writer Tim Miller had travelled in Japan and is a big fan of the culture; he pitched me something he had read in a book of Japanese tales, it was a four-line footnote: 'A young boy training to be a samurai was brought before the Shogun, shown a severed head and asked if it was his father. The boy knew it was not his father but to save his father's life he lied and said it was. To prove it, the boy pulled out his dagger and killed himself. He would rather be dead than live with the shame his father had brought onto the family.' I thought it was such a powerful scene that posed so many questions, I decided that this would be the opening of our film. We would then cut to the father and follow his journey, revealing along the way why he was being pursued, by whom, who was the dead guy etc. In the end the scene comes thirty minutes into the movie. The only thing we changed was that one of the warriors killed the boy, rather than him killing himself. This kept alive a strand of tension during the story.

JW: I wanted to briefly ask about the casting process. You work largely with non-professional actors in the film. What challenges and benefits does this bring?

AK: I spent a lot on time on location looking for actors, I like to use local people, from the area where we will be shooting. I like the naturalism and truth I get from the non-professional actors, the feeling I get by just looking at their faces, the way they carry themselves. An actor from the UK would just look wrong in the middle of the desert. Non-professional actors also get across so much information without saying a word.

The Thief character was a real street-kid; he had lived rough on a train station platform from the age of seven. I learnt so much from him, rather than the other way around. The difficulty is that you need to make sure the actors don't get bored, so you don't over-rehearse. I would often shoot the rehearsals, just in case it was the best take.

I try not to give the actors marks or expect them to be in the perfect position for the lights. The focus puller has to get the image in focus, the operator deal with the frame, I have to tell the story with the shots and in the cut. The actors just have to 'be', the audience need to believe what is happening to them.

JW: Conversely, Irfan Khan is magnificent in the central role. How did he come to your attention?

AK: I worked with the casting director who did Shekhar Kapur's *Bandit Queen*

[1994]. It was the one Indian film that had the texture I was looking for. As soon as the casting director Tigmanshu Dhulia read the script he recommended Irfan. I met him and he had these eyes and a real presence, he was so brilliant. We never considered anyone else.

JW: In retrospect, how would you attempt to sum up the experience of not only making the film but seeing it so well received critically?

AK: I'm really proud of the movie. The best thing is trusting your instincts from beginning to end, no matter how crazy it seemed on paper as a first film; I wanted to make the movie and just kept at it. I feel really lucky to have had the chance to make the film I wanted to make when I did, considering what is happening in the British film industry right now. It would be close to impossible to get a film like *The Warrior* financed in the current climate.

JW: Having had time to weigh up your next move are you able to divulge what we can expect to see from you next?

AK: I'm working on a few screenplays; a ghost story set in samurai Japan, a dark love story set in the UK and a siege movie I'd like to shoot in Mexico.

* * *

Lodge Kerrigan

Writer-director Lodge Kerrigan, born in New York City in 1964, made his feature debut with the engrossing *Clean, Shaven* (1993), an intelligent and stylistically impressionistic study of schizophrenia. Featuring a harrowing central performance from Peter Greene as an estranged, possibly homicidal father in the bleakest of landscapes, the film played at over thirty international film festivals (including Cannes and Sundance) and has been exhibited at the Hirschhorn Museum (the Smithsonian Institution), the American Museum of the Moving Image and has been included in the 'Best of the Independents' series at the Anthology Film Archives, New York City. A film that was as striking aurally as it was visually – Kerrigan conveys the central character's inner turmoil through the use of discordant snatches of sound – *Clean, Shaven* established the director's interest in characters existing on the fringes of society.

Kerrigan's second feature *Claire Dolan* (1998) was an equally accomplished account of a high-price call girl (impeccably played by the late Katrin Cartlidge) whose mother's death acts as a catalyst for change. Shot in a cold, minimalist style to reflect the impersonal motel rooms where the central protagonist plies her trade, the film played in the main competition section at the 1998 Cannes Film Festival.

Keane (2005), Kerrigan's third feature as writer and director, evolved after Kerrigan suffered a devastating experience with what would have been the follow-up film to *Claire Dolan*. Starring Maggie Gyllenhaal and Peter Sarsgaard, *In God's Hands* was scrapped in its entirety owing to what Kerrigan describes as 'technical issues with the negative'. No doubt a traumatising experience, fortunately the insurance covered the disaster and in 2004 Kerrigan was able to return to the fray, shooting *Keane* in 32 days for less than $1 milllion.

Continuing the director's interest in mental illness, the film follows William Keane, an intensely distressed father apparently searching for his six-year-old daughter following her abduction. Veering between days of relentless searching and nights of alcohol and drug-induced extremes of self-destructive behaviour, he seems to be teetering precariously on the edge of sanity. Working in a hand-held *verité* style, director Kerrigan and director of photography John Foster, plunge us directly into Keane's profoundly unsettled universe. Damian Lewis's riveting, visceral performance of a man grappling with the effects of a profound loss, and the decision to shoot in live New York locations, makes *Keane* a complex, deeply humane and unforgettable portrait of turmoil.

This interview took place in late 2005 and appeared in *Vertigo* (vol. 2, no. 10), in spring 2006.

Jason Wood: How much of a spur for *Keane* was the fact that you have a young daughter yourself?

Lodge Kerrigan: It was certainly the impetus. My daughter is now 11 years old and ever since birth she's been very independent and free-spirited and very wilful. I really love this about her but there have been times when we've gone to public places and she's gone off to be by herself and I haven't been able to find her. Like any parent I'd be filled with panic and dread. Eventually I'd find her but that strong visceral reaction was certainly an impetus to me deciding to make a film about a man dealing with the grief of having his only child abducted. I also wanted to try and examine whether it would be possible to come to terms with this on any level. I don't believe it is possible to find peace but I think that as the film progresses William Keane does find some small measure of acceptance.

JW: It's the not knowing that strikes me as particularly painful.

LK: I think that abduction would be even harder to deal with than the death of a child. They say that funerals are for the living and that in order to see the corpse of someone it brings a sense of finality and enables the bereaved to move on.

But for parents whose children who have been abducted there is still some part of them that holds out in the hope of finding them again. There is no closure.

There were also two other elements that I was interested in exploring. The first is that anyone's life can change irreversibly in a very short period of time. In Keane's case this is the four minutes in which his child was abducted. I also have a long-standing interest in mental illness and was really interested in the aspect – and this could apply to anyone of us, and not just those with a mental illness – that if we were isolated from society and was either living on the streets or in a transient motel and was rejected on a daily basis, I think that anyone's mental health would start to deteriorate very rapidly.

JW: William Keane is treated with a lack of compassion at every turn.

LK: I think that it is human nature to try and step away from something scary. People are naturally fearful and don't want to engage with people living on the street or people who are mentally ill. I try not to be judgemental about it because it is understandable but I also think that we live in really critical times and that there is more room for empathy and that people do have different problems from your typical middle- or even working-class person.

JW: We also see aspects of schizophrenia and mental illness in *Clean, Shaven* and *Clare Dolan*. Where does this interest come from?

LK: It's difficult to say though I do have a friend who suffers from mental illness so I clearly have a personal connection to it in my life. When I was younger I travelled a lot as my father worked for the US government. Because I experienced a lot of different cultures perhaps this opened me up to different points of view. I guess it also has something to do with my upbringing. I really also believe that if each and every one of our personal circumstances were different and if we grew up experiencing certain environments then we could be susceptible to suffering from mental illness. The line is very thin, and so I try to put myself in other people's shoes as I could easily be in their place. That doesn't just apply to people who suffer from mental illness but is applicable to people who have different problems in life, such as those in cycles of poverty or who have been marginalised as a whole. I'm not a social filmmaker and I don't want to appear moralistic or self-righteous. This is why I really focus on individuals.

The filmmakers I admire the most are those who embrace the moralistic view to consider what it is to be human and so what it is to be flawed and to have not only great qualities but also to have some questionable qualities. Keane is obviously a good person with loving qualities but he ends up abducting a young child.

This is horrendous and so he is clearly a flawed human being but as a filmmaker I also try to look at what it means to be human, with all the flaws inherent in that. There are so many institutions including religion, politics, celebrity or even sports that are trying to push an idealised version of humanity. I prefer to come from a position of acceptance.

JW: As William Keane demonstrates you strenuously avoid simplistic characters that can be reduced to notions of good or bad.

LK: There are plenty of other people who deal with those. I make challenging films and entertainment is not my priority, I understand that. At the end of the day, and people ask me 'is it a struggle to make these films' and 'why have you made only three films in ten years', life is short and if you don't pursue want you want in your life actively then you are going to only end up pursuing what someone else wants. It's important to be clear about what you are doing.

JW: Is it a difficult landscape for independent productions and the challenging type of films that you make?

LK: I don't really want to talk about that too much because I think that it becomes a self-fulfilling prophecy and every time you read an article about how hard it is to distribute challenging, independent films it only makes it harder. Ultimately, it can be negative and leads the filmmaker into a difficult place.

JW: Was it gratifying to have Steven Soderbergh on board as an executive producer? He's always shown support for directors with distinctive voices, working with people such as Scott McGehee and David Siegel, Greg Mottola, Christopher Nolan and Todd Haynes.

LK: Absolutely. Not only do I admire his work as a filmmaker, he's an incredibly supportive producer. His concern really is to make the best film possible and it's not about an ego play. It really is about the work. He called me up three-and-a-half years ago and said I like the movies you make, how can I help? He's confident in my abilities as a director and doesn't question me on that level or try to instruct on how I should make the film. He's also a very remarkable person. It's rare that you meet someone in life who has had an extraordinary level of success who tries to help other people who maybe haven't had the same opportunities. Of course, having Soderbergh on board it's also an endorsement from someone who is universally admired. How could that be a bad thing?

JW: Let's talk about two specific scenes that strike me as pivotal. The first is the scene in the bar where William Keane keeps asking for the music to be turned up. The second is where Keane recounts his life history to himself in his lonely hotel room.

LK: The first scene is where Keane is clearly hallucinating. In *Clean, Shaven* I would have made it very subjective so that the audience would have heard the hallucinations. In *Keane* I was much more interested in behaviour and observing a person more objectively because I thought that it would have more of an emotional impact. I erred towards realism in the hope that an audience would empathise. If you look he's clearly distracted and is hearing voices so he chooses to play music as a way of trying to drown out these voices. The music is clearly playing very loudly, but not loudly enough to drown out what he is hearing inside his head. I was also interested in the idea of using the upbeat Motown love song ['I Can't Help Myself' by the Four Tops]. It's quite upbeat and I thought it would be really poignant to have it as a counterpoint. It's also important to note that when the bartender refuses to turn up the music any louder Keane gets up an on a chair to get his ear to the speaker but when he's told to get down he does so immediately. Automatic obedience is a common symptom of schizophrenia. The scene also shows how emotionally isolated Keane is.

The scene in the hotel relates to the fact that Keane does suffer from schizophrenia, but equally important is the grief that he is suffering. It's very possible that a lot of his symptoms, such as the hallucinations and breaking down in public, could also come from the grief. There is a connection that means that it is not just a symptom of his mental illness. With the reference to the disability cheque that Keane receives from the government I show that he does have a history of mental illness but his crisis is certainly linked to the ordeal that he has suffered. In the hotel room where he is listing the experiences of his life I feel that what he is doing is trying to hold on to his identity and his sense of who he really is. Keane is losing it at this point so goes over the facts in a list-like fashion of what his life is because he feels a real loss of identity at this point and is beginning to spiral. He speaks in a disassociate manner as if it could really be a biography of anyone. He's desperate and trying to hang on. He repeats information over and over again in an attempt to solidify who he is in his mind. For me personally it is one of the key moments of the film. Surprisingly very few people mention it.

JW: Apart from the Motown song there is very little music in the film and you don't use a score.

LK: One of the director's responsibilities is to find the right aesthetic tone for the movie and I don't think I have a particular style. I certainly don't try to impose a style on every film that I make. However, based on the content I try to find the correct style for each of my films. With *Keane* I felt that realism would have the biggest impact on an audience; if they felt that he really existed they would be really moved by him and overcome their own distance from someone who is clearly disturbed. Once I embraced that there was no room for a score. You can't have a score when you are dealing with realism, it would have seemed self-conscious, manipulative and over-determined. I should say that I am not dogmatic in any sense. I don't come in with rigid parameters that I apply across the board. You use what you need to express what you want to express. I'm actually a fan of scores and have had them in my films before. I do think though that filmmakers tend to rely on scores, using them as a band-aid to fix problems and find emotions that aren't generated in the scene. The real emotional life should come from the writing, the performance and the direction. Sometimes scores and source music is an easy crutch.

JW: Did this also drive your visual approach? You use hand-held camera throughout, shoot on location and work mostly with available light.

LK: Every scene is also shot in one take in real situations. There is no coverage or shots from other angles. The cuts in the film are all jump cuts; it was done in real time. Combined with the live Port Authority locations it's an extremely risky way of shooting. It also presents problems in terms of capturing the actors as you have to capture them at the same emotional point when their energies are at the right levels. With Damian Lewis ['William Keane'] and Abigail Breslin ['Kira'], this didn't always happen until about take fourteen. It's very demanding on the actors to have to repeat three- or four-minute takes in environments over which I very often had little or no control. You could be three minutes into a four-minute take on what is take twelve and all of a sudden two buses arrive and a few hundred people get out and someone says 'hey, are you making a movie?' When this happens I don't have anything and have to go back to zero again. Though a high-risk way of shooting, the advantage was that it gave us so much energy. This hopefully really comes through in the film. I think that Damian really appreciated this approach because he comes from a theatre background and so he was able to try to find his performance within a whole scene as opposed to in the more disjointed and traditional way of shooting a few lines and then cutting.

JW: Damian Lewis gives an astonishing performance.

LK: I'd only seen him in *Band of Brothers* and it was on this basis that I cast him.

Once you get beyond the fact that film is a business determined on attracting the largest possible audience and once you start to look at the pool of available talent, most casting directors look at performers who have performed similar roles in the past. This is somewhat backward looking. I don't take that approach. I look at an actor's level of talent and their command of their craft. When I watched Damian in *Band of Brothers* I realised just how precise he was but there is nothing in that role, apart from presence, that is remotely similar to his character in *Keane*. I met with Damian in London for two days to make sure that we got along because that was essential. All of the films that I've made live or die on the central performance. This is particularly true of *Keane* because Damian is in every shot. It was a collaboration in the best sense of the word and what you see is a result of our work together. I have huge respect for Damian for taking this role.

JW: You allow the spectator to make up their own mind as to whether or not Keane really has got a daughter who has been abducted. Are you keen to avoid being an authoritative voice on the subject?

LK: As a filmmaker I have to have a definitive point of view, I have to otherwise I am being fake and not giving direction. But whenever I've met with people with mental illness and I've heard their stories I'm never 100% sure of whether they're being accurate or not. I don't think that they are deceitful or manipulative but fabrication is a symptom of mental illness. The audience is with Keane. They are with him in his life and as close to him as they can possibly get. They have to decide for themselves whether or not he had a child. They have to determine if they believe what he is saying. The reason I chose to put the audience in that position and not answer it for them is because it is more real that way and so more emotionally impactful. There is no standard objective response to a movie and so I feel that every audience response is valid. For myself, and Damian too, we find it more poignant to believe that he did have a daughter. I think that this is transmitted not through dialogue but through behaviour. When I see the patience and the care that Keane takes with Kira, I believe that Keane is a parent. In life things aren't always definitive one way or another.

***

Andrew Kötting

Not for want of trying, I am incapable of improving on *Vertigo* editor Gareth Evans' description of UK artist and filmmaker Andrew Kötting: 'One of the UK's most intriguing artists, and perhaps the only contemporary filmmaker who could be said to have taken the spirit of visionary curiosity and hybrid creativity exemplified by the late Derek Jarman, he is also a great collaborator, building a community of shared interest around his various projects, while anchoring his prolific production in an ongoing report on the lives of those closest to him.'

Currently the Professor of Time-Based Media at the University College for the Creative Arts, Maidstone, a role that has allowed this restless and endlessly fascinating figure to continue his visual travels and hybrid creativity, Kötting has so far produced two quite astonishing features. The first, *Gallivant* (1996) was a remarkable British road movie in which the director, his grandmother and daughter embark on a 6,000-mile journey, zig-zagging around the coast of Britain. An experimental travelogue and an intensely personal story, Kötting begins the journey to bring Gladys, his 85-year-old grandmother, and Eden, his 7-year-old daughter, together. Gladys's stamina is limited, and Eden has Joubert's syndrome: both are fragile, and the journey is an opportunity which may not be repeated.

Kötting looks not for an essential quality of British life, but for its symptoms: folk culture and songs. He cajoles two old men at Port Carlisle into singing 'Do ye ken John Peel?', one accompanying the other on his mouth organ. At Robin Hood's Bay, folk musician Martin Carthy gives a more professional rendering of 'Sailing Over the Dogger Bank'. In Goathland, a sword dancer explains the dance's pagan Viking roots, and in Hastings a man tells how the Jack-in-the-Green festival has exploded in popularity. The journey ends where it began, in Bexhill-on-Sea, with evidence that Kötting has succeeded in bringing Gladys and Eden closer: the film closes on the two exchanging a hug. The flavour is rather as though a film by Humphrey Jennings had been remade by Richard Lester, with occasional input from John Betjeman and Spike Milligan.

The harsher, grittier side of Kötting's work emerged in his second and so far only other feature, *This Filthy Earth* (2001). Loosely adapted from Zola's novel *La Terre*, the film is set in a rural community somewhere and sometime in the north of England. The melodramatic plot matters far less than the brutal, phantasmagorical atmosphere, a timeless nightmare vision of blood and shit and all-engulfing mud. Kötting described the film as intended to show the landscape in its full beauty and brutality.

Kötting has completed *Mapping Perception* (2002), a short science, film and art project inspired by his daughter Eden. The extraordinary *In the Wake of a Deaddad* can be viewed in *Vertigo* (vol. 3, no.1, 2006).

The following interview took place in 2002 and originally appeared on www.kamera.co.uk.

Jason Wood: Despite the way in which you present the physical hardship of rural existence in *This Filthy Earth* there is a lyrical beauty to the film. Did you want these sequences to exist in any kind of opposition to the other 'spunk and bones' sequences, and did you allow any other films to here affect the way in which you filmed? I was reminded of Malick's *Days of Heaven* [1978] and Alexander Dovzhenko's *Earth* [1930].

Andrew Kötting: I haven't seen the Soviet film *Earth* but I was definitely influenced by Terrence Malick, and that 'magic hour' light that can sometimes seem so surreal. Polanski's *Tess* [1979] was an inspiration as well. The harvesting does read as somewhat elegiac, but there is also something ominous, forever present and, of course, the message of the old versus the new.

JW: What kind of atmosphere was it on the shoot, and when and where did the majority of the shooting take place?

AK: We shot in Dentdale in North Yorkshire for everything other than the girls' abode which was shot in Dent in Cumbria. The atmosphere on set was that of one large and dishevelled spunk-stained family. The cast were always around even if they were not required for many of the days of shooting. Peter Hugo Daly AKA Jesus Christ would wander the Yorkshire Dales in costume, spirit bottle in hand ready to cure the afflicted.

JW: The film has a certain timelessness to it but it still manages to deal very effectively with concerns that affect modern communities, such as the racial abuse suffered by Lek [Xavier Tchili]. Were you keen for the film to have contemporary resonance?

AK: Absolutely, we never wanted to write it large but it was very important.

JW: Newcomer Demelza Randall is especially good, are there benefits to working with non-professional actors?

AK: I was casting intuitively. I had help from casting agents who were responsible for drawing my attention to Rebecca Palmer and Dudley Sutton, but it was a process of pushing and probing at interview stage. It was also about look and how genuine I thought the actors were when I confronted them with the *real* that I was after. It was important whether they baulked at the idea of full penetrative sex or dead animals. We were hoping to cast at the city farm but this proved problematic so we had sides of beef delivered instead. Shane Attwooll is from Deptford – like myself – and it was always his look that I had been interested in. I found his picture in spotlight years before I cast him and it was this image that informed the Buto character. The fact that he can act despite his Buddy Holly fingers was a real bonus.

JW: Do you encourage improvisation?

AK: I am always on the look out for happenstance, whether that be from the landscape, the cast, the crew or the props or whatever. To trust in the cast to improvise is all part of my process.

JW: I understand that you take quite a 'sculptural' approach to filmmaking, describing it as a 'hunting and gathering process'.

AK: Yes, it is very much a sculptural process; contingent, never set in stone, and always an approximation of what you set out to do. Therefore I'm far less likely to be disappointed or dependent on, for example take 66. Albeit that we stuck very closely to the final script on *This Filthy Earth* I was always on the look out for the *other*. This approach can, however, create no end of problems at the editing stage because of all the new possibilities, but that just makes you work harder as a filmmaker.

JW: You obviously work in a variety of media including DV and Super-8. What kind of potentials do these formats present, and how do you see digital filmmaking as influencing the future of film production?

AK: The impact of the new technologies is profound. I think that a lot of the control is now firmly back in the hands of the filmmakers. The power of the labs has been undermined and the industry as a whole is losing its monopoly. It is all very positive, but as far as the different formats within *This Filthy Earth* are concerned it is as much about texture and feel as it is about being cost-effective. I also use DV throughout in a symbolic way, it is meant to represent the eyes of the landscape as seen through the eyeless character of Joey (Ryan Kelly), the feral vagabond. It is an animistic presence and in the wake of Joey's sister's death the film goes into a berserk and apocalyptic freefall where madness is almost kept at bay.

JW: How tough is the current filmmaking climate for directors such as yourself?

AK: The paradox is that although it might be cheaper and easier to produce films, it is becoming harder to distribute anything that is at all wayward and unfamiliar. This is not necessarily true of world cinema but certainly of British cinema. Output seems to be genre driven, generic and rather limp. Filmmakers always erring on the side of caution or accommodation. However, for a few years now there are new arenas opening up which are more about the gallery space or viewing context. I am very inspired to see the works of people like Isaac Julien, Tacita Dean and Shirin Neshat so well disseminated.

JW: What aspirations remain for you as a filmmaker?

AK: I've been collaborating with Mark Lythgoe, a neurophysiologist at London's Institute of Child Health, for a few years now on a project that uses my daughter Eden's Joubert syndrome as a catalyst and focus. We are making a short film and gallery installation from the ideas and footage generated or archived, it is called 'Mapping Perception' and can be visited as a work in progress at www.mapping-perception.org.uk. As far as longer linear narrative pieces are concerned I have a screenplay that I co-wrote for BBC Scotland just after we finished writing *This Filthy Earth* and I would love to get up to the Inner Hebrides and give that a go. If indeed they're still interested in the wake of the last outburst!

* * *

Richard Linklater

Having amassed a consistently intelligent, thoughtful, resourceful – given the miniscule budgets on which he has frequently subsisted – and influential body of work, Richard Linklater now finds himself in an envious position. *School of Rock* (2003) successfully bridged the gap between art and commerce and has facilitated the subsequent balancing of lucrative directing gigs such as *The Bad News Bears* (2005), with more personal, esoteric fare, including the recent Philip K. Dick animation, *A Scanner Darkly* (2006). Interestingly, Linklater is able to work under the aegis of a major studio, retaining almost total creative control.

Born in Houston, Texas in 1961 but for many years a resident in Austin, Linklater was a confirmed cineaste from an early age. A self-taught filmmaker who began working on Super-8, Linklater completed his debut *It's Impossible To Learn to Plow By Reading Books* in 1988. Relatively rarely seen, the film did however establish a number of the director's recurring themes; namely an abiding interest in travel, the restlessness of youth and the importance of living in the moment. It was with *Slacker* (1991) that Linklater truly established himself, and in the process cast a sizeable shadow over the American independent cinema movement that gathered momentum in the early 1990s; Kevin Smith credits the film for turning him onto filmmaking.

A quizzical snapshot of a generation at a loose end, *Slacker* (which helped introduce the word and its attendant spirit into the lexicon of modern language) suffered initial rejection by every major film festival. Undeterred, Linklater acted as his own distributor, screening the film at an on-campus cinema. Sensing the film's zeitgeist factor in its ability to directly connect with the rapidly emerging Generation X-types being heavily hyped by the media, Orion Classics acquired the film for national release one year after its Austin platform. The rest, as they say, is history.

Linklater's subsequent films, including *Dazed and Confused* (1993), *Before Sunrise* (1995), *Suburbia* (1997) and the slightly misfiring but ambitious *The Newton Boys* (1998) all showed an evolution of style and theme whilst remaining true to his own highly singular artistic vision. Crediting his audience with the intellect and sense of intrigue to follow him on disparate stylistic and narrative journeys, Linklater completed two highly experimental works in 2001: *Waking Life*, a hand-animated feature that utilised an advanced 'rotoscoping' technique (again adopted for *A Scanner Darkly*); and *Tape*, a digitally-shot three-hander that dissects perspective by unfolding over a single evening in a motel room. Having taken a leaf out of Steven Soderbergh's book with the aforementioned *School of Rock*, Linklater re-asserted his indie credentials – and earned an Academy Award nomination – with *Before Sunset* (2004), an engaging return to *Before Sunrise*'s older, but not necessarily wiser lovers.

A Scanner Darkly, a dark adaptation of Philip K. Dick's novel, has earned some of the best reviews of the director's career, even satisfying the notoriously fickle Sci-Fi purists. Premiered at the Cannes Film Festival, the starry *Fast Food Nation* (2006) looks set to be equally well received. An intelligent and timely look at fast food consumer culture, the film bravely holds a mirror to contemporary American society, a role Linklater has dutifully performed throughout his diverse and eclectic career.

The following interview took place in New York in 2004 and was made into a short film on Linklater, shown as part of a Richard Linklater retrospective at the 2004 Cambridge Film Festival.

Jason Wood: How did the idea of making a follow up to *Before Sunrise* come about and what kind of ideas and loose threads from the original did you wish to explore?

Richard Linklater: We actually started talking about it a year after we finished the first film and the more we got into it the more we began to forget about the first film all together. In fact, we didn't even re-watch it until a week-and-a-half into shooting the new one. The intention was to see what naturally came up and to let the subtle dialogue between the younger selves and the older selves just organically evolve; we certainly didn't design it that way. I knew that by ignoring it there would be these nice little echoes. We approached it the same way as we did back then and were very demanding of each other. There is certainly a subtle interplay between the two films but I hope that this interplay isn't too specific.

JW: Before Sunset is the result of a very collaborative writing process between Ethan Hawke, Julie Delpy and yourself. How did this dynamic play out?

RL: It wasn't that much different to the first time around. I had an existing script when I cast the first movie but the structure that was always going to be in place was that the two actors were going to work with me to re-write, personalise and internalise to make sure that there were a lot of them in the project. I was very conscious of looking for actors who were also writers and creative collaborators. I needed to get the pitch of honesty I was looking for. Julie and Ethan understood this perfectly the first time and perhaps even more the second time around. Having already established the characters and lived with them this long it made sense that we would work on the characters and the script together.

JW: You described Before Sunrise as 'a romance for realists'. Do you think this description equally applies to Before Sunset?

RL: This was always our goal and my goal certainly in terms of approaching something that I guess may fall into the very broad romantic comedy genre. I wanted to do my own take on it and avoid making another Pretty Woman [1990] or the kind of film that seems to be from another universe entirely because it is so opposite to your own life. I just wanted to take the cues for the film from my personal experience and in doing so hopefully reflect the experiences of many people who may be watching. I wanted it to have an incredibly romantic vibe without resorting to the cliché of having music swelling every time somebody looked at each other. I wanted the romantic core notion of this deep connection between two people and I think that in itself this can be pretty real. I mean who doesn't go through their lives without having some similar experience? It is just how you deal with that and how you treat it and we wanted everyone to seemingly exist in the real world of Jesse and Celine.

JW: I was impressed by the honesty that is extended toward the characters. For example you show the unhappiness of their lives post-Vienna and the fact that Jesse is in a very unhappy relationship and has a young child. This sense

of disappointment is not something that you would ordinarily see in a film of this kind.

RL: To be honest, they can suffer these disappointments and still be intelligent and compassionate people. They are more adult now and the only real thing that is different is that they have nine more years of life and the accumulation of that has perhaps made them better people. It's just the way life unfolds; you can't live a life without disappointments. I don't mean to suggest that all youthful ideals are crushed, that is not it at all; they are perhaps a little more cynical but equally passionate and intelligent as a result of the nine more years that life has given them.

JW: In terms of the film's structure, it unfolds almost in real time, a concept I would imagine that made it quite difficult to shoot.

RL: That was probably the biggest single challenge of the movie but it's also what is the movie. The idea to set it in real time was a challenge both content-wise and geographically speaking; we couldn't cut out anything and had to have it all planned out like a very intricate puzzle. Every film has its big challenges and this was ours. We also wanted to make it seem spontaneous and seamless. I would say that this starts with the style of acting, the idea being that it is improvised and then the style of the film itself. I always felt that the film should resemble a documentary and the kind of documentary that draws absolutely no attention to itself. If people were to come out of this movie talking about specific shots then in a way I think that we have lost something because it is so much more about the spontaneous moment between them and I didn't want anything to distract from that.

JW: This must have been difficult to pull off, making a scripted and meticulously planned film seem as if it were a slice of life.

RL: Well it was but people do believe these people and feel that their lives are unfolding in front of them, and I think that this is a tribute to how hard Ethan and Julie worked. In fact, they were never not working because it had to be so tight before it could be that loose. It was an interesting segue when we went from being co-writers to being actors and director because I think it was then that the enormity of the task ahead really hit them. I'm actually very proud of them.

JW: I like the ambiguity of the film and the ambiguity of the characters. This is the third time we have seen Jesse and Celine as they also appeared in animated form in *Waking Life*. Is it this ambiguity that allows you to keep returning to them?

RL: I think so but also the scene they did in *Waking Life* was almost five years ago – a half-way point as it turns out – and it was just fun to check in with them even in their disembodied cinematic dream-state world. At this point we all realised that we all really liked working together and working with these characters and that the first one wasn't just a fluke. After it had theoretically been put out there by all of us we felt that we simply had to pursue these characters. There is a real chemistry I feel between the three of us; it's a joyful collaboration.

JW: If you look at your films collectively there are themes that recur: communication, the journey from adolescence to adulthood and the attendant choices with which we are faced, generational angst and travel to name but a few. Are these the themes that still interest you?

RL: They do. So many of the films I have made have been based on actual experiences and the various points I have been at during my life but I don't think of these things consciously, it just comes back. I'll wake up and find myself making another film about people just talking and I think this must be who I am; you settle into it, just as you do with life. When I first got into film I thought, 'now I can do this and now I can do that' and then you do it ten or eleven times and it dawns on you that it is only a little piece of the pie that you are interested in. We are all prisoners of our own personalities and our own interests and indeed our own abilities. As you realise what you can do and where you are led the world narrows but that's okay. Just as you settle into the kind of person you are then you also settle into the kind of filmmaker you are, there is no point in battling it. I actually feel in a good place right now and can follow my instincts in regard to what I should be doing. I'm lucky in that I can follow my muse even if this leads me into *School of Rock* or *The Newton Boys* or something that may not ostensibly feel like a Richard Linklater film.

JW: You seem to revel in defying convention.

RL: Again it's not a real conscious effort to go out and defy convention; it's more a lack of interest in convention. For example with *School of Rock* and the genre of the teenage movie I simply decided what it was that I don't like about most teenage movies and set about doing my own version, trying to personalise what teenage movies mean to me. *School of Rock* also reflects the fact that I never did get on with institutional environments and attempts to offer my take on it.

JW: Are the motivations that originally inspired you to begin making films all those years ago the same or have they also evolved with time?

RL: I often think about what motivated me in the first place and the fact is that the core love of cinema is always there. When I first got into film I wasn't positive that I would be a director as I wasn't sure that I had the skills. I felt that I often had films in my head that I could see and view and I'm very thankful that I have got to make films but I still feel that even had I not got to direct I would still be doing something involved with film in some other capacity. In fact, I am involved in other capacities, such as the film society that I run in Austin. To me it's all the same, writing about film, showing films, it's all tied up with the bigger picture: the love of film. If I ever didn't feel that anymore then I simply wouldn't do this.

JW: You could always go back to working on the oilrigs, one of your vocations before you turned to film.

RL: Hopefully not. That was more of a young man's game. I just feel lucky that they keep letting me do this. I have to say the older I get the motivations have become less specific. I've just done what I guess would be officially termed a sci-fi movie, an adaptation of Philip K. Dick's *A Scanner Darkly* – and people think that I ploughed through hundreds of sci-fi moves but in fact I didn't watch one. Laurence Olivier always said that it takes twenty years to internalise the craft of acting and I kind of feel the same way about directing and it is now coming up for twenty years that I first picked up a movie camera. I no longer feel the need to question my artistic choices as to how I want to shoot a movie; I can just show up, I know what I'm doing now.

* * *

Kim Longinotto

One of the pre-eminent contemporary documentary filmmakers, Kim Longinotto is arguably also one of the least visible. Despite a CV shot through with awards and acclaim – she was the recipient of a Human Rights Watch retrospective – Longinotto is a rarity amongst her contemporaries in that she is contentedly remains firmly behind the camera. Renowned for creating extraordinary human portraits and tackling controversial topics with sensitivity and compassion, Longinotto studied camera directing at the UK's National Film and Television School (NFTS), where she made *Pride of Place* (1977), a critical look at the boarding school where as a child she spent several unhappy years. At the NFTS Longinotto also completed *Theatre Girls* (1979), a peek into a hostel for homeless women.

After graduation Longinotto worked as a television cameraperson before forming the production company Twentieth Century Vixen with Claire Hunt. The films they produced include *Fireraiser* (1985), a look at Sir Arthur 'Bomber' Harris and the World War Two bombing of Dresden, *Eat the Kimono* (1990), about the controversial Japanese feminist performer Hanayagi Genshu, and *Hidden Faces* (1990), the internationally acclaimed, collaborative documentary with/about Egyptian women. *The Good Wife of Tokyo* (1992), the duo's film about love and marriage in Japanese society remains a seminal work, forging the template for Longinotto's abiding interest in show-ing ordinary people, most often women, as they attempt to break out of cir-cumscribed roles.

Having completed a series of works on special needs issues for Channel Four, Longinotto, who has continued to make a virtue of collaboration, part-nered with Jano Williams to co-direct *Dream Girls* (1993), another insightful look at gender and sexual identity that examines the spectacular world of the Japanese musical theatre company, the Takarazuka Revue. Williams and Longinotto worked together subsequently on *Gaea Girls* (2000), tactfully ob-serving the gruelling training regime of female Japanese wrestlers. Shot with Longinotto's signature neutrality with the camera as close to the subject as possible, *Shinjuku Boys* (1995) gives an authentic, intimate and unmediated glimpse into the lives of its subjects as it observes three Tokyo women who live as men. Here, as with *Divorce Iranian Style* (1998), a film dealing with the taboo subject of women and divorce in Iran, the emphasis remained the relentless back-and-forth between those trying to maintain control, and those who resist it.

Like *Divorce Iranian Style*, *Runaway* (2001), set in a refuge for girls in Teh-ran that re-visits Longinotto's interest in institutions, is co-directed with Irani-an anthropologist Ziba Mir-Hosseini. A documentarist who remains drawn to humanist subject matter, Longinotto aptly describes her work as having a dis-tinct anthropological bent. Her most recent work, *Sisters In Law* (2005), is an uplifting and enlightening slice of life focusing on justice in the Muslim town of Kumba, Cameroon, overseen by the progressive female legal partnership of prosecutor Vera Ngassa and court president Beatrice Ntuba, who together help women to speak out and fight back against assumptions of patriarchal pr. /ilege in modern-day Africa.

Co-directed by Florence Ayisi, the film represents a natural progression in Longinotto's career and directly evolved from the Emmy-nominated *The Day I Will Never Forget* (2002), a film about the practice of female genital mutila-tion in Kenya. Offering a positive view of African women, *Sisters In Law* is a warm and involving portrait of two remarkable characters and an example of grassroots action at its most effective. It is also that rare thing, a film that makes you believe things might get better.

The following interview took place in August 2006 and appears in *Vertigo* (vol. 3, no. 3) in autumn 2006.

Jason Wood: How did yourself and co-director Florence Ayisi first come to Kumba in Cameroon and to the female legal partnership of tough-minded prosecutor Vera Ngassa and court president Beatrice Ntuba?

Kim Longinotto: *Sisters In Law* followed on from *The Day I Will Never Forget*. That film was about female genital mutilation and was set in Kenya. Even though it is such a harsh subject it was an inspiring film to make as I was able to film young girls and women fighting against the tradition and changing their lives. The film ends with sixteen girls taking their parents to court and putting a stop to their circumcisions. When we were filming outside the court we met a local Kenyan TV crew and, when the case was adjourned, we asked them if they would come back to film the verdict. They said they wouldn't bother as the story wasn't important enough. But, of course, the court case was a part of a real social revolution and we were so happy that we were there to document it and to be able to celebrate the courage of those girls. And the girls were making legal history.

I wanted to make another film in Africa and, as a filmmaker, what you're looking for is an engrossing story with lots of action and drama and characters that you really like. The style of my films is to try and take the audience on an emotional journey where they identify with the people and get involved in their stories. I thought it would be great to film in a predominantly English-speaking country as Mary Milton [the sound recordist] and I had had such language difficulties in Kenya. Sometimes we had to move very quickly to catch things happening and we'd end up somewhere where none of us could understand the language. For example, most of the 16 girls only spoke Kalenjin but luckily three of them had learnt a little English at school so we could talk to them ourselves.

Some time after that, I met Florence Ayisi at a screening of one of my films and I got to know her. Together, we went on a research trip to Cameroon. Kumba is Florence's hometown so we went there at the end of the trip. We were interested in women in the judiciary and so we went to see Judge Beatrice who Florence had been to university with. I still hadn't found a story I felt would make a film. When we were in her office she started to talk to her assistant about Juliana Djenga, a retired court clerk who she and Vera had encouraged to become the first woman customary court judge in a nearby village. Beatrice told us that it had been a long, hard struggle but Juliana was finally going to be appointed that summer. Beatrice said that the women in the village were very excited but the men were creating all sorts of problems. It was really going to stir up village life! This seemed to me to be a great subject for a film. What I had in mind was an absorbing and gently humorous film showing the different forces of change taking place in a village.

We filmed the beginning of Juliana's story that August and got to know Vera while we were filming as she was supporting Juliana all the way. Then, five weeks into filming, we heard that all our rushes had been destroyed by the x-ray machine in Douala. We had paid someone to get the film on to the plane without it being x-rayed but he had put it through anyway. So we had to abandon Juliana's story.

This was when I decided to make a completely new film about Vera's work using her office as a starting point. When I asked her if she would agree to be at the centre of the new film, she just looked at me very calmly and said 'You'd better be here first thing tomorrow morning'. Both Vera and Beatrice see their work as a fight against 'customary thinking' so, even though they are working thousands of miles away from the sixteen brave Kenyan girls, they are a part of the same struggle. Vera and Beatrice are true pioneers. They are heroes to me and the very thought of them cheers me up when I feel low.

JW: In terms of filming the scenes inside the court and the various dressing downs that Ngassa and Ntuba dispense – a mixture of the hilarious and the profoundly moving as evidenced by the residual uncovering of the brutality that 6-year-old Manka has endured – did yourself and Ayisi encounter any resistance or was your presence wholly welcomed?

KL: There were three of us in Kumba: myself, Florence and Mary Milton. Sometimes it would be only Mary and I in the room when we were filming and the main characters were happy to be filmed. In fact, Amina would ask Mary and I if we would be going to film her the following day – for example, when she was going for the divorce she was very scared and she wanted to be sure that we would be there as she knew we were on her side. When she was being pressured by her family to withdraw the case, she was happy that we were in the room with her. So it was more the fact of us being there than the fact that we were filming. It's strange though, as after the divorce court hearing, she goes back to the compound and the women there ask her if she was the only woman in the court and she says 'yes' so she'd forgotten our presence.

JW: It's refreshing that you allow the events and the characters to speak for themselves without the need for voice-over narration.

KL: Most of the films I have made have been without commentary and with very few or no interviews. I want the audience to feel as if they are there in the middle of the action seeing what we saw and experiencing the stories as if they were there with us. I want it to be as immediate and compelling as possible, just as when we watch fiction; you're going on an emotional journey and nothing is coming between you and what you are seeing. Some people don't like this as they want facts and information, but I suppose that in the end we all make the kind of films that we enjoy watching.

JW: Many documentary filmmakers, yourself included, often take great pains to ensure that your subjects actually get to see the film they have been a part of.

KL: Vera and Beatrice both came to Cannes for the premiere. They were cheered after the film and got a standing ovation. It was thrilling to see the whole audience stand up for them. Vera cried which I'd never seen her do all the time we were filming. They took a whole lot of DVDs back with them to Kumba after Cannes and they made sure that everyone saw the film. Vera invited Ladi and Amina to her house to watch it and said they were all laughing and making a lot of noise together. Amina and Ladi immediately wanted to watch it all over again.

* * *

Samira Makhmalbaf

The daughter of famed Iranian director Mohsen Makhmalbaf, Samira Makhmalbaf has become – at an astonishingly young age – one of the world's most lauded directors in her own right.

Makhmalbaf made her movie debut at a very early age, acting in her father's film *Bicycleran* (*The Cyclist*, 1987) when she was just seven years old. At 14, allegedly claiming that her instructors had nothing more to teach her, she quit school and began learning the craft of filmmaking from her father, who established the Makhmalbaf Film House, a family-run film school and production company that has produced films not only by Samira, but her mother Marzieh Meshkini (*The Day I Became a Woman*, 2000), her brother Maysam and younger sister, Hana. *Samira cheghoneh 'Takhté siah' rol sakht*, (*How Samira Made Blackboards*, 2000) and *Lezate divanegi* (*Joy of Madness*, 2003) by Maysam and Hana respectively are video documentaries about Samira's filmmaking activities.

Aged just eighteen Makhmalbaf became the youngest director ever invited to the Cannes Film Festival for her film *Sib* (*The Apple*, 1998), based on the true story of two disabled girls who were kept cooped up in their tiny Tehran home for the first twelve years of their lives. Actual family members were used to play themselves. The film was very much in the Iranian tradition, focusing on young children to make unsentimental and perceptive comments about ritual and Iranian society.

Two years later, Makhmalbaf became the youngest director ever to win the jury prize at Cannes for *Takhté siah* (*Blackboards*, 2000), an ambitious and frequently harrowing film that addresses the condition of Iran's Kurdish population through the adventures of two itinerant teachers. The jury prize success was repeated three years later with *Panj é asr* (*At Five in the Afternoon*, 2003). The first film to be shot in arduous conditions in a post-Taliban Afghanistan, *Panj é asr* comes two years after Mohsen Makhmalbaf's *Kandahar* (2001) and similarly deals with the plight of Afghan women through its focusing on Noqreh, a progressive young woman trying to survive in post-Taliban Afghanistan. Played by non-professional actor Agheleh Rezaie, we follow Nogreh as she goes about her daily life. Girls' schools have now been reopened, but frustrated by a strained relationship with a bigoted but loving father she dreams of becoming President of the Republic. A bitter political statement that tells a harsh and cruel tale, it is also an exquisitely moving and often comic depiction of life after the Taliban.

An outspoken and highly political provocateur, Samira Makhmalbaf also contributed a memorable segment to the portmanteau film, *11'09"01 – September 11* (2002).

The following interview took place in 2003.

Jason Wood: How did *Blackboards* evolve?

Samira Makhmalbaf: After *The Apple* I was looking for a subject that would give me a lot of energy, and whilst I was travelling to Kurdistan with my father that idea really came to mind; the idea of a teacher with a blackboard looking for students, and I thought I am going to make a movie out of this. I thought that it was a very open subject, this can be surreal and at the same time very natural-istic, it can carry so many social and humanistic meanings. So I asked my father to give me the script. But even during the writing, and during the scouting for locations and the actors, it continued to develop, even in the very moment of shooting. I believe that some kind of life came into the life of the movie we were trying to create.

JW: Was the film a difficult one to make, especially in terms of the mountainous region where you shot.

SM: It was hard. Like *The Apple* it was a miracle of a challenge. The location was very near to the border of Iran and Iraq and there were many landmines left there which could have killed many of us. Then again how could we make a movie about these kinds of situations without experiencing them for ourselves? And yes, climbing those mountains was very hard, and the working with non-professional actors was also very hard. But as the process went on it became easier, especially as it was my second movie-making experience. Another thing that was difficult was that I was the only woman there. The other crew members and the majority of the actors were men but they very quickly believed in me as they realised that I would not ask them to do something that I was not prepared to do myself. They learned to trust in me.

JW: The film features such strong performances. How did you find your cast?

SM: I chose them one by one and from different villages. This took a very long time as I talked to them one by one. I did consider a professional actor for one of the roles but he was trying too hard to be real that it just wasn't working out and so I had to ask him to go. It was better with the local people. The location also gave the people a metaphysical energy.

JW: You deal with political and social themes in a humanist way.

SM: It's important the way you look at things. There are more social problems and humanistic problems that occur because of political situations. I'm obviously talking about war and it doesn't even matter which war exactly. I like to think about things in a humanist way; I am very conscious about this approach.

JW: I think this is why audiences are able to connect with your films, and with the films of the new Iranian cinema.

SM: It's a serious problem for humanity, but I think a lot of Iranian directors are able to deal with important issues in a spiritual and poetic way, making them simpler to understand. It goes for the heart and it is so simple.

JW: You also look closely at the complexity of human relationships.

SM: The important thing for me was to deal with the way we fail each other in our relationships and the way in which we relate to each other. Through the processes of making a movie these things become evident; that's why in the new film I thought it was important to make the lead character a teacher. I also want to look at the details of human relations.

JW: Do you feel that people overlook the humour of your films.

SM: There are certainly moments of humour, yes. There can be moments in life, your life, the lives of the characters in the film that are so terrible – the struggles to get back to your own country for instance – that are so terrible and yet sometimes the only reaction is to laugh at such situations. The marriage in the film illustrates this; it is funny and yet it is very painful at the same time because she doesn't even really know her new husband.

JW: You seem to have so much experience of different people and, without wishing to sound patronising, you are relatively young.

SM: It's a skill to be young and to communicate well with people of different generations. I also have developed more of an edge by making movies. Your heart becomes like a mirror; you are able to reflect the experiences and emotions of thousands of other people. You have to really open your heart, ears and mind. It's a good challenge.

JW: You've had a wonderful apprenticeship.

SM: I have acted in movies from an early age, but I really didn't want to act. I wanted to be involved in cinema so much and I begged my father to be involved as an assistant in some way from early on. I also made some shorts, but I must say that there are moments where you feel that you know nothing about cinema but you want to know and you want to articulate what you feel that you have to say; these are sometimes the best moments. With *Blackboards* I did benefit from my experience but I only realised this as I began to make the film. My father experiences the same thing and on the first day on set says that he sometimes feels as if he knows nothing about filmmaking. It is sometimes good to know nothing. You have to be like a baby, seeing everything for the first time.

JW: What challenges do you face as a female director working in Iran?

SM: We have a lot of limitation in terms of written law and unwritten law. Traditionally it is in the minds of everybody that a woman cannot be a filmmaker or an author. It is therefore much harder. When you live in this kind of environment there is a danger that you can start to believe it for yourself. It's a challenge but this situation is now slowly changing in the minds of the people. When you break a cliché the changes can start and so I now very much hope that we can, as we think about freedom and democracy, produce more women directors. I'm optimistic about the future. We also suffer from so much censorship in general terms, as men and as women, but I decided very early on in my career not to practise self-censorship, to not censor myself.

JW: Have state legislations forced you to be more subversive with the way in which you present your ideas?

SM: Yes, you try to find another way of expressing yourself. Also many film-makers start with just an idea and then must find a way in terms of cinematic language to express it. We must also – because the state does not let Hollywood cinema come to Iran – find our own way, a national way of expressing in a very personal manner the thoughts that we have.

JW: Are you self-consciously aware of the current international interest in talent emerging from Iran?

SM: I would have to say that Iranian cinema is a hundred years old and we have produced so many good films and so many good filmmakers that have been lost in the history of Iranian cinema that to me, a good body of work is not anything necessarily that is new. A lot of the really good stuff that we are making these days and a lot of what went before has not been seen outside of Iran, so I do not think that there is necessarily a new wave of Iranian cinema. Also, don't forget that because of censorship a lot of the films by directors such as Abbas Kiarostami have not been seen in Iran so you only become aware of them when you travel.

JW: Having achieved so much already, what aspirations remain for you?

SM: I want to continue making movies, but I also want to live and to continue to learn. I've learned that though it's good to create it is also good not to try to force it, to sometimes not to create and to simply explore.

* * *

Lucrecia Martel

Born in Salta in northern Argentina in 1966, as a teenager Lucrecia Martel apparently did a good deal of filming of her large family, and this eventually stood her in good stead as she blossomed into a distinctive film voice after studying communications in Buenos Aires.

Graduating to features after a period directing for Argentinean television, including, between 1995–98, the children's programme, *Magazine for Fai*, Martel also completed the documentaries *Silvina Ocampo* (1998) and *Encarnación Ezcurra* (1998) before receiving a Sundance/NHK Filmmakers' Award for her screenplay *La Ciénaga* (*The Swamp*, 1999) which precipitated one of the most visually accomplished and transcendent films of its year. Widely assumed to contain autobiographical elements, the film focuses on the apathetic households of two middle-aged cousins over the course of a blisteringly hot summer. Almost impossible to classify (many described the film as existing at the juncture between Jane Campion and David Lynch), *La Cienaga* has an acute sense of suffocating stasis, mystery and faint, though palpable, menace. Another key aspect of the film is the director's attention to sounds: the densely-layered soundtrack introduces further moments of tension and surprise.

Stating a desire to follow the film with an erotic movie about a girl who thinks she is a saint, Martel exceeded the expectations raised by her debt with

La niña santa (*The Holy Girl*, 2004). Executive produced by Pedro Almodóvar and his brother Agustín, the film is produced by Lita Stantic, one of the key figures in the 'new wave' of Argentinean filmmaking. Elusive and feverish, the film is set in winter in a rural, northern Argentinean town, the like of which Martel grew up in. Two friends, Amalia and Josefina, get together in the parish church to discuss faith and vocation, also whispering secretly about kissing. A chance encounter between Amalia and Dr Jano, who is attending a medical conference at the hotel she lives in, allows the young girl to at last find her vocation – to save a man from sin.

An oblique work full of unexpected revelations, the film, a synthesis of the spiritual and the sexual, proceeds through fleeting sounds as much as image. *La niña santa* places Martel at the forefront of a remarkable moment in Argentinean cinema.

The following interview took place at the 2004 London Film Festival.

Jason Wood: You have described *La niña santa* as being about the difficulties of distinguishing good from evil. Could you say a little more about this concept in relation to the film.

Lucrecia Martel: What interested me in this film – and also in *La Ciénaga*; it will probably interest me for the rest of my life – is that contradictory area between what is organic and perceptible, and moral laws, or laws in general, including language. Between these two bodies, one organic and one discontinuous, there are contradictions, and these underlie each character and situation in *La niña santa*. In this sense, the distinction between good and bad is totally pointless. Not the distinction between what is good and what is bad for us, which has much to do with the body and things organic, but moral ideas, good and bad, which turn out to be absurd. The film isn't about differences between good and bad, but about the impossibility of distinguishing between them.

When I write, I don't think of a character as man or woman, adult or child, but as a living thing. A living thing is not contradictory. It's a set of possibilities, and all possibilities are possible. All its actions are possible and equally valid. What permits them or not is an external moral and social structure. What I enjoyed about writing this film was seeing how these moral issues worked as a trap for these very complex beings. It isn't an attempt to judge their actions, but it simply observes these contradictions, without being judgemental.

JW: Catholicism is obviously central, both in terms of Amalia's professed vocation – to save a man from sin, the sense of sexual awakening of the girls, and in terms of the sexual repression that hangs heavy throughout. Why this interest in religion and how deeply did the Catholic religion inform your own way of thinking?

LM: In religious literature there are many allusions to the priest, or whoever administers religion, as a kind of doctor. They're words that are often used together. It also has to do with a series of questions, like the choice of a hotel, which is halfway between a hotel and a hospital. In everything I'm going to talk about, religion and religious aspects are closely linked to things medical.

The realm of the body and illness as a medical concern and moral defects as a religious concern are subjects that are, as a group of words, closely linked. That's my own take on the world. I had a fairly traditional Catholic education, from which I later distanced myself, but that's my background. From the age of 18 until now, nineteen years later, I've been developing my own theory of perception of the world. But that was definitely my background.

Religious education doesn't just mean a lot of repressive nonsense that is so readily associated with Catholicism, but a real vision of the world. If you abandon it, you need to construct another vision. What I constructed for myself when, as a teenager, I abandoned religion, was ... it's not a finished construction. This idea, that I began developing then is the possibility of a social order which is in keeping with the body. That totally changes one's set of values.

For example, to allow hunger would be a moral failure, to allow someone else's pain would be, too. As society stands, those don't appear to be failures. In individual terms, that is. Hunger and pain can only be analysed now from a historical or political perspective but never as something personal, as a personal responsibility.

JW: I admired the performances that you drew. Could you comment on María Alché as Amalia, perhaps also touching upon some of the concepts and concerns that the character represents.

LM: The character of Amalia is based on my own experiences as a teenager. What interested me most was that very powerful aspect of adolescence and also its vast mystery, full of secret plans. This is especially true of those girls who relate so personally to the divine. They're very powerful girls. Those were the reasons behind the creation of the character.

To find Amalia, we saw 1,400 girls, from which we chose 25 to find Amalia and her friend Josefina. I worked with these girls until I found that the best pairing was Julieta Zylberberg and María Alché. It was the first time either actress had worked in film. María had done some theatre work. Julieta had worked in TV, in some rather strange programmes, but she did have a certain amount of TV

experience. Luckily they're more uninhibited than I am. It's a different generation. Things that to me seemed difficult to even discuss ... they made it so much
easier for me. It was the other way around from what you'd expect, they had to
put up with me! I find that actors are a world apart. I can rarely become friends
with them, despite having close bonds with many of the actors in this film. I
find it difficult being friends with them because they are people who are very
daring, and that's not me at all. When someone who's very reserved is with very
outspoken people, there is a constant danger of having to do something I don't
feel like doing. When I meet actors, I need to talk with them at length so they
see my limitations and I can see what they're like, so we can help each other in
making the film. An actor's lack of experience is never a problem. Personality can
be more of a problem. In this regard, they've probably been a lot smarter with
me than I with them.

JW: Mercedes Morán is very impressive as Helena.

LM: I love this actress. She's one of the most extraordinary actresses in Argentina. Mercedes has an exceptional ability to express herself very subtly without
using large gestures. In film, someone like that is a real find. If she heard me
saying that I can't be a friend with an actor, she'd be very upset because we have
a very good relationship. But there's a kind of vertigo that actors feel, and that's
the stage. There's a vertigo that directors feel, and that's the actors. We all like to
feel like we're on the edge of the abyss!

JW: The hotel setting contributed a great deal to the film.

LM: The characters of Elena and her brother are like the children of hotel-owners
who live in hotels and have to get used to making friends with kids who are just
passing through. They develop friendships very quickly, knowing that they won't
last long. That shapes a very special kind of person, someone rather melancholic,
because they know that the end will always be a bit sad.

People working in film experience something similar for a good part of their
lives. What with festivals, film promotions and so on you can easily spend two
months a year living that strange, solitary hotel life. I think the family is a disease.
Falling in love is also a disease. They are vital experiences, they are essential, but
they have positive and negative consequences.

I think the idea of the family contains so much ... exclusion, racism. There
are so many very negative values around the family that when the family is dis-
solved, I don't think it's necessarily a bad thing. What I do think is that a person
can't be disconnected. Whether it's the family as we know it, with blood ties, or

anything else we construct as a kind of community, it's important, but not as the traditional concept of a family, with parents, children.

Coming from a very large family myself, I don't consider it paradise. I think everyone needs a small community but I don't think the traditional idea of the family is the best solution. If one could organise social relations on a much more elemental, physical basis, the concept of the family would also change. It would be unbearable for anybody to see an abandoned child. It would be unbearable to exclude generations because they're old or sick, to exclude them from the core of the family. The way the family is organised now is based on a racist point of view, on blood, and an economic point of view, that is inheritance. I don't find it a very positive institution.

More than 'family', for me it's the idea of community. Not like a hippy community of the 1970s, but the idea of common ties, things you're prepared to share with others, not necessarily a family. It's never deliberate but it always ends up happening.

JW: I found the film to have a timeless quality to it.

LM: It has to do with the film being structured around many events associated with the late 1970s and 1980s, that period of my life. When we talked about the film with the art director, we never thought of it as a period film and we never say it's the 1970s or the 1980s, and yet what we show clearly ends up being a strange period of around that time. The idea of certainty about cause and consequence and the chronology of events are much closer to language than the workings of things organic, especially regarding how memory works, which is very organic. There's something fantastic in the way memory perverts language and time. It perverts these ideas that form the backbone of how we organise reality. When you write a film like this one, based on recollection, memory ends up contributing those things – specific things regarding editing, time as represented in the film, how to narrate events and which details to include.

Certain types of American cinema have so much faith in reality, organising stories in such a consistent way with a cause/consequence structure with a very exact, well-defined chronology. On the other hand, for films strongly based on memory, which perverts ideas of time and space and the idea of cause/consequence, that kind of narrative structure is obviously no good. So, in order to tell a story based on this experience of memory, you need a different narrative form. This involves editing, how space is represented in the film, which details or interplay of details should be used to tell the whole story. In the editing, above all...

JW: I admired the way that the film proceeds through the gradual accumula-

tion of detail and things half-seen or partly concealed.

LM: What got me interested in film was the discovery of the similarity between editing scenes in a film and how memory works, especially with regard to what is edited out. What disappears in a narration, what isn't said, what you'd rather hide … what you don't wish to share with the audience for some reason and would rather not show … What is left out can be as important as what is shown and said, if not more so. But not as a game to make it harder. Some people think it's done deliberately to irk the viewer, but it's not. In order to share complex emotions, you need to discover and experiment with ways of reaching that shared situation.

JW: The use of sound in the film is very distinctive. Was this an aspect to which you played particular attention? I liked the theremin too.

LM: The great thing about the soundtrack – especially when you include the human voice as a sound – is that it demystifies language, it deconstructs the idea of dialogue, even that of music. What's interesting about sound is that it lacks a harmonic organisation, which allows the viewer to predict feelings and anticipate events. The interesting thing about sound is that … let me try and explain. Music, like the plot and like language, always allows the viewer to anticipate and even prejudge what's next. Conversely, sound only allows the simultaneity of the experience. That's very important when you're trying to share emotions. It only allows you to face what you are seeing at that moment. In a horror film the music tells you that something terrible is about to happen. You are prepared for it. It's the same thing with a romantic scene, music works that way. A film's plot works the same way, too.

When you see a film with a very strong plot, you know who the good guys are, who the bad guys are, and how the film will evolve. Sound, on the other hand, understood as a soundtrack with no music, allows much more uncertainty. I find that fascinating.

What I like about the theremin is that its sound is very humorous, and, for our generation, is closely associated with B-movies.

JW: How did Pedro Almodóvar's El Deseo production company become involved in *La niña santa*?

LM: Pedro Almodóvar is so generous, in that he is passionate about cinema; when he likes a film he has no hesitation in saying so. He said he'd liked *La Ciénaga*, so we thought he was the ideal person to send this second project to.

It caught his interest and he got his production company involved immediately. It was great for the film's production. Because the production company started out as a director's production company, they're people who have enormous respect for the writer's decisions about the work. They never intervened or tried to change anything in that regard. It was an extraordinary experience for me, especially as I admire him as a director. To our generation, he's an iconic director. So, as well as a great experience, it was a huge honour.

JW: What parallels exist between *La Ciénaga* and *La niña santa* and what were the main lessons and experiences you drew from that project when working on your second feature?

LM: What I learnt most was that there are things you can never know. Such as that it's very difficult to see the film as a whole once you start filming. The last time you have a narrative idea as a whole is the day before you start filming. After that, it's an act of faith. During shooting, it's the closest thing to religion there is! You have to believe in that vague memory of the film as a whole. This time I enjoyed shooting much more, I had fun ... I still always manage to have great fun in the situations I've had to live through. In this film in particular, it was such fun. You can tell when that happens. People had such a good time in the film that afterwards there was party after party where almost all the team would meet up. That's the most important thing I learnt, that that's how it is, that the film as a whole becomes lost, that you're never going to see the film. The film is something that only the audience sees. Perhaps in twenty or thirty years time I'll be able to watch it as a film. I find seeing what I do very off-putting. I only see the problems and things I'd liked to have done differently. There's little chance of seeing it as a whole. Above all, it is knowing that the maker of a film is under no obligation to watch it!

* * *

Scott McGehee
and David Siegal

Former students of the University of California in Berkeley, Scott McGehee and David Siegel began making short films in San Francisco. Sampling a single frame of one of the three features thus far directed by the duo offers evidence of the striking visual aesthetic that defines their work.

A frequently thrilling synthesis of composition, editing and design (visual and aural), *Suture* (1993), *The Deep End* (2001) and *Bee Season* (2005) has seen them imprint contemporary American filmmaking with an indelible signature style, including visual motifs and colour-coding.

Completed under differing circumstances to previous features and under the aegis of a studio, the move-up in division that *Bee Season* undoubtedly represents may have given those that have followed McGehee and Siegel's career cause for concern. And yet, both thematically and technically, all is as it should be. The film retains the pair's intelligent explorations of fractured families, human dynamics and inchoate desires and, from its photography by Giles Nuttgens, design by Kelly McGehee, editing by Lauren Zuckerman and score by Peter Nashel, represents a feast for the senses. Unfairly maligned on its release in the UK, the film is ripe for rediscovery.

The following interview took place in 2005 and a version originally appeared in *Sight and Sound* (vol. 15, no. 12). The interview was conducted via written correspondence, and the response to the questions were delivered jointly.

Jason Wood: The genesis of *Bee Season* was different for you as the producers brought you aboard a project that was already set up. Given your independent sensibilities did you have any concerns?

Scott McGehee/David Siegal: This is the first time we've not written and produced our work, and yes, we did have some concerns about the prospect. But Albert Berger and Ron Yerxa [co-producers] were very respectful of both our process and our creative team. Our director of photography [Giles Nuttgens] and our composer [Peter Nashel] had been with us on *The Deep End*, and our editor [Lauren Zuckerman] and designer [Kelly McGehee] go back to *Suture* and beyond, so our process creatively wasn't so different from our earlier films. We like producing our work because it puts the responsibility and control of how money is spent on our shoulders, and we find that allows us to make decisions more effectively. But of course this was our first 'studio' film, so we had a lot of learning to do.

JW: What particular aspects of Myla Goldberg's novel and Naomi Foner-Gyllenhaal's script secured your involvement? The dealing with themes of identity and the interior lives of characters strikes me as being a particular attraction for you.

SM/DS: The producers had actually shown us the book a couple years before we got involved as directors, and we had liked it and talked about what a script might look like, but we were busy at the time with another project that eventually never happened. Things changed, and a couple of years later we were re-approached, now with a draft of the script. We were, quite honestly, a bit trepidatious about even reading it. We figured the chances were better than not that we would be disappointed by the screenplay's translation of the book. But we were pleasantly surprised. Naomi Foner-Gyllenhaal had managed to preserve what we thought was the spirit of the book, and her changes were really smart. We've joked that it was like having elves come in while you sleep and do your work for you. We worked with her a bit on a subsequent draft, then did a draft of our own, but her script was a really great blueprint for the film.

We were attracted to the material for a number of reasons. There are certain themes that always seem to interest us: how families work, and how identities are defined and differentiated in the world. But the spiritual story in *Bee Season* – the story of these people all struggling toward some kind of relationship with God – was something really new, and was handled in a way that we found exciting. Myla Goldberg's idea of putting spelling and Kabbalah together seemed so clever to us, managing at once to talk about language and something beyond language. About communication, really. In so many different ways, and all very intimate, and sort of familiar, and familial.

JW: How did you respond to Goldberg's evocation of the thirteenth-century Kabbalistic practices that Saul introduces to Eliza? Also, did it – and the film's other Judaic concepts – allow a connecting thread between the spiritual yearning, the sibling competition and the spectre of mental illness that almost destroys the Naumann family?

SM/DS: Obviously, Myla put a lot of thought into the web of signifiers she was weaving with Spelling Bees and the word-based Jewish mystical traditions that Saul talks to Eliza about, and even Aaron's interest in Hare Krishna, a religious practice that focuses on chanting the name of God. This was all very interesting to us, especially in a story about a family that finds it hard to communicate.

We also really responded to another idea Saul talks about, that the world is a kind of broken vessel, something created by God that is then shattered into fragments, unable to contain the magnitude of His divine light. We were excited about the visual connection with Miriam's kaleidoscope in the story, and we enjoyed exploring that visual idea throughout the film. But there was also something within this story that connected for us with how we think about the filmmaking process itself. The way a film is built, the relationship of the piece to the whole within a film story. It's been very rewarding terrain to spend our time within.

JW: You use the spelling bee as a metaphor for using words but failing to communicate with them. Having visited numerous spelling bees, what did you find in terms of human emotion and dramatic impact?

SM/DS: We went to the National Bee in 2003, and were really impressed. There's something irresistible about kids spelling words that most of us have never even heard. And the environment at the real event is quite sweet and much more 'educational' than we expected. There's less of the high-pressure, aggressive parent, win-or-die mentality than we had feared. There were lots of people in the audience writing their best attempt at a spelling word in their programs, just to try their own skills against the kids. There were also lots of supportive families and lots of camaraderie. This isn't to say that the kids weren't under a huge amount of pressure, or that there wasn't a real desire on each of their parts to win.

Our favourite speller was a little girl from Jamaica who would stall endlessly by asking question after question of the pronouncers: What's the language of origin? Could you use it in a sentence please? Would you repeat the word please? Again, please? Is that three syllables or four? On and on until everyone was fed up. We would be sure she must be stumped, but she'd finally get it, every time. She made it all the way to the top five.

JW: I was initially sceptical about the casting of Richard Gere. Could you talk a little about the casting choices in terms of the need to create a palpably real family?

SM/DS: We think Richard is a terrific actor, obviously, or we wouldn't have cast him. We really thought he could capture the essence of this character: a well-meaning but ultimately overbearing guy, a bit self-involved, a bit distant emotionally, despite the outward charm. Richard really understood the character perfectly, and we all had fun poking and shaping the nuances of Saul's character, his narcissism, really. None of us wanted him to be a simple villain in the drama; his good intentions interested all of us. We were also intrigued by the dimension that Richard's well-publicised personal spiritual life could play in filling out the character.

Miriam was originally written as a Jewish American woman, but when we thought of Juliette Binoche for the role, we both were very taken with the idea. Miriam spends a lot of time by herself in this film, and we knew we needed an actress who could really communicate a complicated interior life without much dialogue. We started kicking around the idea of making her a Catholic woman who converted to Judaism when she married Saul, and we liked the narrative that this created about their relationship, her taking on his religion, acquiring it, using it in a way to make sense of the world.

One of our producers, Albert Berger, suggested we take a look at Max Minghella for the role of Aaron. He had gotten to know Max when he was working with his father on *Cold Mountain* [2003], which he was also a producer on. We were very impressed with Max when we met him, but our first reaction was that he was far too beautiful to play Aaron, who was written as a bit of a misfit. But because we had been so taken with him, we kept turning the idea over in our heads. He felt like he belonged in the family we were putting together, and it wasn't as if Richard's Saul and Juliette's Miriam were likely to have a really homely son. Ultimately we came upon a version of Aaron who was sort of in his head a bit, and awkward, without being the more goofy nerd Aaron that was originally written. We were all very impressed by Max's performance in the end. It's his first time on camera, and he came to acting so naturally; he seemed to walk right into his American accent. We asked him to stay within the accent during the course of production (on set and off), thinking it would help make the dialogue more second-nature, and help him develop a different kind of persona for the character, which he did. He really surprised the crew at the wrap party when he started talking like himself again.

We found Flora Cross as the result of a big national talent search that was organised by our casting director Mindy Marin. Mindy ran ads and had a website, and ultimately received – and watched – thousands of tapes from every corner of America. But as Mindy sagely predicted before the whole process ever started, Flora was one of the first tapes we looked at. She had never before acted, and we just fell in love with the very shy, very natural girl on that tape. We hadn't started casting the Miriam role yet, and joked about the physical resemblance between Flora and Juliette Binoche, about how perfect Flora would be if only Juliette were playing her mother.

Months passed, and we looked at many more girls. Lots of really talented young actresses. But there was something about Flora that held our attention. One thing is the way she speaks. She's got quite an interesting background: both of her parents are American, but she was born in France, learned to speak French before English, attended the Lycée in New York for a while, has always been educated in French, but has lived in quite a few places, including Israel, Panama and currently Argentina. She's essentially trilingual with English, French and Spanish, and really doesn't use her English that much in her normal life. We think the care she takes getting her mouth around English words is part of what we found irresistible about her, something tentative and thoughtful in her speech. But there is also something so deep in her face. Her eyes seem to convey a whole world of possibilities. We think she's very special.

JW: Albert Berger and Ron Yerxa have described their desire to work with you as being a response to your distinctive visuals. Could you talk about *Bee Season*'s visual approach and the various textures that you sought to create? The cinematography – and I'm thinking of Giles Nuttgens' imagery of kaleidoscopes, permutated letters and mosaic manipulation of layers of shadow and light – is especially striking.

SM/DS: We were under the impression that Ron and Albert chose us because of the expensive meals we bought them. Of course, it was great to work with Giles again. He's so talented, and approaches his work from a very story-oriented place, which makes him a great collaborator. And we just love the way he lights. Subtle, yet dramatic and clean. He's just got a great eye for light. In a story about enlightenment, we thought that was important.

Many aspects of the film's visual tapestry came from the process of making the film itself, starting with the location scouting. Kelly was with us for many of the scouts and we were all impressed by the density of the worlds within the libraries that we saw. The colours, the textures. All this went into our thinking about the Naumanns' house, their clothes, etc. We wanted the characters to feel like they belonged in the same place yet somehow were individually separated from each other, much as books sit on a shelf. The craftsman-style architecture that the Berkeley area is known for helped us to convey this idea as well. How each character was illuminated, and from what source they are illuminated was also a big concern. But more than in our previous films, we avoided a strict programmatic approach. There were themes we kept circling back to – most importantly this idea of fragmentation – but we found the visual world generally emerging quite organically from the story as we were telling it.

JW: The film journeys into Eliza's thought processes as she sees words and their essences spinning into being around her. Here you introduce a magic realism aspect, something that you've perhaps not done as overtly as this before. Were you excited by the prospect of digital effects?

SM/DS: We did, in fact, have one digital effect in *The Deep End*, when Margaret comes into her kitchen and we see her whole world upside down and backwards through a drop of water on her kitchen faucet. This was a scripted shot that we had planned to get photographically, but it proved too time-consuming. So we sort of backed into our first digital shot.

We were definitely intrigued by the more extensive possibilities for digital work in *Bee Season*. We liked the idea of these child-like, very organic fantasies of letters forming. And we decided early on that it was important that we see Eliza within her own imaginings rather than picture them as cut-away worlds inside her head. That was the one big global decision about approach. We worked with a smallish visual-effects company in Los Angeles called Black Box Digital, and it was really in partnership with them that the working out of the shots was done. We would come up with ideas to try, and we'd run the ideas by the team at Black Box, and they'd tell us what they could do well and what, in their estimation, they would have a harder time doing well. Once we had a list of things they were game to try, we went ahead.

JW: You must get asked this all the time, but how does the dynamic of the directing relationship work? In other co-directing partnerships one finds that one person handles the cast and the other handles technical duties. Are such divisions of labour and creativity as clear-cut here?

SM/DS: We don't divide up our directing chores systematically at all. We really just do it together. In the ideal version, we are one brain with two bodies; a funny sort of economy of means. We plan things carefully, and take a lot of care while rehearsing and shot-listing our day so that we really understand one another before the shooting starts. Post-production, similarly, we stick together and work things out as we go.

JW: How do you feel audiences will react to *Bee Season*? Are you hoping that they'll come away having more than learned to spell a difficult word or two?

SM/DS: If anyone learns to spell anything watching our film, we'll be surprised and disappointed.

* * *

Pawel Pawlikowski

Born in Warsaw in 1957, Pawel Pawlikowski came to Britain as a 12-year-old refugee, an experience that would later form the basis of what is widely considered his breakthrough film, *Last Resort* (2000). The recipient of numerous newcomer awards for the film, including a BAFTA, Pawlikowski had actually been making documentaries for the BBC since the late 1980s. Defined by their integrity and interest in figures somehow ostracised from their communities, keys films from this period include *Lucifer Over Lancashire* (1987), *From Moscow to Pietushki* (1990) and *Serbian Epics* (1992).

The Stringer (1998), Pawlikowski's fiction feature debut is rarely seen and has been summarily dismissed by its director as being unrepresentative of his work. His featurette *Twockers* (1998) offered a marked improvement. A film concerning child burglars that was originally conceived as a documentary but which organically evolved into a drama, the film's naturalistic performances, minimalist aesthetic and acute sense of time, place and character provided the template from which Pawlikowski's two subsequent features were forged.

The first of these, *Last Resort*, was shot for the BBC for just £320,000. Filmed on location in Margate, the film follows Tanya, a vulnerable and naive young Russian, who arrives at Gatwick airport with her 10-year-old son to meet her English fiancé. When he fails to show up, a distraught Tanya claims political asylum and finds herself virtually imprisoned in a nightmarish refugee holding centre in a lonely seaside resort. Desperate to escape, Tanya forges an unlikely alliance with amusement arcade manager Alfie, which soon develops into something more.

An affecting and poetic love story that paints a picture of Britain as a cold and inhumane nation founded on administrative ineptitude, *Last Resort* perceptively comments on refugee status and those that are forced to subsist below Britain's poverty line. Never resorting to didacticism, Pawlikowski's shooting methods inform what is seen on screen, the director preferring to cohabitate with a minimal cast and crew throughout filming and vehemently resisting input from financiers, script supervisors or other superfluous industry lackeys.

Pawlikowski's *My Summer of Love* (2004) came into being after creative differences led to the director choosing to depart from the production of the Sylvia Plath biopic, *Sylvia* (2003). A characteristically insightful, restrained and intoxicating look at obsession and desire, *My Summer of Love* also returns to the territory of *Lucifer Over Lancashire* in its consideration of the struggle for faith in a world where it seems impossible. Again completed after extensive rehearsals with the cast of relative newcomers and working from a script that evolved from workshopping and improvisation, Goldfrapp's dreamy, mysterious music sets the tone for a lyrical exploration of one summer in the lives of two Yorkshire teenagers who hail from very different sides of the tracks. Mona is instinctive, inquisitive and poor, living in an empty pub with her born-again Christian brother Phil, while Tamsin is mannered, well-spoken, lonely and fond of playing Edith Piaf and quoting Nietzsche. The combination is entrancing. The pair meet on a sun-kissed country road and never seem to part – living, sleeping, wandering and exploring together for the rest of a charmed summer, only interrupting their capsule existence to wonder at Phil's strange and suspect religious obsession.

I have interviewed Pawlikowski a number of times over recent years, mostly for on-stage discussions after screenings of his work. The following interview took place in 2003; I cannot recall the location, but I suspect it was at the Curzon Soho.

Jason Wood: How did you find Nathalie Press and Emily Blunt and how did you instil the intimacy between them?

Pawel Pawlikowski: It was a very long casting process because I didn't want known actors; I wanted to cast the film with originals. We didn't have much money so it was long, but low-level research. I looked at professional actors and non-professional actors and spent a lot of time up north looking at Mona-type working-class girls in places like Leeds and Manchester. A lot of them were fine but I couldn't help feeling that there was always something clichéd and televisual about them; by and large they tended to conform to very broad types and I needed someone more complicated and contradictory, someone who could do more than one thing. What I really wanted to avoid was making one of these so-called gritty realist films about contemporary Britain or contemporary youth. Neither interests me very much. I needed characters that were more interesting and timeless.

People go on about how real the characters in my films are, but honestly realistic acting is not my great ambition. Of course, you should try and avoid false notes, clunky exposition or emoting; that goes without saying. But the thing I really want to see on the screen are interesting characters, people who are a bit surprising, who I can engage with.

So we went on looking back in London and eventually we came across Nathalie who immediately stood out. She had a great presence in the room, a strong aura. There seemed to be this tension in her or a contradiction – she was clever, witty, spunky, cynical and yet she had something romantic about her and this rather intense interior. Sociologically Nathalie couldn't be further away from a northern lass – Nathalie is from North London – but psychologically there were parallels with Mona. Once I saw Nathalie and had done some tests with her, I knew I had a bit of firm ground under my feet, I knew I had got to the first rung of the process. The next stage was to find the Tamsin character. Again we went through a lot of young actors, including some bigger stars, but we did not find anything that interesting. Then I came across Emily and she had these striking lively eyes. She could do the posh, confident, horsey type of girl with ease, not that she is this type of person, but she knows that world and understands how it works. But she had these mischievous eyes, which could animate suddenly and a really quick mind. We auditioned a few other girls after Emily but I kept coming back to these eyes and when I put the two girls together – obviously I had to test people as couples – there was a real spark, in an opposites-attract sort of way. Both had good energy, looked and sounded good together and moved well as a pair.

JW: You described the film as being 'sculpted' in that you shot without a script but rather worked on moulding the film with the help of your actors and your chief technical crew. How did this contribute to the rapport between the two leads?

PP: I did have a script of sorts, and a pretty clear structure. In fact many scenes were shot more or less as written, after some tweaking in the rehearsals, especially scenes which were driven by Tamsin. But in many other scenes, I sketched in several possibilities and kept things open to the process. The point and the subtext of these scenes was fixed and some of the lines and gestures too, but we kept trying things out in different ways, to weed out false notes and to generate something more alive and interesting on the screen. This open approach allowed me to mould the scenes and performances throughout the process, in workshops weeks before filming, or the day before, or in the lunch-break, sometimes even during the take, when I slipped ideas to the actors while the camera was rolling. Frustratingly for some, my brain never stops, I keep fiddling with the material and the process is never-ending. This sort of thing can only work, of course, if you have actors, a director of photography and art department who really participate and also a producer prepared to go with you on this journey.

JW: How much of the source novel by Helen Cross did you retain?

PP: Not much. What I kept was mainly the characters of the two girls. The book was a much busier, more populated affair. I remember Mona had a proper family, a father, a stepmother, an older sister and an obese stepbrother. Their pub was very lively, very northern, with a crowd of characters. There was also a creepy paedophile lusting after Mona and there were two murders and the whole place was in the grip of the miners strike – the year was 1984 – ah ... and the Yorkshire Ripper was on the prowl terrorising the population. It was all too specific and at the same time too generic and the plot was a little contorted and fanciful. What was brilliant though was Mona's voice – the story was told in first-person – which of course we couldn't use in the film, but it was really strong and memorable. I loved Mona's mixture of intelligence and naivety, cynicism and yearning. Tamsin's character is also from the book. The born-again brother, played by Paddy Considine, I invented from scratch.

The world in the film is a little abstract. I wanted a more timeless and elemental world, one in which the sort of emotions I'm interested in could occur. The landscape I'm talking about has little to do with the surface of contemporary Britain, where we are so swamped with images, information, endless noise that it's hard to respond to anything in a fresh way, to look into someone's eyes and fall in love.

JW: Phil's character was based, was it not, on an earlier documentary you made about evangelical Christians?

PP: Loosely inspired would be a better way of putting it. In 1987 I came across this evangelising preacher in Lancashire who wanted to plant a twenty-metre crucifix on top of Pendle Hill, where famously some witches were hanged in the seventeenth century. He convinced his followers that the whole area was once more under threat from witches and Satanists and he wanted to reclaim it for Christ. Unfortunately the local council didn't give him planning permission for the cross; they thought it would have constituted a 'new development' – that's England for you! So my film – *Lucifer Over Lancashire* – didn't really take off either. After that I went to make films abroad.

JW: I feel that there is very little fat with your work.

PP: The final result may seem that way, but the process is more complicated, it's full of digressions and waste. What usually happens is this. First I need to get really excited about something, a character, a theme, a story. And this is the most difficult bit. I am extremely lazy, so I really need to get worked up about something to make me want to get out of bed every morning for a year or two. Once I've stoked up this fire, I start throwing all sorts of things into it – personal stuff, memories, people I knew, characters from favourite books, photographs, strange stories from the papers and all kinds of terrible, pretentious ideas, motifs, stuff from my previous films (the moped with no engine, for instance, is something I stole from Trevor in *Twockers* [1998]). I also start driving around looking for landscapes, meeting people, taking photographs and writing notes. Once I've amassed all this stuff, I try to sketch out the story outline, see what fits and what doesn't. I keep trying the different versions of the outline on people – my wife, my producer, whoever will stay with me in the room and listen. It's trial and error. A good writing partner would help of course; someone like-minded who could bring stuff to the table and spur me on in some way. I'm still looking for that.

Once the outline and the characters are broadly there, the paring down begins. It's mainly a matter of finding the balance between character and plot, between the unexpected and the believable, between information and the image. So you start stripping away all your bad ideas, clever motifs, weak lines, exposition, obviousness. What can help in this process is casting and screen-testing. Even meeting actors who are wrong for the part can help you focus. And when you met someone who is right, then that's a huge step forward.

So I keep trying things out, distilling and slowly the characters firm up and the hidden shape of the film emerges. This can last right up to the first day of filming and sometimes, I am afraid to say, even beyond it. The main thing is not to tread water, not to rely on clichés. Sometimes you can't avoid them, of course, but what you want is to get to the heart of something. Just make sure there is a heart to start with. The key thing is the initial impulse.

When it comes to directing I also try to keep things simple. I try to stay close to my characters. The perspective tends to be limited. Of course, big wide land-scape shots, with interesting light and framing, that's a different matter. You need them to create the universe. You can never have enough of these. But otherwise I keep it small. I always feel there is just one good angle from which to photo-graph a scene and there's no need for what's known as coverage. Unless you're really struggling, which sometimes happens.

I generally avoid tracks or crane shots. It's partly because I don't work with big budgets and these sorts of things take time to set up. But also I find that very few filmmakers know how to use these things well. Usually these sorts of operations seem to be there just to draw attention to the fact that the director is directing. In fact, what they actually draw attention to is the fact that the film is missing a heart or some other vital organ. I remember on *My Summer of Love* we came up with some complicated shot for a very simple scene. We had the track laid and lit it, then I looked through the viewfinder and said to my director of photography: 'God Ryszard [Lenczewski], this is beginning to look like some … movie.' Which was anathema. We axed the shot immediately.

JW: Did the 'sculpting' approach that you adopted cause you any concerns? Were there moments where perhaps you felt that the project was in danger of drifting away from you?

PP: There were ups and downs. I did shoot a few *non sequitur* scenes. There were a couple of others – we had to shoot them out of chronology and they weren't pinned down very well – which had the wrong tone or wrong emphasis. So I had to re-shoot them. But the emotional structure of the whole was pretty firm. Basically, when you have a set of good characters and relationships, the right actors to do them, a decent beginning, some strong turning points in the middle and a possible ending – and when you know what the whole story is about – then you know that you have strong foundations.

JW: And what were these turning points? I thought that the cello scene was key as it indicated to Mona a beauty and culture her class had denied her.

PP: For me even more important was the scene where the girls dance to Edith Piaf and Tamsin tells Mona this complete fairytale about Piaf's murdered hus-bands. Mona is totally out of her depth here and totally gripped by Tamsin's yarns and Tamsin realises she can take Mona wherever she wants. Another key moment is where Tamsin tries to seduce Phil. I was always looking forward to shooting that scene. I knew it was going to be great, and it really twists the story and makes it go somewhere new. Then you have the moment where Tamsin's supposedly dead sister crops up – a real kick in the face – where Mona realises that everything Tamsin has told her is probably a lie. However flexible my methods, I have to have such key scenes worked out from the very beginning to know I've got a film.

JW: The ending also comes as quite a shock.

PP: I toyed with the idea of Mona going the whole way and murdering Tamsin, but this would have been a bit too literal. Also, to have concluded the film in this way would have been horrible. Where can you go after murdering someone? Also I am generally scared of murder and blood-spilling. So we left the ending a bit more open. Mona re-emerges from the forest with a spring in her step, while Tamsin is left deflated and empty. What will happen to Mona is hard to say. She's definitely the stronger character at the end. I am sure Tamsin will be OK too; she'll bounce back from this misadventure, go to back to her boarding school, then to Oxbridge, and have a brilliant career in the media. Some of the financiers didn't like the openness of the ending. They wanted the audience to leave the cinema 'with a smile on their face' and begged me to show Mona enjoying a new life in Paris or somewhere nice. I had to put my foot down.

JW: And what about the beginning of the film, an image we later return to of Mona drawing a portrait of Tamsin on her wall. How did this originate?

PP: I was racking my brains for what she could be doing in that room, where she was being held captive for such a long time. Then I remembered that between takes Nathalie kept making these obsessive drawings: faces and angular shapes. This is where the idea came from. I decided not to rehearse this scene and explained to Nathalie that we should launch into it and do in real time. I asked her to be intense, but also calm and tender, in love with her drawing. When Nathalie started drawing on the wall, the atmosphere in the room went really strange, magical or maybe demonic. Her intensity, her face, the movements of her body were amazing; just a girl, a pencil and wall in an empty silent room. I had shivers running down my spine. What was also amazing was the way Ryszard managed to get into Nathalie's rhythms with his hand-held.

JW: The landscape really contributes to the overall tone of *My Summer of Love*.

PP: I really like this ambiguous landscape you get in that part of Yorkshire, where nature and post-industrial decay overlap. But I wanted to shoot this very English landscape in a new way. Because of the light you get in this country, most films tend to capture the landscape in greens, browns and greys. I wanted strong saturated colour, no half-tones. I wanted the landscape to be strong, elemental, more in keeping with the story and characters. For that we needed the sun. To everyone's horror, the place I'd set my mind on happens to be in the rainiest part of England, so it was a huge gamble. But we got away with it.

JW: Do you feel more pressure given the critical acclaim accorded *Last Resort*?

PP: The critical hype around *Last Resort* didn't affect me that much. I mean the film was what it was. I liked it, but it seemed to me that some critics, who professed to love the film, hadn't actually seen it. The film was this rather personal story about a mother and son thrown into a strange, scary world, which again was slightly abstract. My 'political' contribution was mainly to show two foreigners with a degree of empathy, from inside, as interesting people, and not the way they're shown in English-speaking films, as incomprehensible gangsters or victims to be pitied. But despite what was there on the screen, these critics just went on about the film's gritty realism, about it being a searing indictment of the asylum system. And then, rather comically, a pompous right-wing critic was spurred into action and declared that the film was a piece of shit.

The same sort of thing could well happen around *My Summer of Love*, so one shouldn't get carried away either way. What was great, though, was to see the audiences in Edinburgh, Toronto and other screenings. They just went with the film and seemed to genuinely like it. As for critics, I have a pretty good guess what some of them will write: 'After bravely confronting the issue of immigration in his uncompromising *Last Resort*, with its echoes of *Dirty Pretty Things* [2002], *In this World* [2002] (and any other films involving immigrants they can think of), Pawlikowski has now tackled the genre of lesbian coming-of-age movie, paying homage to...' and here they reel off a number of other films which I don't particularly like or haven't even seen.

***

Carlos Reygadas

Born in Mexico in 1971, Carlos Reygadas trained in international law at the University of Mexico. After completing his studies he relocated to London to take a Master's degree. From there he began working for the Mexican Foreign Service at the United Nations, preparing work for the International Penal Court. In 1997 Reygadas decided to quit his profession and moved to Brussels where he discovered a passion for cinema, visiting a cinematheque and voraciously viewing films by directors including Rossellini, Dreyer and Bresson. Rossellini would exert a mammoth influence in terms of allowing the reality of the filming environment to shape and inform the narrative. Bresson would likewise prove instructive in regards to working with non-professional actors and the adoption of a naturalistic approach to sound. It was Tarkovsky's films, however, that would really open the relative youngster's eyes.

Whilst preparing the necessary materials to gain entry to film school Reygadas met Diego Martinez Vignatti, an Argentinean director of photography who would work with the Mexican on a number of shorts and, later on Reygadas's remarkable two features, *Japón* (*Japan*, 2002) and *Batalla en el cielo* (*Battle in Heaven*, 2005).

Completed with a team of newcomers, *Japón*, Reygadas' self-produced debut feature was presented at the 2002 Rotterdam and Cannes film festivals. One of the most outstanding and audacious films on the Croisette that year, the film received a Special Mention for the Camera D'Or. Coming soon after Alejandro González Iñárritu's *Amores perros* (*Love's a Bitch*, 2000) and Alfonso Cuarón's *Y tu mamá también* (*And Your Mother Too*, 2001), the film was heralded as developing a major renaissance in Mexican filmmaking. Shot in Super-16 'Scope and making phenomenal use of the natural habitat, this parable-like tale was also remarkable for a final tracking shot set to Arvo Pärt's 'Cantus'. Critically acclaimed for its uncompromising aspirations to a transcendental form of filmmaking, the film also established something of a pattern for Reygadas in terms of its enigmatic title and inflammatory cross-generational sex scene between Alejandro Ferretis and Magdalena Flores.

Described by its director as 'a Mexico City-set existentialist drama dealing with moral corruption', *Battle in Heaven* screened at Cannes to a chorus of controversy and acclaim. Marcos and his wife kidnap a baby for ransom money but the plot goes wrong when the infant dies. Seeking spiritual salvation, Marcos confesses his crimes to the prostitute Ana, and so sets himself down a path of reckless abandon.

Presenting a characteristically uncompromising vision of human folly, Reygadas's compelling second feature is also remarkably open to the possibility of redemption and grace. Again Reygadas almost exclusively casts non-professionals, claiming that his requirement for the most natural performances possible necessitates a total lack of acting from real people who don't try to communicate meaning. Reygadas has since refuted charges that he exploits non-professional actors for his own artistic purposes, pointing to the trust that exists between himself and his players. The film again deals with moral and spiritual themes that are irrefutably universal, but the closing pilgrim's procession to the Basilica of the Virgin of Guadalupe seems to suggest a more concrete grappling with the notion of Méxicanidad, a consideration of national identity and what it means today to be Mexican. This is a subject that continues to fascinate the emerging band of contemporary Mexican filmmakers.

Currently preparing his third feature, Reygadas also recently produced Amat Escalante's *Sangre* (*Blood*, 2005).

The following interview took place in 2003. Excerpts appear in *The Faber Book of Mexican Cinema* (Faber, 2006).

Jason Wood: How did your initial career in film originate?

Carlos Reygadas: I was alone in Brussels finishing my law career when I decided I wanted a career in cinema. I started going to the Museum of Cinema to see three films a day and I realised that I had to go to film school to find the human team and the materials and to generally have access to things. While I was preparing for the exams I met Diego Martinez Vignatti, an Argentinean director of photography who went on to work on three of my shorts and indeed *Japón*. It was Diego who persuaded me to do a short that I would be able to present as part of my entry credentials and he also offered to provide me with access to a Super-8 camera and film stock. The next day I had a storyboard and a completed scenario and had chosen the actors; in fact everything was prepared. I had so many stories I wanted to tell and so many ideas in my head. I also acted as my own producer, as I have often do, because I realised the need, especially in the beginning, about being realistic about what I could and couldn't achieve with limited budgets and means. My first short still remains amongst my favourite works and I then completed three further pieces in a similar way. Following that, I made another short film entirely by myself because I wanted to learn and understand the whole process.

I then began working on the scenario for *Japón*. It was a practical and relatively easy film to make because it's set in an area I know well that's close to Mexico City and the house of my grandparents who live in the area. I prepared the script and the storyboards and decided that the film would have to be very practical and well prepared and consist of 300 shots. In fact it turned out to be 302. I worked with the team I had worked with on my shorts and we had to work very hard in an organised manner to make it.

JW: You talked about the three films a day you watched whilst studying. Which films or film-makers were particularly influential?

CR: You never know what influences you in life but you do know what you like. Speaking very broadly, I like Roberto Rossellini very much and the conditions in which he had to shoot, with the matter that was there. This was especially true of *Rome, Open City* [*Roma, città aperta*, 1945] and the situation was in some ways similar for me on *Japón*. Everything that goes through the camera is real and you can go to where we shot and see it exactly as it is. Nothing was constructed though the form of course is fiction. Rossellini was a master in this; using the world as it is to create everything he needed for his stories. For me Dreyer and *Ordet* [1954] are also great. *Ordet* is one of the most moving films I've ever seen in my life and a miracle of film. Bresson, though I am now influenced by him less and less, is also a master, especially for the way in which he works with actors and uses sound. *A Man Escaped* [*Un condamné à mort s'est échappé*, 1956] is a personal favourite. Tarkovsky was the one to really open my eyes. When I saw his films I realised that emotion could come directly out of the sound and the image and not necessarily from the storytelling. For the first time I saw in cinema that emotion need not come from a plot-driven climax; just the sound and the image could release so much power and beauty. The first films of Carlos Saura are also very dear to me as are, for different reasons, Ozu and Kurosawa.

JW: Much like recent cinema coming out of Iran, *Japón* strikes me as a film based upon seemingly minor incidents and details that are then minutely observed and expanded upon.

CR: Yes, definitely. And to stray from your question slightly, when I first saw Iranian films some years ago I was struck by geographical, political and religious similarities, though Islam is perhaps more roughly applied there than Catholicism in Mexico but socially the presence of religion is very similar. I was impressed by the work of Abbas Kiarostami and to return to questions of form, his decision to use very long takes with few cuts. I also appreciated that there was in fact lots happening within the scenes and within the little details. It is such details that I am also interested in. I am not interested in the operations of MI5 and such; these are things that are so far away from me. Rather than taking the spectator to live vicariously through someone else's experience and then coming out of the cinema thinking 'what a beautiful dream where I could forget about life for two hours before going back to my miserable existence', I would rather respect the spectator and realise that a good spectator comes to the cinema to live, not to forget about life.

JW: This is in effect what happens to the central male character in the film; he has his sensuality awakened by Ascen.

CR: That is what happens but I don't want to be moralistic about it and say 'yeah life is really worth it, you might as well live it'. I think it's a great human capacity to be able to end our lives of our own choice if we want to. In the case of the film it's more about not a reawakening but more a confusion about what we want when perhaps we want something different. It's also about our sub-conscious being more aware of what we want than our intellect.

JW: Alejandro Ferretis is amazing in the central role.

CR: Yes he is. He was actually a friend of my parents and has been for a very long time. I knew him since I was a very little boy and he always appeared as special to me. He lived through the 1960s in a very combative way, voraciously reads and has a tremendous gift for languages. He was always asking me complex, stimulating questions, often from a Marxist perspective, which we would then endlessly debate and discuss. So when I was writing the script I was always thinking of him, especially as he had often expressed his admiration for Arthur Koestler. When we actually started shooting he started to glamorise himself a little bit as if he thought we were shooting a French perfume ad. However, he soon learned that I didn't want any of that and that I actually wanted him to do very little, which reminds me again of my earlier point about Bresson.

JW: Had Ferretis acted previously?

CR: No, never before.

JW: And the actor who plays Ascen, Magdalena Flores?

CR: No she had never acted before. In fact all the cast are non-professional actors.

JW: Was it a conscious decision to work with non-professional actors?

CR: Yes, it was a deliberate decision. I wanted to work with pure, real matter, largely for the sake of authenticity. I cannot imagine any actress in the world performing the role of Magdalena. This sense of authenticity was especially important for the sexual scene in which Magdalena is really afraid and really modest but at the time has so great a sense of honour that she has to fulfil the promise that she has made. This very real intellectual and spiritual fight she is having would have been impossible for any actress.

JW: Did you speak with professional actors about the part?

CR: Yes, and most I met were sick with narcissism. One actress said that she would have done the nude scenes when she was younger but that an audience would vomit if they saw her naked now. I actually saw around 300 women for the part of Ascen and there was always something more powerful about the peasant women I auditioned for the role. Magdalena was unaware of the fact that she wasn't beautiful because she is unaware of popular conceptions of beauty. It was an ethical and cultural problem concerning her nudity, which was overcome by mutual trust.

I had actually found another woman to play the part of Ascen and worked very closely with her but one week into the shooting period she simply vanished, leaving a note saying that she had broken her hips. In Mexico this simply means that she was afraid so I didn't try to look for her in any hospital. We found Magdalena when we were shooting the slaughter of the pig as she had come to buy some meat, and of course she initially said no when approached about the part but finally consented after we went to see her family and developed the relationship naturally. Magdalena Flores is a very intelligent woman and did beautiful work. She did not even have a script but simply took direction on a scene-by-scene basis.

JW: The sex scene is pivotal. Was it difficult or in any way traumatic to film?

CR: Zero traumatic and very simple. It's a bit like virginity. Girls are told about it and what is going to happen for years and then when it happens they think, 'all that shit for this?' Given Alejandro's liberal sensibilities I anticipated that he would have no problem with the scene but as often happens in life, at the hour of truth it was maybe harder for the man than for the woman. For Magdalena she had nightmares before but when the day came it was a very small, intimate crew and after some tequila she was very tranquil. I also kept the directions very simple to both Magdalena and Alejandro. As it was, it was much like in the film; Alejandro was supposed to be in control but became more hesitant as he became nervous.

JW: What has been Alejandro and Magdalena's reaction to the finished film?

CR: I showed it to the people in the village but I had to unfortunately cut the sex scene because I was worried that Magdalena might suffer abuse and teasing because of the scene; there is a saying – 'little town, big hell'. The film will come out in cinemas so we will see. You know, Mexico is a very special place; some of the population is Western and some of them are not. In terms of the cast, the only one with Western sensibilities was Alejandro so it is hard to really gauge what they feel and how they react to the film. I know that they really laughed at the scene involving the screaming of the pig; in fact, anything involving animals prompted laughter, which is certainly not the reaction you will get here in the UK. It is not even the reaction you might get in more highly populated cities in Mexico.

JW: The film repays repeated viewings, largely due to its many subtleties.

CR: I think this is the basic analysis of film. There are so many films that I have watched the first time and thought they were great and then on second and third viewings thought that I must have been drunk when I liked them. The fourth time I would turn the film off after ten minutes. Good films go the other way around. The pleasure increases each time you see them as do the number of new things and nuances you discover in them. It's for other people to say whether *Japón* also does this but these are certainly the sorts of things that I am interested in.

JW: You must get asked this so many times but you gave the film an enigmatic title.

CR: Yeah, so I suppose its my fault. I should have just called it *Magdalena and Alejandro in the Canyon* or *Love at Last Sight* or something like that. It's obvious but titles are a necessary evil and ideally wouldn't exist but we have to give it a name so that people can refer to it. Paintings for example don't have titles. I wanted to do the same with my film and leave it untitled. I then thought about calling it *untitled* but that would just be pretentious. I always give the titles to things I have made at the end and so I wondered what is this film about after all and for me it is partly about the cycle of light coming again after night. I was struck therefore by the notion of the sun rising which of course has connotations with Japan. I could have called it Korea or Taiwan but these counties are more closely associated with microchip technology. People also often associate other characteristics with Japan such as Haiku poetry, a respect for the elderly and the repression of feelings. There is also the culture of the Samurai and in many ways Alejandro represents this with his veneer of toughness and the impression he gives that he is totally in control. Of course, all he really wants is to cry with his mother holding him. This is perhaps what most of us men really want.

JW: The film does go against some of the popular conventions of society and particularly perhaps in Mexican society the idea that the man is dominant and strong, the elderly are weak, and indeed women are weak. You subvert these slightly.

CR: It's a subversion of ideas as opposed to a subversion of reality because even in our society these are conceptions and not perhaps realities. It's more looking at things as they are in my opinion. I wanted the film to be open to actuality, specifically in regard to pleasure and pain. There are also contradictory ideas in the film. People have interpreted Ascen's act differently. Some believe that she does what she does because there is a force that compels her to save him; other people believe that she does it because of ideas relating to Christian sacrifice. There are also those that interpret Ascen as simply realising what may perhaps be her last opportunity to enjoy physical pleasure. All those things are and can be there depending on the way that you personally look at the film.

JW: Can you explain the technical process behind the film?

CR: It was shot on ordinary 16mm but in front of the primal lens a special anamorphic lens was introduced so that the actual frame is a standard 1:85 ratio but the images are squeezed. The blow up to 35mm was a standard blow up by photographical process. There are few 16mm scope films but it's actually quite a simple process that gives a very grainy look, which I like. I actually got the contact for the process after watching Gasper Noé's *Seul contre tous* [*I Stand Alone*, 1998]. I had already decided that the film had to be in Cinemascope but if I hadn't shot the film in the way that I shot it I would have had to do it on 35mm Panavision film and equipment which is both expensive and heavy.

JW: The filming conditions must have been difficult.

CR: They were very difficult and the cameraman especially did a very good job. Everyone was so committed and the job they did is even more remarkable when you consider that every single one of them were debutants in terms of feature film.

JW: I was impressed by the use of music, especially during the final shot revealing the tragedy.

CR: That's Arvo Pärt and it's an amazing piece of music. When we talked at the beginning of the interview about inspirations I forgot to mention Arvo Pärt. That piece of music in fact influenced very much the ending of the film and suggested the images and gave me the key and the clue regarding how to shoot the last shot. The sound in general is also very important and I sometimes believe that sound design is almost half of cinema, especially in terms of expression. Sound can be objective or subjective. I would say that Tarkovsky is a master of subjective sound and Kiarostami is a master of objective sound; I try to use both.

JW: There currently seems to be a critical and commercial vogue for Mexican cinema due to the success of films such as *Amores perros* [*Love's a Bitch*, 2000], *Y tu mamá también* [*And Your Mother Too*, 2001] and the work of Guillermo del Toro. Has this impacted in any way upon your own work?

CR: Not at all. This is interesting actually. There are always these waves. Most of these directors are maybe ten years older than me but we are from the same generation: the crisis generation. Since we were born there has always been shit around us. Although we have different things in our heads we all share the need to express ourselves. All the films you mention are also made by people who believe in themselves and want to express themselves outside of the system. These people certainly opened the door for me and I hope that in turn I will also open the door for others.

For a so-called 'wave' to exist, a certain number of values have to be shared by a large number of people. The Mexican system concentrates on producing a few big films each year. I think it would be much more interesting if it were to also concentrate on making smaller films. In Argentina, for instance, people are doing a lot of films on 16mm, video and 35mm. But the average budget is much lower than that of a Mexican film. I think this policy would allow a genuine 'movement' to form as opposed to just a passing trend.

JW: Finally, I know it's early days but I believe that you have already started work on a follow-up film. Are you able to reveal anything about it?

CR: It will be titled *Batalla en el cielo* [*Battle in Heaven*], and it will be a Mexico City-set existentialist drama dealing with moral corruption through the relationship between an elderly chauffeur and the daughter of his wealthy boss.

* * *

Nicolas Roeg

Born in London in 1928, Nicolas Roeg entered the film industry as tea-maker and clapper-boy at Marylebone Studios before working his way up to camera operator on, amongst others, Ken Hughes' *The Trials of Oscar Wilde* (1960) and Fred Zinnemann's *The Sundowners* (1960). Roeg also contributed to scripts for Cliff Owen (*A Prize of Arms*, 1961) and Lawrence Huntington (*Death Drums Along the River*, 1962). However, it was as an inventive cinematographer that Roeg first attracted critical attention, especially on Roger Corman's *The Masque of the Red Death* (1964), François Truffaut's *Fahrenheit 451* (1966) and Richard Lester's *Petulia* (1968).

Intriguingly, each of these assignments anticipated aspects of his own feature films, *Petulia* especially foreshadowing the complex time leaps and splintered narratives of Roeg's mature work; while its depiction of 1960s permissiveness disintegrating into despair and violence finds resonant echoes in *Performance* (co-directed with Donald Cammell, 1968). *The Masque of the Red Death* features a 'Red Death' figure that re-materialises in a different, even more sinister guise in the disquieting *Don't Look Now* (1973). The cold, futuristic surface of *Fahrenheit 451* re-emerges in *The Man Who Fell to Earth* (1976), with its penetrating, alien vision of the emptiness of modern life.

Eschewing the normal rules of commercial entertainment, Roeg's films deal in raw emotion, shaking our preconceptions about civilisation and cinema. His aesthetic is founded on a masterly montage of time and space and elliptical narratives through which his characters are cut adrift from their usual moral and physical surroundings. Frequently involving journeys into self-exploration on behalf of both his characters and his spectators, Roeg's estimable credits also include *Walkabout* (1971), *Bad Timing* (1980), *Eureka* (1982), *Insignificance* (1985) and *The Witches* (1989).

Having seen a number of his finest films suffer at the hands of uncomprehending distributors, and a number of admiring young directors steal his best ideas, Roeg is a director who has always been ahead of his time. Thankfully, time is catching up, and after being absent from our screens for far too long he will return next year with *Puffball*.

Roeg can be considered to be responsible for, at a conservative estimate, at least four of the greatest films of the modern era and remains my favourite contemporary British filmmaker.

The following interview occured at the Hay-on-Wye Literary Festival and originally appeared in the *Guardian* on 3 June 2005.

Jason Wood: Let's begin by talking a little bit about your passion for cinema and how you originally came to work in the film medium. You have a very long history.

Nicolas Roeg: Well, in the words of *Star Wars* [1977], it was a long, long time ago, in a galaxy far, far away... I knew nothing about the cinema. When I went to the cinema as a boy, when I saw a war film, I thought the general was the star, and that Cary Grant was an extra. I had no idea about the structure of film, but I loved going to the cinema. I'd go with my sister, who loved to see them twice – it was continuous performance in those days. Film and the cinema in England at that time was not thought of as it is now. It was not one of the arts – it was the movies.

Many years later, I sat on a censorship committee and I said, they've just stopped censorship for the theatre – Lord Chamberlain's office had just finished – so why are we discussing it for film? And one of the people in the committee, I won't say who it was, but a politician said, 'You must understand, the theatre is a mandarin tradition in England.' What do you mean by that? He said, 'Anybody can just walk into cinema, but in theatre, you make a conscious effort and it's part of the culture.' When I started, I'd tell my girlfriends' mothers that I was studying to be a lawyer or something in the city, in business. It was somehow shameful to be in the film business.

There were no film schools or anything, so I got a job with a man who owned a little studio that had been making war films, documentaries and things. So I started making tea for people who were doing these semi-documentaries after the war. And I discovered things. I thought this is a fantastic thing – it wasn't known to me then, it was a very secret affair. Now everything is known; they do documentaries about how things are done, all these special effects and things. Then it was a tremendously exciting mystery, just to be around it. I didn't know anything about who was the boss on the set, or what was happening, but it was extraordinary.

JW: Did you feel like you'd entered a magical world?

NR: It was just that. Gradually, I got a job in a cutting room. There wasn't a union then. There was an editor, Gladys Brimpts; her husband started the union. Terrific, I suddenly thought this is more than writing. I just couldn't understand why people didn't think this was one of the most wonderful things in the world. In the lunch hours, in Wardour Street, we'd run films backwards and forwards, make a man sit on his head, fall down, get up … It was fantastic, the ability to do that. It was a place with linguists, De Lane Lea, where they dubbed French films into English, and I saw masses of films. It fascinates me now that film has become a university subject; I can't believe it.

It rather shattered me today when I went to see Eric Fellner's talk – it was fascinating, and he's probably one of the most successful producers right now in England. He talked about how his films are ordered and structured and market researched. In my day – and I was lucky that way – it was still a showman's place, a 'walk right up' kind of thing. There was something vagabond-like about it, at the same time it was growing secretly. And the idea of photography as an art was ridiculous. But that was my life, in a factory setting.

After De Lane Lea, through Gladys, I got a job at MGM, who had a studio here at Borehamwood. I went to see the chief loader and was introduced to Freddy Young, who was the chief cameraman; brilliant Freddy, who got two or three Oscars. Going with the chief loader onto the floor, I just thought everything was fantastic. Everything was being revealed; there were no books, no information – certainly not in England; but there was a bit more information in France, Germany and America, which had a tremendous history of film as art. Here in England, with the war, it was all documentaries and propaganda films, but film hadn't emerged as a whole other discipline of the arts. Children's finger-painting came under the arts, but movies didn't.

JW: Was it through working with Freddy Young that you decided that cinematography was going to be your next discipline, which you went on to have a long and distinguished career in?

NR: I had no idea about photography. I didn't think, 'Ooh, I must be a photographer.' I thought it was about loading magazines of film, standing around on set, then going back to the loading room. I stayed at MGM for about two years, and in that time I became part of the camera crew and worked my way up to be a focus puller. I worked with a man called Joe Ruttenberg, a great American cinematographer, who gave me the best tip in the world – it was amazing, just a simple thing. This was the man who had photographed *The Philadelphia Story* [1940] and *Gigi* [1958]. I told him that I was thinking of taking a photographic course, and he said, 'Just stay on the set and watch and be a part of it; anything you want to know, I'll tell you.' He was talking one day to Dick Thorpe, the director, and he said, 'Cinematography is completely different from photography. You're never going to win the Royal Photographic Society award, and don't try to do that. It's the scene that must be served.' You make the movie through the cinematography – it sounds quite a simple idea, but it was like a huge revelation to me. Curiously, it sank for a while when video and commercials came in. Because they had very little story to tell and they just had one thing to sell, they could have magnificent photography but not great cinematography. So quite a lot of people who've come into cinema from the commercials world have had to learn the very fact of what cinematography is over again.

I was shooting *Doctor Zhivago* [1965] and someone from MGM said to me, you only need one more shot to get the Oscar for this. Oscars are won with two or three shots only, because if it's really beautifully photographed, you don't really notice it until the astounding moment emphasises it. So I gradually learnt that, and became an operator and a cinematographer. It wasn't through a love of photography, but rather through my love of film, and the telling of stories through film. And later I thought, I can't think how anyone can become a director without learning the craft of cinematography. I was very glad later when I was directing that I wasn't in the hands of a cinematographer and hoping that he would do it well. I would know what he was doing, and we could discuss how that scene would look. It was just lucky in a way that I didn't go to film school and just learnt all this on the floor.

JW: Did you work with directors who were influential upon you? I know that you hold Truffaut and his *Fahrenheit 451* in very high regard, and also Roger Corman's *The Mask of the Red Death*, which we see very clearly in *Don't Look Now*. Were there people you think you learnt from, that you still would cite as an influence?

NR: Of course. In life, we all learn from everyone. But if you like and admire someone tremendously, perhaps because they think the way you do, or like the way you think, then inevitably you do. With François, I liked his attitude in life. The rules of filmmaking can be taught in five minutes; that was what Orson Welles was told. The rules are learnt in order to be broken, but if you don't know them, then something is missing. François had his thoughts and his attitude in life was very special. One thing I did learn from him: he told me, 'I always like going into the projection box on the first night – mostly because I don't like to sit in the audience to see what they're feeling. But also because I like to watch the back of their heads – I can tell more about how they like it from there than if I sit among them.' And I've done that many times – and from there I sometimes think, 'What's wrong with you there in the third row?'

JW: I believe that you acted as cinematographer in your first two films, but one of the defining characteristics of your work, apart from them looking fantastic, is that they've also been edited very well. Your approach of using these mosaic-like montages and these elliptical details which become very important later on has become very influential. I just wondered if you could talk a bit about that because I was at the National Film Theatre interview with Steven Soderbergh, and he basically admitted that he'd taken the love scene in *Don't Look Now* and replicated it for *Out of Sight* [1998]. I've often heard filmmakers talk about your influence on their editing approach – are you aware of this influence?

NR: The construction of the story is gigantic. I shoot a lot of film, a lot of scenes. Some people are very lucky, and have the story in their heads. I've never storyboarded anything. I like the idea of chance. What makes God laugh is people who make plans.

If we're supposed to head for the beach to shoot a scene where a pair of lovers are taking leave of each other, and she gets up and walks off into the sunset, and they pass some other happier people on the beach, but if when we arrive there and it's raining, the assistant director would say, 'I know, get the camera out.' Because that chance is telling you something. They'd planned to say goodbye on the beach, it's raining, and there's nobody on the beach. There's a fourth hand, telling you something better.

Years ago I had a house in Sussex. It was like Arcadia, with an old Victorian bridge, a pond and the Downs. There was a village watercolour society and they'd come and paint in my field. I watched them from the window, the way they would struggle this way and that to find the perfect moment. God has made every angle on that beautiful, and I felt that tremendously.

I was listening to Philip Pullman talking about how he constructs the storyline – with me, I can't get out of the fact that it's chance. That's why I shoot a lot. Afterwards in the editing process, with the loads of material, you live the film again. You shoot the bookcase to see what the characters have been reading. Maybe the scene calls for the person to lose attention for a moment and glance away at something, because our attention is never singularly focused; we drift.

JW: It's good that you mentioned that because I wanted to ask you about your approach to scripts – you've worked with some very good scriptwriters and from some very good texts, for instance Du Maurier for *Don't Look Now* and Conrad on *Heart of Darkness* [1994]. You've also worked with writers like Paul Mayersberg and Dennis Potter. But one of my favourite stories about you is about when you went to scout for *Walkabout* with your son Luc. And when you returned, your scriptwriter said: 'I've finished the script – I think you'll be rather pleased.' And he handed you 14 pages of handwritten notes. I think your words then were: 'That's perfect.'

NR: Mind you, the writer was Edward Bond. It was pretty good.

JW: It seems to me that the script, for you, is just a catalyst, something on which to hang your imagination. Is that accurate?

NR: Yes. Movies are not scripts – movies are films; they're not books, they're not the theatre. It's a completely different discipline, it exists on its own. I would say that the beauty of it is it's not the theatre, it's not done over again. It's done in bits and pieces. Things are happening which you can't get again. I forbid anyone to say 'Cut', the soundman, the operator, or whatever.

They think something's gone wrong, but in *Don't Look Now*, for instance, one scene was made by a mistake. It's the scene where Donald Sutherland goes to look for the policeman who's investigating the two women. We had an Italian actor there who couldn't speak any English at all, not even 'Hello'. Through the interpreter, I told him to say 'Hello' when he heard Donald knock on the door. And I saw him walking around the set practising. So when it was time for Donald to knock on the door, the sound operator told the Italian actor, not realising that he didn't speak any English, to stay where he was. So Donald walked down the corridor, knocked on the door and opened the door into an empty room with a big lampshade. Donald hunted around, and the sound operator said 'Hello?', and from behind the lampshade came a reply, 'Hello!' It was fantastic. Because it was such a tense film, it set the tone – the detective instantly became strange. That has often been remarked on.

On *The Man Who Fell to Earth*, we had a scene where David Bowie first arrives on Earth and walks into town; it's completely empty, things blowing. I couldn't believe this, but there was a children's fairground, with a big bouncy clown thing bouncing around. We had David cross the road and we followed him from behind, and this bouncing clown lost its cables and started bouncing towards him. I looked sideways, and there was a man who'd been lying in one of these torpedoes in a fairground ride. He staggered out of the torpedo towards David and kind of belched in front of him. And that was Mr Newton's first contact with human beings. Fantastic. He was completely baffled. I used that belch at the end too. You can't write that stuff in. So I shoot a lot of stuff. I think that's probably come from not having gone to film school. Things work themselves out. You've lost the showmanship thing, the fairground barker, the 'come see what's inside' aspect of filmmaking when you try to plan everything for the audience.

I had a furious row with a studio executive once: he said, 'They won't get it, Nic' and I said, 'No, they'll get it; it's you who's not getting it, because you're trying to force something that's different into being the same.' People usually arrive to see something with an open mind. I want to make them feel something emotionally, but not by planning how to get them there. That would almost be like the communist days when newspapers told people what to think – when there was no competition with *Pravda*.

JW: Your work is like a visual and aural assault and has always polarised people. But you've always said that your job as a director is to put ideas out there and for people to respond to them. Is that something that you abide by today? Do you just want people to have a reaction to your films, even if they don't necessarily like them?

NR: Well, I hope that they like them. I made a film called *Bad Timing* that I thought everybody would respond to. It was about obsessive love and physical obsession. I thought this must touch everyone, from university dons down. But it had a curious effect on people – I sort of understood afterwards why it wasn't good for the company. Funnily enough, while it was being made, someone said to me: 'You know, they're not going to get this Nic, because you're scratching surfaces that people probably don't want to have exposed.' It was only towards the end, when we were cutting it and we showed it to the musician, who looked at the rough cut, and said: 'Three years ago, I wouldn't have been able to work on this movie because I kept seeing myself on screen there, I was in that trap, in that hole.'

JW: *The Man Who Fell to Earth* deals with the subject of alienation. This, to me, seems to be a subject that recurs in a lot of your films. You like to take characters and put them in strange situations and see how they deal with it. Is that an accurate statement?

NR: Yes, that's a raw thought, but in detail, I like the idea of human terms of alienation. But it's also about human secrecy. The lover's oldest question is: 'What are you thinking, darling?', then 'What are you really thinking?' In that scene, Mary Lou [Candy Clark] and Mr Newton had been together for a while, and though she thought that he was a bit strange and odd, she had no idea where he came from. Sure he was an alien, but he wasn't a monster. She didn't know that on his planet it had been planned that he would come to Earth and be among humans, but that they didn't get things quite right with his body. And so when she says that he can tell her anything, which in the human context means 'You can tell me anything and I'll still love you', and he shows her his method of making love – by exchanging bodily fluids on a grand scale – of course she recoils.

Then afterwards, when she approaches him on the bed and he starts oozing again and she recoils again, then he goes back to being human and keeps the secret. And it interested me tremendously, especially with David Bowie. People said, he's an extraordinary artist but, and producers were especially interested only in this one thing, can he act? He is Mr Newton. He's a tremendous performer, he's sung on stage in front of 20,000 people. But it suddenly struck me, when he told me that it was a very important step for him and asked what I wanted for the role, that the best thing I could tell him was that I didn't know who Mr Newton was either. So I told him, 'You'll help me by not knowing either. Just do it, say the part.' And it was strange – it was better than acting. He was it. He may have been slightly clumsy, and somebody else might have been more together but training would have stopped it. It wouldn't have had the authenticity of the alien, without anything except who he was. It especially worked with the CIA people and the politicians in the film – he didn't know what they were talking about. You can't learn everything by watching TV. So the alien does not appear to be alien, but is in fact more alien than if he'd had a big head. So the throwing away of the alien disguise was rather like exposing yourself emotionally.

JW: Casting-wise, you've always done quite well with pop stars. *Performance* featured Jagger's best performance, and Art Garfunkel is great in *Bad Timing*. You've done really well with them.

NR: Well, they're terrific performers. Another thing was happening: with a lot of the film stars, especially American ones ... Gene Hackman for instance had been a reporter and in the Marines, and he took acting classes with Dustin Hoffman because he thought he could pick up chicks there. It wasn't to become a big film star. The great difference between screen acting and theatre acting is that screen acting is about reacting – 75% of the time, great screen actors are great reactors. When it comes to film, the director tells the audience what to look at. That doesn't happen on stage. When the dialogue stops, people don't know where to look.

JW: A band called Big Audio Dynamite actually wrote a tribute song to you called 'E=mc²', and your son Luc directed the video. I think you're probably the first director to have a song written about him and his work. But you've always used music, and sound in general, in a very interesting way. I'm thinking in particular about the beginning of *Track 29* [1988] where you've used John Lennon's 'Mother'. In *The Man Who Fell to Earth* you used John Phillips; and then of course in *Performance*, the music is fantastic, and Tom Waits in *Bad Timing*. Is it something you're very aware of? Are you always looking to create an interesting synthesis between image and sound?

NR: Actually, I generally don't like them to match, I like them clashing, doing a different job from just illustrating the picture. We're selective about sound, we tune out things, or maybe you overhear something – and that's an area that's as yet totally unexplored. They sent me a DVD to approve a scene, of *Bad Timing* as it happens, and in it there's a scene where a couple meet again and they're talking, but in between their dialogue, in their heads, the soundtrack has their thoughts, but they had cut that down.

* * *

John Sayles
and Maggie Renzi

Born in New York in 1950, John Sayles began his career as a novelist with the publication in 1975 of *Pride of the Bimbos*. He soon made the move into screenwriting, working for Roger Corman's New World Pictures. Early screenwriting credits include *Piranha* (1978), *Battle Beyond the Stars* (1980), *The Howling* (1980) and *Alligator* (1980).

Using the money he earned writing 'creature features' (and he has continued to function as a screenwriter for hire), Sayles financed his first film as writer-director-editor, *Return of the Secaucus Seven* (1979), a bittersweet look at a reunion of 1960s political activists. The film, with a production budget of only $40,000, gained a national theatrical release, won the LA Film Critics Award for Best Screenplay and is now seen as precipitating the first post-Cassavetes wave of American independent filmmaking. Sayles' follow-up, *Lianna* (1982), was one of the first American movies to deal with a lesbian relationship in a non-exploitive manner, and set the template for Sayles' crafting of strong female roles and protagonists largely ignored by the mainstream.

Following a relatively unhappy studio experience on the mid-1960s-set coming-of-age drama *Baby It's You* (1982), Sayles returned to independent productions with the African-American sci-fi allegory *The Brother from Another Planet* (1984). Filling a three-year filmmaking hiatus with theatre work and directing pop promos for Bruce Springsteen, Sayles made *Matewan* (1987) and *Eight Men Out* (1988). Respectively dealing with a bloody 1920 West Virginia coal miners' strike and the story of the 1919 Black Sox baseball scandal, the films continued Sayles' interest in corporate greed. Subsequent films such as *City of Hope* (1991), *Passion Fish* (1992) and *The Secret of Roan Inish* (1994) similarly furthered Sayles' grappling with issues relating to community and race.

A director who likes to travel when working, using the landscape in which his films are set as 'characters', the Texas-set *Lone Star* (1996) elevated Sayles' career to new heights. A time-spanning murder-mystery, the film garnered Sayles his second Best Original Screenplay Academy Award nomination (*Passion Fish* giving him his first). Sayles would subsequently travel to Mexico for the Spanish-language *Men With Guns* (1997), Alaska for the offbeat thriller *Limbo* (1999) and Florida for the witty and acerbic corporate-tourism comedy *Sunshine State* (2002). *Silver City* (2004), his fifteenth and perhaps most overtly political film to date finds the director in Colorado for a timely and toxic look at the state of the union in the wake of the 2004 Presidential election.

Thematics aside, the cinema of John Sayles is characterised by the stock of repertory actors he has accumulated, including Joe Morton, David Strathairn, Chris Cooper and Kris Kristofferson. Also, despite only paying Screen Actors' Guild-scale wages, Sayles attracts the cream of America's acting talent to his projects, all of whom are drawn to his naturalistic dialogue, sense of equality in the workplace and no nonsense approach to filmmaking. Finally, Sayles' work must also be viewed in conjunction with the collaborations he has established with figures such as composer Mason Daring, cinematographer Haskell Wexler and his producer and long-term partner Maggie Renzi.

The following interview took place at the 2005 Cambridge Film Festival to mark the UK premiere of *Silver City*; Maggie Renzi was also present.

Jason Wood: When did *Silver City* begin to form in your mind and what external elements forced it into being?

John Sayles: When making *Sunshine State* one of the things we kept hearing from the crew was this question about what's going on with the national media in the US? They're talking all about the 'hanging chads' and the voting irregularities like they were just mechanical things, but the real story down here is how many African Americans didn't get the vote. They tried but were told they were felons or were stopped and had their driving licenses inspected to see if they had any outstanding parking violations and were then misdirected to the wrong place to vote. By the time they got to the place where they were supposed to vote the polls were closed. How come that was not a national scandal? I started thinking about what had happened with our mainstream media and just how embedded and corporatised they were and I started thinking about what would be a good movie forum to use for a character who was reacting to that. I think the most famous movie with this kind of format is *Chinatown* [1974], and there's a whole genre of American detective fiction and thriller fiction where basically the protagonist is someone who still has some glimmer of moral fibre but has been burned so many times that they've lost their motivation. Humphrey Bogart used to play this kind of character a lot. What happens in the process of an investigation is that they discover that the game is rigged and that their own employers are using them as a pawn and that they're in over their heads and that they can't trust the people who are employing them, whether it's the police or politicians or just wealthy people who hire them. And then my next step was to decide if this character should be a detective, which is a kind of retro thing that Polanski used. What do private detectives do now? It must be kind of boring. Or, should he be a journalist? So I finally compromised and made Danny O'Brien an ex-journalist who was now a very bad detective because he didn't care about the job. One of the things it allowed me to do was that in the arc of the movie he gets to be a more sympathetic character as he builds a sense of moral outrage and he gets to be a better detective because he finally finds that he cares about something that he's looking for, whereas when you meet him he doesn't care if he's getting facts for the prosecution of the defence or even what the case is about. He just goes and files his report and forgets about it.

JW: I understand that the intention was to get the film into theatres in time for the upcoming election. I know you are very exhaustive with your research and being a low-budget filmmaker you are used to working fast but you had to allot yourself a fairly short pre-production time. What effect did this have?

Maggie Renzi: Well we allotted ourselves not enough time to raise money for the film, so I would say to John today, 'When the journalists talk to us about this film I want to say I ruined my health for this movie.' It was really hard to get money for *Silver City*. It's pretty hard to get money for movies in the States now anyway that are about anything and it's hard to get money for movies that cost more than about a million dollars because the distributors can pretty much just bottom feed off home-grown movies. So we're in an odd slot, John and I, and we're committed to making union movies and that means they cost a certain amount of money. So we couldn't believe that we couldn't get money from the usual institutions for this movie with an incredible cast and on the hottest of subjects. So we just got started and we got deeper and deeper into it and we still didn't have any money. I'm laughing now but it was awful and we ended up putting all of our own money into the film in order to make it.

JS: But what it did mean was that we did have enough time to do the pre-production to make the movie and it was a very ambitious movie to make in six weeks. Luckily we'd made a lot of movies before and so we were able to do that and we were working with very good people, but the part where you spend a lot of time looking for the money, Maggie was having to do that while we were basically already in production.

MR: But the exciting thing was that we got to make the film and it was exhilarating to make it with all these people who were starting to feel like they were involved in something that might make a difference. The next year we toured with what we called the 'Silver City Express' and we used the movie to get at the voters and we were among people such as REM and Bruce Springsteen going around the country trying to get the vote. We did a fantastic job and nearly beat the bastards. And so that's the part of me that must remember to never regret the extreme thing we did. Obviously the conversation is not over because we are into a second term but I'm delighted to see the movie has a life after the state of emergency in which we made it.

JW: **John, you've described how Danny Huston's central character has something of an epiphany. Did you also intend the film to show the general American public that politics is important and that there needs to be a certain coming to consciousness in this regard?**

JS: I think a lot of people took it as a kick up the butt, including as lot of the critics.

MR: It's a movie that totally berates the press, and what they actually do…

JS: In the US there is a real resistance, critically and in general, to content in movies at all. It's considered cheating, or there's something wrong with a movie that's about something. And why are you bothering us with something that might actually happen. And for me, making a movie about something that was not actually about something that was going on … I'm a screenwriter and write a lot of stories for Hollywood and very often what I'm asked to do, implicitly or explicitly, is to walk all the way around the block to avoid something that's really going on because that will complicate the movie in a way they don't want to complicate the movie. So what I usually feel like doing when we make our own movies, if they're contemporary movies especially, is that I'm not going to ignore anything that's right in their path and that's part of their lives whether it's racism or economic problems or whatever, by being part of the characters. And it seems crazy to be making a movie about the media and politics without including characters who are very much like the people who are running the country at the moment. And that's not just the Republicans. A huge part of the problem is that both parties are so thoroughly bought by monetary interests and corporations that their constituents are not the American people anymore. They are the people who put them into power.

MR: Do you think he's on a list?

JS: Certainly not an important one. But I did feel like·I have to make this character that Chris Cooper plays obvious enough so that people will know who we're talking about. But it is, finally, about a 'gubernatorial' race and it's local politics and based very much on George Bush when he was running for Governor of Texas for the first time and was totally new at the job, and where his handlers understood that you couldn't let him adlib questions. I don't know if you've heard this here but at his rallies before the last elections, to get into them, to be one of the fans at the rally or be one of the people who might be there to ask one of the questions, you had to sign a loyalty oath to say you were a supporter of his and of his policies. And then you were basically only allowed to ask a question if you had been approached by one of his staff who had said, 'Well here are some questions you might ask.'

And you could pick one of those questions and they'd say, 'Oh, we've got you down for number three' and they'd rehearse you a little bit and then you could ask that question. And generally there were only about ten questions because that's about as many as he could remember the answers to.

JW: I've always been fascinated by your approach to character because you write very extensive biographies for all the characters with speaking parts. How do you feel that feeds into the characters you create and how the actors who play them approach those parts?

JS: I don't have rehearsals for our movies. All we really get is a blocking rehearsal so we know where the camera is going to be and then we start shooting and very often I see how an actor is going to play the character or wants to play the character on the first take of their first day of work. Although we've talked about it I send every·one a bio of the characters which is sometimes literal information

– 'this is what you did and this is how long you've been married and this is who you are to this character' – and sometimes is much more a free association like 'here are three pages in the mind of this complicated character'.

What it encourages in the actors, and is something I really look for in actors, is the ability to play a text and a subtext. The text is what they're doing on the surface and the subtext is what they are really worried about or what they really want. Chris Cooper's character in *Lone Star* is a sheriff who is ostensibly investigating a murder that happened 27 years ago, but really because his father, who is no longer living, is one of the suspects, every question he asks is 'what kind of human being was my father? I only knew him in a certain context, you knew him in a different way. Who was he?' And Chris is a very good actor with playing a subtext.

In this movie, David Clennon, who plays the character of Mort Seymour who is this chipper guy who is trying to build this Silver City thing, his text is 'I'm really excited about this project, this is going to happen'; his subtext is 'Everything I've touched has failed, my wife supports me, I'm a loser and if this doesn't work what's going to happen to me?' So there's a little bit of desperation in his sales pitch all the time. And that's the kind of thing you put into the bio and that the actor has to draw on and that you, quite literally, don't have to talk about on the set. Time and money is blowing away from you, you've talked about it over the phone or they've thought about it before they got there.

MR: And it makes them feel special when we keep the budget as low as we do because we pay the actors the union minimum and it's a sort of self-selecting club; the actors who think that's not the way they should work don't come. But we have this nice camp of people who only want to be there and I'm happy to say it's a camp that more and more people would like to be in. And they do like to compare their bios because they certainly can't compare their trailers.

JW: There are certain people who are known to work in your productions who have gone on to become stars – Chris Cooper, David Strathairn, Angela Bassett are just a few of the names. But despite working in the independent sector you've increasingly attracted 'name' actors, or 'stars' to your projects. This must be quite gratifying.

JS: The biggest compliment we get is that people say 'Yes', and we're just offering a good part and scale and an interesting movie and you don't get a trailer.

MR: But you know, it's what most of them got into it for. I'm not sure that still it's quite so true but the opportunity to be a celebrity just wasn't available to that many people and you had to put a lot of time into the business for that to happen to you. Most of the people who want to be actors do so because they actually want to explore a character, they want to explore the text and extend their instruments; that ambition doesn't go away. Richard Dreyfuss still really wants to work on a part and that hasn't changed at all. So when you offer them something that is worth to them what they trained to do, they're delighted. They have such a good time with each other and there's this whole world, when I'm doing my job right, that's just all of them getting to work together and then they have dinner together and hang out.

JS: We learnt a lesson when we were casting *Matewan*. We felt like no one who is well known is in this movie and we'd never get someone like James Earl Jones to agree to participate so we were looking for a James Earl Jones-type. And there just aren't that many actors who are that good and a James Earl Jones size who have his presence. We had already been shooting in West Virginia a couple of weeks when finally we decided, 'What the hell, we'll just ask James Earl Jones; all he can do is say no.' And about two days later Darth Vader is on the phone and he wanted to do it. And so from then on we've always at least asked. We were also told on *Limbo* that Tom Waits would never let us use one of his songs because his ex-manager, who he really hates, would make some money if we did. In the end we just asked him and he grumbled, 'Ah, what the hell, just use it.' And so we got to use the song.

JW: Your liberal sensibilities are also imbued in your productions. Maggie, you've worked very hard to have fair working conditions where people don't work longer than 14 hours. You've really made sure that people aren't exploited and I think that gives both of you and air that you're going to be listened to. It's gives you an authenticity.

MR: I think after a while I noticed not everyone was doing it and so that made it pretty special. But it seemed pretty sensible because no one can work more than 14 hours because it's a great stretch for any of us to work safely or well. I mean America's famous for this right? This kind of crazy working twenty hours a day bullshit. It's a problem for us now because we are a country, rather like your own, where the unions are struggling to stay relevant. In fact, IA, which is our film union, is a terrible union. In truth they work us like shit but I still have to try to support them. Because I support the work I have to support the union. When the rules are arbitrary then it's not up to me to break them. And so if we have a standard then it keeps people from having something genuine to complain about and also from whining. And I just can't handle whining.

JW: Apart from the fact that you've worked together since the 1970s, there are other partnerships you've forged, not just with the actors but with people like Mason Daring who has composed most of your scores and Haskell Wexler who's shot four of your films.

JS: We first worked with Haskell on *Matewan* and the main thing Haskell brings is a very high quality to speed ratio. When you're making a very low-budget movie you don't have a lot of time for lighting and many cinematographers who are used to many more pieces of equipment and more time like to wait for the sun to be at a certain position and they just don't want to work under those kind of four-week, six-week conditions. They did it when they were young and they're passed that. Haskell, if he really believes in the movie, says he'll try to make the movie look as good as he can even if the light really sucks right now and I'll do what I can with it. And his experience means that depending on what time of day we're planning to shoot something he's just going to look at it and say 'here's where the sun's coming from and we have to shoot it at 4 o'clock because that building is going to block the sun out and it won't match with the rest of the things'.

Haskell is also someone who actually knows something about the world and about politics and so he's a great co-worker in that way. He understands what the movie is about, and many cinematographers don't actually care what the movie is about; they're worried about the pretty pictures.

MR: Our work has that appeal to people we have worked with over and over but it really is about what John wants and that's what an auteur is. It means that we have final cut, we have control over the music, we have control over the look of the film. And 'we' really means John with the support of all the people he works with. And that just doesn't happen that often where you have a mature authority in charge where it isn't a committee-led decision, and increasingly that is obviously less true because if there are so many views on a film then it is increasingly a committee-led film. I think one of the reasons we can get people like Mason and Haskell to do their very best work is that they're not hassled by the dissonance of too many voices.

JW: Another defining quality of the films is that you lend authenticity to characters whose sensibilities and opinions may be polar opposites to your own.

JS: I think it's as much to do with the way I see the world in that I tend to at least see that a lot of the conflict is because people have a lot of totally different worldviews and that they might not even all be in English. But I use my background as an actor even more because what actors often do is play someone who is completely different to who they are and the way they see the world. When I finish a draft of a script I tend to read it out playing all the parts and feel that if I had to play all these parts, is there enough there that I understand who this character is? If there's one more line that will define this person even though it's a small part then it's worth looking at. And when that character walks into the room what do they see?

When I was working in the theatre I acted in two different productions of *Of Mice and Men*. In one I played this old guy who, in the days before social security, is afraid he's going to get fired and starve to death and he's worried about losing his job. And in the other one I played Lenny, the large retarded guy who only cares about his pet mouse. And you walk into the same bunkhouse and as one character you feel totally different things to the other character. And it's something I'm always aware of when I write characters, they have different ways to express themselves and they also just see the world differently and they want different things. So somebody who seems evil to you, that character doesn't think they're evil, he thinks he's practical.

JW: You like to travel with your films. *Silver City* **is set in Colorado and we've also had West Virginia, Florida, Texas. You've also worked extensively outside of America in Mexico and Ireland. You are jokingly referred to as the** *Fodor's* **of filmmaking.**

JS: I think that we're more the *Rough Guide*.

JW: Places become characters for you.

JS: The places are part of the character. One of the things I think about when I'm writing a movie is where does this take place and how does this affect the characters? Does the place have a personality of its own? I did a book tour when I had a novel out in Britain and I had a very different ride around London, Manchester and Bristol and I didn't spend more than two days in any of them. But there was a very different ethnic mix and you really learnt about the history of the different places and the feelings of those towns and the lives of the people who lived there. And certainly in the US that's true regionally, even though we're homogenising very quickly.

Passion Fish was a movie where I had the ideas for the characters in the story and for years I had this idea, and I told Maggie about this woman who was a patient who had been paralysed and a nurse and there was a class difference and a race difference but I didn't know exactly where it should be set, which is one of the reasons I didn't pursue writing it. We were with some Australian friends on a rock 'n' roll tour of the South West and we ended up in Louisiana and a friend invited us to his parent's house on this lake in Louisiana and we woke up and said, 'This is the place for the movie about the nurse.' And it just struck me that I needed a place that would seduce you out of your cocoon. If you decide to roll in a ball and die because you've been paralysed this place wouldn't let you do it. It brought the movie alive. So sometimes the place really is a character in that it's the last link that I need to know what the movie is about.

MR: Also, when you're making a low-budget movie, one of the great things is to have the place itself fill in all the spots that you can't fill in with money. Authenticity is a fairly expensive and difficult thing to buy, but if you go to the right place you get it back in spades.

JW: So where are you both off to next?

MR: We're doing a little movie called *Honeydripper* and basically we're raising the money; it's looking good. It's set in rural Alabama in 1950 and it's about the first night in this little blues club where the people heard the electric guitar for the first time.

* * *

Elia Suleiman

Born in Nazareth in 1960, Elia Suleiman relocated to New York City in 1981, frequently serving as a guest lecturer at universities, art institutions and museums. During this time Suleiman directed a number of shorts, prominent amongst them *Introduction to the End of an Argument* (1990). Moving to Jerusalem in 1994, Suleiman was asked by the European Commission to initiate a film and media department at Bir Zeit University. Two years later he completed his first feature film, *Chronicle of a Disappearance* (1996), which won the Best First Film Prize at the Venice Film Festival. Largely composed of seemingly unrelated sketches, the film presents a surrealist yet poignant comment on the Israeli occupation of Palestine.

Divine Intervention (2002), Suleiman's second feature, again encases its provocations in a protective layer of fantasy, presenting the Arab-Israeli conflict as a succession of Jacques Tati-style sight gags. In Nazareth, under a guise of banal normality, the town embraces folly. Under pressure from his failing business, a man takes matters into his own hands and tries to break a chain reaction of petty feuds. He breaks down himself. The man is E.S.'s father. A love story takes place between a Palestinian man living in Jerusalem and a Palestinian woman from Ramallah. The man, E.S. (a resolutely deadpan Suleiman), shifts between his ailing father and his love life, trying to keep both alive. Because of the political situation, the woman's freedom of movement ends at the Israeli army checkpoint between the two cities. Barred from crossing, the lovers' intimate encounters take place on a deserted lot right beside the checkpoint. The lovers are unable to escape from the reality of occupation. They are unable to preserve their intimacy in the face of a siege. A complicity of solemn desire begins to generate violent repercussions. Against the odds, their angry hearts counter-attack with spasms of spectacular fantasy.

Interviewed during the 2004 London Film Festival where *Divine Intervention* received its UK premiere, the following transcript originally appeared in *Enthusiasm 06* in spring 2006.

Jason Wood: You use a subversive humour to approach a very personal and difficult subject.

Elia Suleiman: This is I suppose a cliché but also true: I love to laugh at my own jokes, luckily some other people laugh at them too. With this also comes a more complex and conceptual and intellectual baggage that I have carried with me through the years, and the nourishment of criss-crossing all the different cultures and countries that I have lived in. With that also comes that this is not just an ephemeral joke and there is also choreography of a particular kind. I like the fact that you describe the humour in my film as subversive. Historically, there is something resistant about humour and even if talking in terms of a wider discussion of just my film, when people live for instance in a ghetto and when they produce black humour, irony, etc, I think this is a way to deter finality in some respects and I think this is a way of producing hope. I think humour can be a poetic sight with a poetic dimension and this is something that cannot be captured by the dominant order.

To negate all that, however, I must say that the humour is not a strategy; all that it takes for me is a notebook and a pen since cinema for me is not a profession but a way of life. I write whatever tickles me in terms of both what makes me laugh and also in terms of depicting through choreography the banality of daily life. I seem to be someone who is tickled a lot by ironies and absurdities.

With this film I also add an analytical element because in the first part of the film Nazareth is a ghetto and the humour comes from dealing with a population living in a claustrophobic state of stasis, an impotent inability to change the face of their reality. Unable to dislocate or shift the dominant power ruling them they eventually unleash their frustrations against each other. Added to this is the filmmaker, that is I, who has a particular sensibility towards these moments that I am picking up. I transform all this into a biography or a self-portrait, if you want, which is the aestheticised, media-ted territory which you see in the film. I work very hard, sometimes in utter euphoria and sometimes in angst trying to add multiple layers to the frame and the tableau until a moment when I feel that it pigments and matures. When this process is complete I feel that I have a scene which I then put to one side and begin another one. When I feel that I am completely in control of all of the elements inside of the frame then I feel I can throw myself into the risk of departing the image in the film.

JW: Some of the more bravura moments such as the release of the balloon are extremely imaginative. Did such moments directly evolve from the writings in your notebooks?

ES: Well, I never saw a balloon flying over a checkpoint. But I can say generally that almost all of the film comes from a departure point of something that happened. The balloon, for example, comes from me buying a balloon for fun many years ago during a period when there were numerous gadgets produced with Palestinian symbols on. At the time when I was writing the script in France I opened my draw of gadgets and there the balloon was. Arafat's face had melted because of the heat and I thought that this could be funny because of the structure.

JW: In terms of both the structure of the film and the execution of the visual sight gags there are similarities with the work of Jacques Tati and Buster Keaton. Your performance in the film is also redolent of Keaton. Were these inspirations?

ES: It's very flattering to hear these comparisons now but I have to say that neither acted as inspirations to me. It's ironic that some of the people that I was inspired by have none of this humour. In fact I only heard of Jacques Tati when I was shooting *Chronicle of a Disappearance* and my soundman said you have to see Tati because what you are doing is similar. I do see the similarities and its not so odd that people have similar sensibilities.

The people I was inspired by are not known for their humour. Robert Bresson – whose work I do detect humour in actually – for example, and Hou Hsiao-Hsien. Both these directors emphasised to me the point that I could do what I felt or desired. From Bresson I took a lot of the tension of the frame and to this day I am fascinated by how tense and liberating Bresson's framing can be.

JW: *Divine Intervention* certainly has a precision and visual economy. Do you see yourself as a particularly visual director?

ES: I think that I have recently caught the thread of what it is that I should rely on to make a good image or a punchline to deliver a comic moment. You obviously gain experience in trying to translate and express yourself both filmically and technically, though I still envy some of the shorts I made in *Homage by Assassination*, one of my earliest shorts. When it came to *Divine Intervention* I felt very confident in terms of expressing myself totally uncensored. So, in this film there is a minimalist choreography and static framing but also the appropriation of commercials. There is also obviously the action scene at the end of the film so I approached the film from a variety of angles.

There was a lot of self-searching when I approached this film but I found myself coming back to what I consider basic values that long ago I shied away from because I considered them too simplistic. And so I realised that the thread that I mentioned is that if you are utterly sincere to yourself and take out all the convoluted emotions, the camera position is where it is exactly. The relationship between the moment of truth that you capture and the moment of truth that the spectator captures is incredible. This is what I consider the godliness of communication. I still don't fully understand and I prefer not to analyse it, the notion that given that we are not living in any form of uniformity, how is it that between Palestine, Norway and the United States people are laughing at exactly the same moment in the film?

Lately I feel like I am beginning to understand at least that in order to make a good image it means to better myself, I need to feel good, generous and loving to myself to release this to others. I must not shy away from these values and so I am going to rely on that for the meantime. I have perhaps resisted slogans such as 'make love not war' but I am now considering redefining the term because I feel it is worthwhile. This is partly why I have negations in the film and why I have the two lovers at the checkpoint. The checkpoint is a place where soldiers identify and love has no identification, it leaks and seeps and goes through any kind of checkpoint. I have discovered that if the spectator catches this moment the truth then he or she may leave the screening room extending the pleasure beyond the one-and-a-half-hour feature-film length. Having appreciated this moment of pleasure that will want a continuum and *de facto* may become more tolerant and will perhaps make love and not war. They see that it is precious to live this moment. This is perhaps what culture can do for us.

JW: The politics of life in day-to-day Nazareth and the restrictions imposed upon its people are dealt with in a very humanistic and non-didactic fashion.

ES: Many have reflected on this and I think this again has to do with a universality that I think the film has. A member of the audience in a screening in New

York told me that she felt that my Nazareth was very much like her Los Angeles. I think that the spectator associates with a universal image in a self-reflexive fashion and participates with it. I think I attempt a kind of democratic reading and I want the spectator to react and feel according to his or her own emotions.

JW: With all due respect to the spectator in New York who empathsises, you depict a situation concerning people whose lives are being lived under enforced military occupation.

ES: I am not asking people to empathise with anything; this is not a demand or a desire. The first thing for the spectator to do is have pleasure. The fact that they go and aestheticise a life beyond the film is for me an expression of support for the Palestinian people. I feel Israel is a microcosm of occupation and I think that the world is being globally occupied and this adds to a self-reflexive reading on the part of spectators all across the world who relate to it through their own personal experience. There are illusionary checkpoints in Los Angeles. The film is not directly talking about Palestine, it is talking about that which imposes itself to negate and capture and protest love. Spectators relate to it because we all want freedom to eat, sleep, make love and live better without imposition.

JW: Could you reveal a little more about Manal Khader who acts alongside you in the film?

ES: I have actually just come back from a screening in Ramallah which I think is one of the most memorable screenings and moments in my life. The people there are living a similar and much worse experience to that depicted in the film. They are privileged in that their laughter and angst is much more intense than that experienced by anyone anywhere else in the world. It is the only place in all the screenings that I have attended that the audience begins to clap at the exact moment that Manal's foot crosses the checkpoint; for them it is a very intense and physical experience. When the tower falls they are in euphoria. I wrote this scene ten years ago inspired by a moment when Manal and I had a rendezvous to have a coffee in Jerusalem. She wanted to defy the checkpoint and a soldier pointed a rifle at her, she said 'Go ahead and shoot, I'm crossing.' They didn't shoot. She is not an actress; she is a journalist who told me many of the stories and incidents that you see in the film. Ninety per cent of the people that you see are non-professional actors. When I first asked her to be in the film her initial reaction was that I must have been joking.

JW: I was interested to read about the casting process involving the Israeli

actors who play the soldiers at the checkpoint.

ES: I cast in Tel Aviv and naturally what I wanted was Israelis that had served in the army. Most of the people I looked at were not actors; well they were more than extras but not professional actors. I asked those that auditioned if they had served on a checkpoint and if they had used a gun. My casting took on an interrogative form as I began to ask if they had not only checked ID's but also hurt and even shot people. Some of them had and some of them shied away from telling me the severe acts they had committed because they wanted the role whilst others exaggerated because they too wanted to act in the film. I became a little sadistic in my questioning of their moral standards.

JW: I enjoy the way you use music in the film.

ES: I think that sound and music are parallel to image as far as I am concerned. I use it for the humour and there is a second-degree use of kitsch music but I had a sense of the type of music I wanted often before I shot particular scenes which is why there is no original soundtrack, because I like to compose or re-compose the songs of others myself. I detest filmmakers who bring music because of their insecurity concerning the image; I prefer to have it as a parallel track. Sometimes telling its very own story. I also think that sound is so vital in the telling of the story. This film uses very particular bird sounds in certain sequences. If you listen closely there is a very sadistic bird, a 'mocking' bird whose sound appears every time the father opens the letters.

JW: What practical problems did you encounter when filming?

ES: One could be dramatic but in terms of filming *Apocalypse Now* [1979] then the making of *Divine Intervention* is not so dramatic. There were of course difficulties. Given the situation in which we filmed and the locations in which we filmed there were often other television crews filming. It was also not a particularly good ambience in which to film. It was also often difficult to get permission to film and we had to shoot several scenes on a hit-and-run basis. The authorities, of course, also detected the mocking aspect of the checkpoint sequences and didn't like it very much. But generally I really loved making this film and if I understood them correctly the crew also enjoyed making it. Sometimes we even added an extra take because it was just too funny. We laughed a lot. I truly did this film with love.

***

Jan Švankmayer and Eva Švankmajerová

Invoking the poetry of Lewis Carroll, the sinister horror of Edgar Allan Poe and the claustrophobic paranoia of Franz Kafka, the films of Czech animator and director Jan Švankmajer are bizarrely beautiful: a witty blending of the perverse, the macabre, and the child-like.

A crafty alchemist, Švankmajer has pursued many styles: live action, clay modelling, puppets, traditional animation, stop-frame special effects and object collages, breathing life into vegetables, toys, rocks and trees. An influence on filmmakers from Tim Burton and Terry Gilliam to the Brothers Quay, who made the short *The Cabinet of Jan Svankmajer* (1984) in his honour, Švankmajer has never been completely comfortable with the label of animator, claiming that story comes before technique and that animation is used only when certain objects need to be brought alive through metamorphosis.

Born in 1934 in Prague, the son of a window-dresser father and a dress-maker mother, Švankmajer received a toy puppet theatre as a Christmas gift in 1942 – the beginning of a lifelong obsession with marionettes and puppetry. He trained at the Institute of Applied Arts from 1950 to 1954 and then at the Prague Academy of Performing Arts (Department of Puppetry). Švankmajer soon became involved in the Theatre of Masks and the famous Black Theatre, before entering the Laterna Magika Puppet Theatre. Here he first encountered film and directed his first short, *Poslední trik pana Schwarcewalldea a pana Edgara* (*The Last Trick*) in 1964. The film resulted in Švankmajer being banned from filmmaking by the Czech authorities for seven years. It was followed by a series of increasingly surreal and wickedly ironic shorts, including, amongst others, *Byt* (*The Flat*, 1968) and *Zvahlav aneb Saticky Slameného Huberta* (*Jabberwocky*, 1971). In 1970 Švankmajer met his wife and future collaborator, the surrealist painter Eva Švankmajerová, and the late Vratislav Effenberger, the leading theoretician of the Czech Surrealist Group. Švankmajer remains a card-carrying surrealist.

Švankmajer did not direct his first feature-length film, *Neco z Alenky* (*Alice*) until 1988 but the film's impact was seismic, bringing the director a new legion of international admirers. The subsequent years' *Jídlo* (*Food*, 1992), *Faust* (1994) and *Spiklenci slasti* (*Conspirators of Pleasure*, 1996) confirmed that Švankmajer's vision remained as characteristically witty, subversive and inventive as ever.

With a new feature, *Sílení* (*Lunacy*, 2005) recently completed, Švankmajer's last release for the time being remains *Otesánek* (*Little Otik*, 2000), a wonderfully wicked comedy adapted from a traditional Czech fairytale in which a couple who long for a child carve a tree-stump into a baby-like shape. A characteristically dazzling blend of live action and animation – the director's preferred mode of working in recent years – the film dissects the destructive aspects of humanity's procreative urges. It was during the release of *Otesánek* that this interview took place. Eva Švankmajerová was also present.

Jason Wood: You seem to often work from myths and fairytales. How did the tale of Otesánek first come to your attention and what was it about it that made you feel that it was suitable for a film treatment?

Jan Švankmayer: I first started work on this particular myth in the middle of the 1980s when I wrote a story based on the myth. But even earlier than that, the story was brought to my attention by my wife Eva. Eva wanted to make an animation film from the story and it was a story that I too liked very much. It is true that I often work from old fairytales, which are narrated cosmological myths. This myth of Otesánek is a very old and basic myth of civilisation that goes as far back as Faust and maybe even earlier. It concerns the rebellion against nature and the tragic consequences of that rebellion. I do not criticise that rebellion because you cannot live any dignified life without rebellion but I am just making sure that people understand the tragic dimensions of this particular rebellion. However, it is an imaginative film and I do not dictate the interpretation of the film. With this film and all my work, all and any interpretation is possible. I do not make films as theses; I do not simply have an idea that is present at the beginning that I then develop to its logical conclusion. Because the subconscious and the unconscious works throughout the film, at the end of the film I want to be like the viewer, looking at the work and thinking what have I done here? What is this about?

JW: In your diary of the making of *Little Otik* you describe in vivid detail many of your dreams. Your subconscious is a huge influence on your work.

JŠ: Absolutely. It is a priority. I actually prefer the term non-conscious. Whatever comes out of my subconscious I use because I consider it to be the purest form; everything else in your conscious being has been influenced by reality, by art, by education and by your upbringing but the original experiences that exist within you are the least corrupted of all experiences.

The real creation starts with the actual shooting of the film and obviously I do write a script and I do prepare, but this is all very rational. When the filming process actually starts, then for me I am with the topic 24 hours a day – when I sleep, when I eat and when I am dreaming – and that's when things first start truly coming. I don't shoot exactly according to the script; obviously I use this script for dialogue etc but it is during the shooting process that I can begin to incorporate these elements from my non-conscious – these elements are released into the work and I feel enrich it. So everyday when I start shooting I will look at what I had originally written and then basically write a new script for the day. Everywhere there will be new notes and new bits of paper. When you write the script you do not have the benefit of seeing the actors or of being on the set on the morning of the shoot to experience the mood, the make-up, the clothes that the actors are wearing. To only work from the original script would be a cold experience, it is only during the actual working process that you can truly create a film. If you are simply following script directions – even if they are your own – then it is simply process by numbers, you may as well be a civil servant.

Obviously, during the political climate in the 1970s and 1980s in Czechoslovakia the script had to be approved at an early stage but of course the finished film would differ vastly from what was approved, which obviously caused problems with the authorities. Thankfully, the change in the political climate means that this approval process does not apply anymore.

JW: I wanted to ask Eva about the 2D animation fable that Alzbetka reads and what she feels this contributes to the film in a wider sense, and how she feels about Jan 'stealing' her idea?

Eva Švankmajerová: He didn't really 'steal' it. He took it and developed it. I always had a need to tell really scary fairytales. I had already worked on an earlier project of this nature – which to this day many children, including my own, still find too scary to look at – and Otesánek felt like perfect material. I gave the story to Jan to read and he liked it and was able to incorporate it into the wider fabric of the film.

JW: The fairytale I feel helps contextualise the story, especially in terms of both defining and developing the Alzbetka character.

JŠ: The fairytale is of course important in that while Alzbetka reads the tale she is the only one who knows the future and where the story is going. The myth has risen from the depths and brought itself to life, Alzbetka is trying to stop it, she wants to alter the outcome of the story – which is why she hides the old woman's hoe – but she is unable to alter it. The myth will proceed to its logical dimension. The film is also about the very power of the myth, and how we are still acting out and struggling with myths. The old lady is the only other one who reads the fairytale so she also takes on the role of fulfilling that myth and goes to do what the myth requires her to do. However, I wanted to have something of an open ending, leaving some doubt as to whether she was able to fulfill the myth or not.

JW: Obviously you are best known for your integration of animation and live-action but I think *Little Otik* differs from your other work slightly in the emphasis the film places on the performance of the actors. How did the actors come to your attention, particularly Kristina Adamcová who plays Alzbetka?

JŠ: I used many of the same actors for *Alice*. For the little girl I had a very specific image in mind, I wanted the girl – and the actress playing her – to look like Eva when she was eight to ten years old. To find this girl I visited many schools with my photographer and Eva and screen-tested very many people. I decided after my experience on *Alice* that I definitely did not want a trained child actor because they are already compromised and corrupted by mannerisms. On the DVD of *Little Otik* there are many scenes of the tests with Adamcová that show how hard I made her work and how much better she became by the time she came to actually work on the film.

JW: I remember reading in your diary that you made her slog.

JŠ: (laughs) Sometimes I could have killed her!

JW: Jan and Eva's work together is obviously very collaborative.

EŠ: We are very happy to work together. Jan is lovely to work with and, to be honest, I would not want to work with any other director.

JŠ: I rely very much on Eva's work in terms of design and art in my films. For example we pulled up many tree stumps from many forests looking for what would be our Little Otik. We could not quite find what we wanted and had to go through various processes to arrive at what we wanted. Having said that, I would have been happy to use without any alteration a natural stump if we could have pulled one from the ground that exactly resembled what we wanted. Eva provides an authentic touch; this was very much in evidence with the puppets she helped create in *Conspirators of Pleasure*.

EŠ: The only downside of our working together, of course, is that Jan gets to see things when I am still in the process of making them and not strictly speaking when they are ready for his inspection. I did previously work with other directors but I never truly felt their reactions to what I had produced mattered. Jan's feelings have always mattered and meant a great deal to me.

JW: There are many themes that recur in your work and in the work of surrealists in general. I'd like to concentrate on that of food and cannibalism. How do you feel that *Little Otik* expands this metaphor?

JŠ: You are right to notice that food is indeed one of my recurring themes. It is something of an obsession. I believe that obsessions are not to be repressed; they may often be all that we have. My obsession with food goes back to when I was a child because I was a non-eater and was sent to various feeding camps where they tried to fatten me up. It's funny, but when I showed *Faust* to my surrealist group one of them exclaimed 'for crying out loud, food again!' and I replied 'where?' as I had not even realised that food was so evident in the film. *Little Otik* is obviously in many ways about what is the absolute eater. It is important to notice that Otik does not just eat everything, he absolutely devours it and therefore it is a symbol about how our civilisation feels the need to devour everything: ethnic groups, cultures. This film is about food, but it is more about devouring.

JW: I've stopped eating since I began watching your films. I particularly enjoyed the faux commercials that appear in your latest film. They make a strong point about the consumer culture in which we live.

JŠ: I believe that the consumer society is the final stage in civilisation. The society can continue for another hundred years or so but I completely believe that this utilitarian, devouring way of life signals that civilisation is ending. I am not saying that mankind will die out but we are now watching the consequences of the end of the civilisation that we have. Terrorism is nothing more than a consequence of the absolute inequality that we have in this cycle of civilisation. Black humour is important and must remain one of the essences of the civilisation. I mean the Americans are currently dropping bombs on Afghanistan and then immediately afterwards they are dropping food parcels.

* * *

Bertrand Tavernier

How best to summarise the life and career of Bertrand Tavernier as an introduction to the following interview which took place in 2001 around the time of
the release of the director's twentieth feature, *Laissez-passer* (*Safe Conduct*)?
It is frankly an almost impossible task.

Undoubtedly one of France's premiere directors, screenwriters and producers, Tavernier is renowned for making dramas encompassing themes as
diverse as familial relationships, World War One and contemporary social ills.
Regardless of the subjects they explore, Tavernier lends his films great intro-
spection and humanity, something that has established him as not only a fine
filmmaker and renowned cineaste, but also a compassionate and progressive
thinker.

Born in Lyon in 1941, Tavernier grew up with a love of film and wanted
to be a director from the age of 13. He was particularly influenced by such
American directors as Joseph Losey, John Ford, Samuel Fuller and William
Wellman, and – during a spell at the Sorbonne, where he studied law – he
became involved in the film industry as an assistant director for Jean-Pierre
Melville. By his own admission, he was not very good at the job, so Tavernier
became a film critic, working for prestigious publications such as *Positif* and
Cahiers du cinéma.

One of the few exceptions to Woody Allen's 'those that can't do, teach' rule, Tavernier directed his first feature *L'horloger de St. Paul* (*The Watchmaker of St. Paul*) in 1974. The tale of a clockmaker and his complex relationship with his violent son and the bourgeois society that has produced him, it cemented a long-lasting working relationship with actor Philippe Noiret and garnered Tavernier international acclaim and a Special Jury Prize at the Berlin Film Festival.

It is impossible to mention every subsequent Tavernier feature in the space available here but each is linked by a superlative sense of craftsmanship and an almost insatiable thirst for knowledge and understanding. Brief highlights from an almost impeccable career could however include, from the 1980s, the sci-fi *La mort en direct* (*Death Watch*, 1980), a disturbing reflection on voyeurism and the dark realms of the human psyche; and *Coup de torchon* (*Clean Slate*, 1981), a film noir-infused adaptation of Jim Thompson's *Pop 1280*. It is also impossible to leave out *Un dimanche à la campagne* (*A Sunday in the Country*, 1984), a film focusing on the relationship between an ageing painter and his children and grandchildren. Two years later, Tavernier had possibly his greatest international success with *'Round Midnight*, his elegy to Jazz. Starring Dexter Gordon as a self-destructive American saxophonist living in self-exile in Paris, the film was a moody portrait of the friendship between the saxophonist and the French fan who becomes his caretaker. Martin Scorsese also featured.

Tavernier began the 1990s by turning his attention to the problems and social issues facing contemporary France, his *L.627* (1992) offering a timely observation on drug abuse and HIV/AIDS. Two films expressing anti-war sentiment also stand out: the Algerian war documentary *La guerre sans nom* (*War Without a Name*, 1992) and the quietly terrifying *Capitaine Conan* (1996), the tale of a World War One captain whose proclivity towards killing people becomes something of a problem during peacetime. Tavernier then returned to the themes of *L.627* in *Ça commence aujourd'hui* (*It All Begins Today*, 1999), a social drama revolving around the efforts of a schoolteacher to bring change to his demoralised, largely impoverished community.

And so back to *Laissez-passer*. Paris, March, 1942. The victorious German occupying power demands that France pay a colossal financial contribution – 400 million francs a day – to the German war effort. 'Continental Films', a German controlled production company founded in 1940 in Paris by Albert Greven (Christian Berkel), is a snare similar to the one into which the French nation has already fallen. Should French technicians agree to work for Continental? Is it a hiding place 'in between the wolf's fangs, where it cannot bite you', or is it equivalent to collaborating with the enemy? Drawing on their real-life experiences, the film is the story of two men, Jean Devaivre (Jacques Gamblin) and Jean Aurenche (a man with whom Tavernier had previously collaborated as a writer and whose memoirs inspired the film, played here by Denis Podalydès) whose lives converge and interweave. Dedicated to those who lived through this time, Tavernier included the following statement in the film's press release: 'Were things as black and white as people subsequently made out? Where do you draw the line between collaboration, survival and resistance? No film has ever dealt with these issues. *Laissez-passer* is set during the German occupation but it is not a war film. The dramatic tension comes from the energy, rhythm and multiple contradictory sentiments – comedy, tragedy, emotion – that ricochet off each other within a single scene. The story is full of paradoxes. Firstly, because everybody at the time was on thin ice. They never knew what the next day would bring. So, we have scenes that start out as comedy and then we're suddenly reminded that there was always the danger of being rounded up or killed. All against the background of people trying to make movies for a German company.'

The following interview took place in 2002, but was first published in *Enthusiasm 06* in spring 2003.

Jason Wood: How did you originally conceive of the idea for *Laissez-passer* and what research did it entail?

Bertrand Tavernier: I wanted to do a film about the period from the first moment that I worked with Jean Aurenche. I missed one thing, I never asked him to write a screenplay about himself. We started to write one about the Occupation using some of the things that he knew but I regret now not asking him to write a kind of autobiographical story. I knew what I wanted to use from the stories that he told me but I knew that I was missing something. It was when I met Jean Devaivre and when he started to tell me what he did that I suddenly thought here is my second character and we started working on those two characters. Both characters were totally opposite and had only one link, the desire to resist. When we started to work on the screenplay I was inventing that relationship because they never met. We were trying to make them meet but each time we did this it simply looked contrived and artificial. What they were doing meant that them meeting was unlikely because cinema was very hierarchical at that time; I mean to have a screenwriter meet with an assistant director when they are not working on the same film? I had an idea which I relayed to Jean Cosmos, this was to make a virtue of the problem. As they cannot really speak to each other we have to organise the film in such a way that the audience will themselves organise that confrontation, that the audience will see that the doubts of Aurenche reinforce the determination of Devaivre and that the lack of analysis of Devaivre is explaining the more intellectual approach of Aurenche. I wanted to write a screenplay that was totally free of the normal Hollywoodian rules of construction and be more like a chronicle and have moments where it goes in other directions so that you could never predict what would be the next scene and the next shot. This seemed to me to be very true of the period.

JW: Could you talk a little more about your co-screenwriter Jean Cosmos? I understand that the film relates in a very personal manner to his experiences.

BT: Jean Cosmos is a very dear friend and, I think, a very gifted screenwriter with a wonderful ear for dialogue, especially the dialogue of people that really work. He knows the dialogue of the working class and was a great help on *Life and Nothing But* [*La vie et rien d'autre*, 1989] and *Captain Conan*. He also knows the vocabulary of the time and the words of the period and uses them naturally, dramatically and poetically. He was twenty during those years and was in fact two streets away from Devaivre during the bombing which forms the first scenes in the film. He was only 200 meters away from Devaivre! Jean Cosmos put a lot of personal memories and touches in the film, most particularly perhaps the obsession with food. Jean said that we were always talking about how to find a way of getting a little more food, a little more bread. As he says, we were starving. He gave me all these elements and physical details concerning the trafficking of food. Cosmos was generally a great, great help in the film and I think it is one of his best works.

JW: I very much enjoyed the scene where the bombs are landing in the Seine and the grips are catching the floating fishes.

BT: I loved this story. First it showed the desperation for food because I can tell you that fish from the Seine are not very good. The flesh is poor and they are full of bones. Imagine how they taste when they are boiled! Secondly it shows how astute people in the film crews were. When there was a problem they could always find a solution and it is a tribute to the great intelligence of the French film crews. They were able to often, through crazy means, solve problems that even the American film crews with all their money could not. I have witnessed this even now when shooting. I love this moment and I also love going from the horror of the bombing where people are being killed to the aura of the film world. It is two worlds that are parallel. I think it is both funny and also very true.

JW: The film stylistically reflects the uncertainty of the period and you switch tones. I'm thinking specifically of the dinner party scene where the tone darkens from the guests casually observing a man catching cats to realising that he is hunting them for food to then watching him being viciously beaten.

BT: Again, that is something that I love about the film. I always remember something Aurenche told me and that was that we never knew what was going to happen in the next hour nevermind the next day. When somebody knocks at your door it could be a friend but it could also be the police; you are on shaky ground. This can sometimes be very funny and absurd, for example there is a producer – played by Olivier Gourmet – who mistakes Mussolini and Hitler. In the next scene we see Aurenche walking and he finds himself in front of a little girl forced to wear a yellow star. In one minute we switch from comedy to drama and I like the fact that we have this constant surprise. There is also the fact that you can never believe what the people are saying. Greven tells Aurenche that he will protect Jewish writers but then you have also seen the Jewish composer being expelled and forced to hide. The instigator of this is the same man. It is this complexity that I wanted to show. That, and the courage of the people who fought.

JW: You also present, primarily through the characters of Devaivre and Aurenche, contrasting attitudes to the act of Resistance.

BT: They are totally different. Devaivre is in the Resistance without ever analysing his opinion when he is asked why he is doing it. He wants them simply to leave, that is all. Aurenche is the opposite. He is very analytical and thinks that he would not be good in the Resistance. He is not a coward, especially after a few drinks. It is when he is writing that we see his act of resistance. He does not want to write one line that might look as if it is endorsing the values of Vichy or the Nazi regime. Even when he was writing a comedy there were lines fighting against the church, against bourgeois society. He wrote a wonderful comedy called *Love Letters* [*Lettres d'amour*, 1942], which is set during a small town during the reign of Napoleon III, but it is really about a class struggle between the people and the society and the aristocracy. Among the people is a young woman working for a stagecoach company who is attacked by the church and by society because of the fact that she has a job. In a small way the film is very feminist because it defends her right to work. Remember of course that Vichy was not at all a feminist regime and believed that the place of the woman was in the home. There is a brilliant, witty line where Napoleon III asks the woman for how long has she been a widow. The woman replies I was married for three months and have been a widow for three years. Napoleon states then that she has had three months of happiness and three years of sorrow. 'No.' says the woman. 'Three months of sorrow and three years of happiness.' This is typical of a challenging dialogue that even on small details refused to offer endorsement. It was a smuggling of ideas.

JW: I love the distinction Devaivre makes of not working for the German-owned Continental but of working with them. His idea of resistance is also to do his job professionally.

BT: Yes, and for some people this was the main way of resisting. You have to remember that the country had been totally defeated in a few days and people were subjected to the most shameful and idiotic propaganda. In that atmosphere where people were beaten up, lost and humiliated, people would take their work seriously. It was something that was incredibly important for people when they saw the films and they revealed intelligence and pools of talent. There is a very beautiful and underrated film by Sasha Dietrich from an original screenplay titled 'Give Me Your Eyes'. In one of the first scenes from the film one of the characters shows to another a room at a museum filled with great works of art. It is revealed that all the works were completed in the year of 1871, the year of the defeat of the Franco-Prussian war. It is an extraordinary scene that the character uses as proof that the people were not completely beaten. It's what I also wanted to show in the film when Devaivre comes on the set and is full of admiration for the work of his production designer who built a beautiful set out of absolutely nothing. I too am full of admiration for these people, they who were able to create beautiful and expressionistic images just through the intelligent use of shadows on a screen. It took me three days to find out how they did these. We could not understand how they did it because we are no longer used to being astute when we make films. In fact, the way it was done was very simple. The fact that these people were still working was the first step of resistance. The second step was to not only work but to go against.

JW: What can you say about your two central actors?

BT: I rarely work with a casting director as I love to meet with the actors and cast them myself. I very much wanted to cast Jacques Gamblin because I knew from all the comedies I had seen him in that he had a great sense of timing and a great sense of rhythm. I had never seem him confront the notion of heroism and I thought he gave that notion a slight vulnerability and a grace which I find quite moving. He does not look like Devaivre and is in many ways a fictional character. In fact Devaivre felt that I gave the character too many moments of weakness and also raised objections to the scenes where he embraces his wife, something he claims to have never done. Too bad for him! Gamblin was also great with a bicycle, which was of course also essential. He is a very experienced rider and does all these scenes himself. In fact he was quite insulted when I asked him if he could ride.

Like Gamblin, Podalydès does not look like the character he plays, well perhaps only a little more. I wanted Denis because I knew he would capture the essence of Aurenche: his great intelligence and always on the move. It was Aurenche who told me that life is a very good screenwriter and you have to have experienced it to capture this. I knew that Denis would capture the inertia and charm of Aurenche and the fact that he was something of a lothario. Of course in the film Aurenche always gives the women he is with his luggage to carry which was a habit of Aurenche's in real life. I wanted to show at the end one of his most famous screenplays, *La Traversée de Paris* [1956], in which two characters have to carry two very heavy suitcases full of pork in occupied Paris. A wonderful film; it is the journey of the two people carrying the cases which Aurenche describes as his way of gaining revenge on the two suitcases he had to carry during the same period. Denis perfectly captured and understood this and the fact Aurenche was insecure and yet always wanting to seduce. I worked with Aurenche when he was 74 or 76 and still he was like this, always between different neighbourhoods and to and from different women. The son of Aurenche said he saw his father totally on screen. Devaivre also admitted that Gamblin captured the truly important things.

JW: What has been the general reaction to the film from others that lived through the period?

BT: I have had wonderful reactions from many, many people from the period and from film historians who specialise in the period. A costume designer who had done six films at Continental wrote to me to say that the film was totally accurate with regard to how the films were made and the movement and energy on the set. It was also interesting in that her letter revealed that she did not at first even realise that Continental was a German company! She was in the Resistance so this proves that the situation was very complex. People have a tendency to think that if you worked at Continental then you were a collaborator but she revealed that it was only after two months when she found herself in Greven's office and saw the bust of Hitler that she realised. She spoke of the trust between the crew and the fact that the only distrust was levelled at the production manager and the people who were in the administration, who were collaborators; these people did not dare to speak very much in front of the crew. She also revealed that people would try to take the wood that was sometimes laid between the cobblestones to use it as wood for fires to produce heat. I am only sorry that I did not put this observation in my film.

JW: We are almost out of time but I wanted to ask about the situation with the writer Charles Spaak who was taken from his cell in prison each day to the set and then returned to prison at the end of the day. Did this actually happen?

BT: Yes it actually happened. I invented only one thing. Spaak's memoirs revealed that someone from Continental offered him food if he continued writing. We decided that it was Greven even though we have no proof. It is more interesting if it is Greven but I truly do not see who else it could be. Also, it's quite funny that Spaak originally asked for cigarettes but forgot to ask for matches so for two days he had all these cigarettes but no matches. Spaak did not want to speak to the German guard in German and so for two days he resisted asking for fire. Eventually he cracked. But after that he did not want to ask again so simply lit one cigarette continuously from the other. He smoked so many cigarettes in this way that he nearly fainted.

JW: In closing, I was struck by reading your comment that you make films to learn and not to teach.

BT: All my films are about subjects that I know little about but wish to discover. With *Life and Nothing But* for example I wanted to know about the Unknown Soldier buried beneath the Arc de Triomphe. I made the film to discover that and explore the notion of what is a missing person. For me film is an exploration in which I am going into a semi-unknown country to share with people I do not know the things that make me laugh and make me angry. I do not like films that are like organised tours.

***

Bruce Weber

A dynamic force in fashion and photography for over two decades, Bruce Weber, born in Milwaukee in 1946, has photographed for virtually every major magazine. With 19 books to his credit, Weber's iconic images have also been exhibited worldwide.

Weber is perhaps better known to cineastes for his sumptuous film work. So far he has produced a total of four feature-length pieces, beginning with *Broken Noses* (1987), an experimental work about machismo focusing on professional boxer, Andy Minsker. A collaboration with jazz vocalist and trumpeter Chet Baker, the unforgettable *Let's Get Lost* (1989), offers a profound meditation on redemption and loss. Nominated for an Academy Award, it introduced a whole new generation to Baker's timeless elegance. *Chop Suey* (2000) continued Weber's interest in male identity, tracing Peter Johnson's metamorphosis from boy to man. Mixing film, archival footage, still photography and setting it to an eclectic soundtrack, it is a deeply personal work and a homage to the things that Weber loves most. Narrated by Julie Christie, *A Letter to True* (2004), Weber's most recent feature, offers a beguiling advance on the artist's scrapbook aesthetic. An open love letter to the eponymous True, one of Weber's five beloved golden retrievers, this cinematic collage is an ode to pets and their owners.

Equally in demand as a commercials director for clients including Ralph Lauren and Calvin Klein, and as a director of pop promos for the Pet Shop Boys and Chris Isaak, Weber has also produced eight striking and deeply personal shorter films. These offer candid views of everything from Weber's early perceptions and experiences (*Backyard Movie*, 1991 and *Gentler Giants*, 1995) to incisive considerations of rock 'n' roll culture (*The Teddy Boys of the Edwardian Drape Society*, 1996).

The following interview took place in July 2005 to mark the screening of *A Letter to True* at the Cambridge Film Festival.

Jason Wood: What were some of the original inspirations for *A Letter to True* and what were the particular themes and concerns that you wanted the film to cover?

Bruce Weber: I think, simply, that everybody wants to make a film about their dogs. And that was my first intention. Then 9/11 happened and my neighbourhood in New York City changed. And my heart was sad. So I decided to write a letter, something that most people don't do anymore, to someone near and dear to me and I decided that that worldly creature would be my dog, True. Our film, *A Letter to True*, is about starting something in your life and then doing 360° and opening your eyes to what's really important in a place you call home.

JW: The film has been described as the work of an enthusiast as opposed to being simply the work of an essayist or analyst. Is it essential that your work excitedly communicate your passion and enthusiasm for your subjects?

BW: I always wanted to make films that described my world at large and what was close to my head and heart. I wouldn't call myself an enthusiast. I would call myself an interpreter of my commitments to things I hold dear.

JW: I did, however, detect a slightly stronger political angle to the film though. I'm thinking of the condemnation of the US government's response to 11 September and the look at the treatment of Haitian refugees. As an artist do you feel a responsibility to respond to world events and issues?

BW: My world of taking pictures for fashion and portraits of actors, artists and musicians is one that I'm very proud of; but as I get older I felt a need to understand my government and their actions. When I was a kid the only thing I ever voted for was class president. Now I have to vote for a man or woman who will tell me we have to go to war. That would make anybody feel the urge to understand.

JW: As one has come to expect from your film and photographic work, *A Letter to True* is a triumph of composition and visual beauty. I just wondered if you could comment on your visual aesthetic and perhaps also mention your chief collaborators such as editor Chad Sipkin and directors of photography Pete Zussarini and Evan Estern.

BW: I always start my films by taking photographs. When I was working with Pete Zuccarini, Even Estern, Shane Sigler and Theo Stanley I tried to find out how they felt about what they were seeing and if it meant anything to them. The scene in the movie when Julie Christie is reciting the Rilke poem happened by chance. Theo and Shane were staying at my house in Montauk, NY and the moon came over the water. Neither one of us said anything at first, but soon both men ran out the door over the cliffs overlooking the moon on the water. Without my asking they had their bolexes in hand and were filming what most people would call darkness. It's one of my favorite parts of the film because in this darkness I see my dogs wagging their tails in the moonlight. My editor Chad Sipkin is like a chef at a first-class restaurant. Even though he's like a great French chef, I still come in asking for matzah-ball soup!

JW: The narration oscillates between various personal passions and reflections on the state of the world. As such the film veers between unabashed joy and a palpable melancholy. Would you agree that this is something of a recurring motif in your work? It is perhaps most previously discernible in *Let's Get Lost*.

BW: I like the decisions of filming to be made during pre-production, the actual filming and post-production. Therefore, it expresses an honesty about what my life is really like at the time that I'm making my film. If it seems sometimes melancholy it's because I was surrounded by a lot of sadness with the effects of 9/11 and sharing in the disappointments with my Haitian neighbours. I don't think it's so discernable in *Let's Get Lost* as it is in *Chop Suey*. During the filming of *Chop Suey* my sister was very ill and dying of cancer. All I could think about was finishing the film so she could see it. I see the film *A Letter to True* about hope. And that's positive.

JW: Narration is always an important aspect of your films and in this instance you have Julie Christie and Marianne Faithfull on board. Though no stranger to working with icons, how gratifying was it to secure their involvement?

BW: Never in my life, growing up as a kid, did I think after watching Julie Christie in *Darling* [1965] that I would be working with her some day. Or that she would send me the most beautifully written postcards to my house. Marianne and I became close while filming my movie about Robert Mitchum many years ago. She has a good sense of humour and I really find her intelligence to be one of the reasons she's still so beautiful. Marianne cried when she saw our film and said, 'Bruce, I could use a drink.'

* * *

FILMOSOPHY
DANIEL FRAMPTON

2006
256 pages
1–904764–84–3   £15.00 (pbk)
1–904764–85–1   £45.00 (hbk)

Filmosophy is a manifesto for a radically new way of understanding cinema. Daniel Frampton explains and elucidates the cinematic ideas of such influential twentieth-century thinkers as Hugo Münsterberg to Gilles Deleuze to build a radical yet practical concept of 'film-thinking', arguing that cinema conveys poetic ideas through a dramatic intent towards the characters, spaces, and events of film. With discussions of contemporary filmmakers such as Michael Haneke, Béla Tarr and the Dardennes brothers, this timely intervention into the study of film and philosophy will stir argument and discussion among both filmgoers and filmmakers alike.

'An extremely daring book. *Filmosophy* does not present a philosophy of film, nor does it explore how film contributes material for philosophical interpretation. Rather, in a lucid and clear style, Daniel Frampton argues that film *is* philosophy; it is itself, aesthetical and philosophical expression – a medium for thinking-with or an accompaniment to thought. In conceptualising film as an 'organic intelligence', Frampton draws from the lessons of both Gilles Deleuze and Stanley Cavell to propose one of the most original film philosophies of the last thirty years.'

Prof. D. N. Rodowick, Harvard University

'A provocative and significant intervention in the contemporary dialogue about the cinema as manifest philosophy, expressed in both thought and action. Frampton's expansive rhetoric is refreshing, his film references eclectic and his prose a pleasure to read.'
Prof. Vivian Sobchack, University of California, Los Angeles

'*Filmosophy*, a sprightly treatment of the ways that cinema make us think, tells us why cinephilia is deeply rooted in perception and reflection. When Frampton tells us 'the thinking of a film should be seen as free and fluid' he brings his readers to the threshold of creative criticism. Every reader will appreciate the energy, force and breadth of the author's appreciation of cinema.'
Prof. Tom Conley, Harvard University

'The link between philosophy and cinema is one of the most fertile areas of contemporary film studies. *Filmosophy* establishes a vocabulary and an original perspective for understanding that link. New cinematic forms require new ways of thinking; indeed, this book suggests that these forms are new ways of thinking. Powerfully and provocatively, *Filmosophy* revises what we thought we knew about cinema, and asks us to look again at what cinema might know about us.'
Prof. Colin Davies, Royal Holloway, University of London

'*Filmosophy* offers a sympathetic and persuasive argument in favour of a new engagement with film which sweeps aside the shibboleths of current film studies and returns the spectator to a position of empathetic involvement with the filmgoing experience, mapping out a poetic-philosophical approach to film so different from the prosaic aridity of much film studies. There is no doubting the originality of *Filmosophy*, or the fact that it constitutes a major contribution to the philosophy of film.'
Prof. Geoffrey Nowell-Smith, Queen Mary, University of London

'Frampton's concepts of 'film-thinking' and the 'filmind' strike me as brilliant, as timely (in response to contemporary cinema), and as evocative and explanatory ... Gritty, impassioned and engaged, *Filmosophy* challenges its readers to think afresh their experience in the cinema.'
Emma Wilson, Corpus Christi College, Cambridge University

'An ambitious attempt to outline a new way of thinking about cinema, *Filmosophy* also gives a sympathetic and often perceptive account of Deleuze's position, seeking to justify his contention that film is a form of thought. Its publication will make a valuable contribution to the debate about contemporary understanding of cinema.'
Prof. Ian Christie, Birkbeck College, University of London